An Introduction to Bibliographical and Textual Studies

An Introduction to Bibliographical and Textual Studies

THIRD EDITION

William Proctor Williams
and
Craig S. Abbott

The Modern Language Association of America
New York   1999

For information about obtaining permission to reprint material from MLA book publications, send your request by mail (see address below), e-mail (permissions@ mla.org), or fax (212 477-9863).

Library of Congress Cataloging-in-Publication Data

Williams, William Proctor, 1939–
   An introduction to bibliographical and textual studies / William Proctor Williams and Craig S. Abbott. — 3rd ed.
     p.   cm.
   Includes index.
   ISBN 0-87352-267-2 (cloth). — ISBN 0-87352-268-0 (pbk.)
   1. Bibliography, Critical. 2. Criticism, Textual. 3. English literature— Criticism, Textual. I. Abbott, Craig S., 1941– . II. Title.
Z1001.W58 1999
010´.42—dc21   99-14326

Printed on recycled paper

Published by The Modern Language Association of America
10 Astor Place, New York, New York 10003-6981

CONTENTS

ACKNOWLEDGMENTS

For permission to reprint pages from their works, we thank several authors and publishers. Figure 4 is reprinted from *Principles of Bibliographical Description* by Fredson Bowers © 1949 by Princeton University Press. Figure 6 is reprinted from *A Bibliography of the English Printed Drama to the Restoration*, volume 2, by W. W. Greg © 1951 by Oxford University Press. Figures 14a–14e are reprinted from *The Dramatic Works of Thomas Dekker*, volume 3, edited by Fredson Bowers © 1958 by Cambridge University Press. Figures 15a–15d are reprinted from *The Plays and Poems of Philip Massinger*, volumes 1 and 4, edited by Philip Edwards and Colin Gibson © 1976 by Oxford University Press. Figures 16a–16g are reprinted from *Mardi and a Voyage Thither*, edited by Harrison Hayford, Hershel Parker, and G. Thomas Tanselle, volume 3 of *The Writings of Herman Melville* © 1970 by Northwestern University Press. Figures 17a and 17b are from *The Complete Works of Washington Irving: Journals and Notebooks*, volume 1, 1803–1806, edited by Nathalia Wright © 1969 and reprinted with the permission of G. K. Hall & Co., Boston.

WILLIAM PROCTOR WILLIAMS
CRAIG S. ABBOTT

I N T R O *1* U C T I O N

*You find the old bibliograph in some corner of the room, amidst a
heap of books.*

— *Joseph Hatton,* Valley of the Poppies *(1872)*

The twentieth century has seen great advances in bibliographical and textual scholarship, but the subject dates back to the great library at Alexandria
(founded c. 323 BC), which was formed primarily so that scholars might engage in textual criticism. Although the texts changed as time passed—first the
Greek classics, then the Bible during the Middle Ages, and finally the Bible and
the Greek and Latin classics from the Renaissance on—the methods employed
were concerned with a manuscript textual tradition for which a long history existed. In the nineteenth century, when English literature began to be established
as an academic discipline, it was only natural that those scholars who took up
English studies should apply the methods of classical textual criticism to English texts, for they had all been educated in a traditional classical school system. But a few nineteenth-century editors of the English classics practiced a
seemingly whimsical eclecticism, and their method sometimes resembled
Lancelot Andrewes's preaching as described in John Aubrey's *Brief Lives:* "he
did play with his Text, as a Jack-an-apes does, who takes up a thing and tosses
and playes with it, and then he takes up another, and playes a little with it.
Here's a pretty thing, and there's a pretty thing!" (7). At times their editorial
work consisted of picking a convenient previous printing and then adding their
commentary notes. The nineteenth century did witness some notable attempts,
such as the Variorum Shakespeare, to prepare sound editions based on the best
methods of the times. Although most nineteenth-century editors were sincere
and diligent, Stanley Wells's assessment of eighteenth- and nineteenth-century
work on Shakespeare is not unjust:

> The work of these early editors was carried out in relative ignorance of the
> theatrical and printing conditions that prevailed in Shakespeare's day; [. . .]
> the emendations they made were governed by literary, grammatical and lin-
> guistic standards of their time and by the stylistic and theatrical tastes of

individual editors [and . . .] while the "good" and "bad" quartos received a
great deal of attention and use, scholarly opinion had not really crystallized
into any settled view of their varying claims to authority.   (*Shakespeare* 13)

On the less austere side of things were editors like Henry Morley, who claimed
he had edited the many hundreds of works reprinted in the 209 volumes of
Cassell's National Library (1888–89).

At the beginning of the twentieth century a group of scholars—W. W.
Greg, R. B. McKerrow, F. P. Wilson, A. W. Pollard, and others—began to study
the texts of Shakespeare and his contemporary dramatists in a way that came to
be known as the New Bibliography. This new methodology was grounded on a
firm and ever more thorough understanding of the book as a physical object
and involved studying the operation of the book trade, the technical procedures
of setting, printing, proofing, binding, and selling books. The New Bibliographers rediscovered what the classical and biblical textual critic had always
known: in the real-time history of a text, the only moment that reveals any information about the correct form of the text is that moment when it moves
from one form to another and from which the later form survives. This is the
case whether the transmission involves a scribe listening to the dictation of a
text by a fellow worker and moving an inked pen across sheets of parchment or
a compositor looking at an author's manuscript and placing individual pieces of
type into a composing stick from which they are transferred to a chase and then
to the press for printing. Where some earlier English editors had gone wrong
was in neglecting the ways texts have been transmitted and in viewing the text
as an abstraction with a life of its own outside of real time and space.

With the rapid growth in the study of English and American literature in
the years following World War I, this examination of the text, the physical documents that contained it, and its history and genetics gradually spread beyond
the confines of English Renaissance drama into almost all literature in English
and, to a lesser extent, literature in the other modern European languages. This
expansion in bibliographical studies and their application to textual criticism
were certainly spurred by the discovery that many major works suffered from
textual corruption. Scholars sought to recover texts the authors wrote, purged
of the corruptions inherent in hand copying or typesetting and those willfully
introduced by families, friends, and well-intentioned publishers' editors.

With the rise of New Criticism in the 1940s and 1950s, bibliographical and
textual scholarship, while developing apace, found itself no longer a dominant
concern in literary study. But it was granted its function as preliminary to the
real work and supposedly higher calling of literary criticism. Thus René Wellek
and Austin Warren, in *Theory of Literature*, advised that this scholarship "should
not be overrated," for it could "only lay the foundations for an actual analysis
and interpretation as well as casual explanation of literature" (57, 69). The re-
striction of bibliographical and textual criticism to a foundational role also

found expression in a 1963 collection of critical studies of A. A. Milne's *Winnie-the-Pooh*, which ended with a paper by Smedley Force entitled "Prolegomena to Any Future Study of *Winnie-the-Pooh*." Force's paper, written for a section of the Modern Language Association, is an old-timer's defense of scholarship and a complaint against "premature" criticism:

> Surely you will agree, gentlemen, that criticism is only possible after certain preliminary matters have been agreed upon. Having screened all your applications for admission to this Section, I know you understand that criticism must be postponed until the text has been definitively established, the lacunae surrounded (but not replaced) with a sufficiently broad range of conjectured readings, the variorum footnotes, appendices, bibliographies, and concordances compiled. (Crews 140–41)

Turning his attention to Pooh, Force points out a textual crux: while Milne's text of the North Pole chapter refers to a sign reading "DISCOVERED," the accompanying illustration by Shepard presents the sign as "DICSOVERED." "Which," Force asks, "is correct?" And he notes the need for scholarship preliminary to criticism:

> All further remarks about this chapter must wait upon the publication of Milne's complete correspondence with Shepard, Shepard's with Milne, Milne's with the publisher, the publisher's with Shepard, Shepard's with the publisher, and everyone's with the printer. I am not saying that this will clear up the difficulty; but I do mean that our hands are tied, critically speaking, until such time as this is done. (Crews 145)

Force's paper and the others in *The Pooh Perplex* (with such titles as "Paradoxical Persona: The Hierarchy of Heroism in *Winnie-the-Pooh*" and "Poisoned Paradise: The Underside of Pooh") were parodies by Frederick Crews. They more or less reflected the state of literary studies in the early 1960s, including the curious arrangement between critics on the one hand and scholars (including bibliographers and textual critics) on the other. Smedley Force seems to have accepted, with a vengeance, his role of taking care of the preliminaries to criticism.

More recently, critics and scholars increasingly recognize that this view of bibliographical and textual scholarship neglects the extent to which such scholarship itself is critical as well as fundamental. In part, this recognition results from the meeting of criticism and bibliotextual studies at the level of theory, as in the discussion of such topics as textual instability and the nature of authorship and authority. Even some of the terms literary theorists use generally or metaphorically—such as *margin, border, gap, erasure,* and *inscription*—are bibliographical in their more specific or literal sense. In 1977, when Jacques Derrida said, "Iteration alters, something new takes place" (175), he was saying anew what the bibliographer W. W. Greg had said fifty years earlier: "the process of transcription is characterized by variation" (*Calculus* 8). Because bibliography and textual criticism are historical disciplines, their rapprochement with criticism has also gained impetus from the historicizing movement in literary studies, as in new historicism and cultural materialism, and the corresponding shift in the orientation of textual studies away from authors and toward social construction and historical contingency, toward textual production and transmission as social phenomena.

Still, the value and methods of bibliographical and textual studies have not gone unquestioned. Even so sophisticated a critic as Edmund Wilson attacked the way textual criticism was applied to the works of American authors in the Center for Editions of American Authors project. (See Center for Editions of American Authors for a response.) And since then some of the strongest questioning has come from bibliographers and editors themselves. These questions and the resulting debate, if they have generated some confusion, have also had the beneficial effect of forcing scholars to examine their assumptions, aims, and methods. Moreover, even those who have questioned particular editorial methods have benefited from the wealth of information discovered during the editorial process—information bearing on authors' styles and methods of composition; on the evolution of particular texts; on the profession of authorship in various periods; on economic, political, and technological influences on texts; and on literary history generally.

In attempting to provide a brief introduction to textual and bibliographical studies for both the beginning student and the more advanced scholar who has missed or avoided the subject, we have sought to write neither a how-to book nor a manual but rather a guide to how this sort of scholarship has recently been and is now conducted and how its insights, methods, and products can be applied to other branches of scholarship. Further, we do not provide a history of the book trade or of book production; for those subjects the reader can start with Philip Gaskell's *A New Introduction to Bibliography* or with other more specialized works listed in our reference bibliography. We do not assume that most readers of this book intend to become bibliographers or textual critics, but we do assume that they are among the principal beneficiaries of bibliography and textual criticism and that all those whose object of study is transmitted by or embodied in books and texts are inescapably involved in matters bibliographical and textual-critical.

We do not take a particular methodological or theoretical stance; rather, we try to describe how bibliographical and textual scholarship has been practiced and applied during the twentieth century. For example, we present extensive discussions of the traditional approach to the question of authorial final intention because it has been basic to critical editing since the early years of this century. But on this question and on similar issues, we also try to indicate current trends, and we provide in the notes, texts, and reference bibliography citations to major documents in the scholarly debate. Similarly, the examples that conclude the sections on descriptive bibliography and textual criticism illustrate various methods of presenting these two subjects. Although absolute neutrality is probably impossible, we attempt to provide a road map rather than a specifically plotted route so that those who use this book may recognize areas of agreement and disagreement.

In describing the aims and methods of bibliographical and textual scholars, we are engaged primarily in summary and description, not in relating personal discovery. Throughout, we rely on the work of many scholars. Although we provide citations for some references within our text, we cannot possibly cite every important piece of scholarship bearing on what we present. While our notes can acknowledge some specific debts, they cannot acknowledge many greater and more pervasive ones. We recommend further reading from the works listed in our reference bibliography.

Documents and Texts

The basic commodity for a literary scholar is the text, which is physically embodied in letters written, impressed, or transferred onto a surface or encoded in digital form, that is, in a manuscript, book, computer file, and so on. It is not possible to speak of versions of self in Donne's verse epistles, cross-gender characterization in Mary Shelley's *Frankenstein*, rhetorical fusion in the fiction of Toni Morrison, or the literary criticism of Edmund Wilson unless one starts with the marks on the paper (or sounds on the tape or images on the screen) that present the text. No matter what else we may know about authors, we must always refer our views back to the texts they have left us and to the physical forms that have embodied them. Hence, although bibliographical studies are popularly thought to be distinct from critical studies, the two are in truth sides of the same coin. One does not normally perform extensive bibliographical work on the *Guinness Book of World Records* or the New York City telephone directory, because these are not texts normally subjected to critical study. Indeed, until recently one did not perform extensive bibliographic studies on historical or philosophical texts, though it would appear that this neglect is being remedied.

Texts have lives. They are the products of people's minds and hands and are thus in a real sense historical, whether we are dealing with the life of Shakespeare's *Othello* (from the First Quarto of 1622 to the most recent paperback published for classroom use, over none of which the author exercised any direct control) or with that of Marianne Moore's poem entitled "Poetry" (which began its public life in 1919 as thirty lines, went through stages of thirteen, fifteen, and twenty-nine lines, and then appeared in 1967 as three lines, Moore herself evidently being responsible for all these alterations). Certainly the student of Shakespeare or Moore ought not use just any text that comes to hand, ought not merely browse through the library or bookstore stacks and take the copy that hasn't been checked out or sold, nor should the teacher select just any textbook for use in class. Few of the many classroom anthologies that print Moore's "Poetry" indicate that there are other versions of other lengths. Similarly, in Auden's later editions of his "complete" poems, one will not find his "September 1, 1939." And then there are the almost supernatural vicissitudes of chapters 28 and 29 of James's *The Ambassadors*, which were reversed in the first American edition in 1903 and in all subsequent American editions until 1955. At this point the publishers, Harper and Brothers, announced that theirs would be the first American edition with the chapters in the correct order, but it was not. In 1957 Harper finally published an edition in which chapter 28 came before chapter 29, but in 1958, after Harper leased the rights to Doubleday, the Doubleday Anchor paperback came out with chapter 29 again ahead of chapter 28. And then, in 1992, it was argued that the "reversed" order was actually James's order. (The error is pointed out by Edel and disputed by McGann ["Revision"].) It probably also makes a difference whether in Joyce's *Ulysses* one of Stephen Dedalus's first thoughts is "No mother" (as in printed versions) or "No, mother!" (as in the manuscript) and whether Linco in Richard Fanshawe's translation of *Il Pastor Fido* says "Leave, leave the woods, leave following beasts, fond boy, / And follow Love" (as he does, correctly, in the 1647 and 1648 editions) or "Love, leave the woods, leave following beasts, fond boy, / and follow Love" (as he does, incorrectly, in the 1664, 1676, 1692, and 1736 editions). (See Gabler 18; Staton and Simeone.)

Texts, as we have said, have physical embodiments. Certainly the literary work begins in the mind of the author, but since that form is inaccessible, the author must set pen to paper or fingers to keyboard or must dictate for an amanuensis. Errors will result from the making of this first physical embodiment of the text (the manuscript, typescript, or digital encoding). Almost all authors will then produce revised manuscripts, drafts, recastings, foul papers, fair copies, and the like. Eventually, if a work makes its way to the printer and publisher, further textual alteration will occur. Before English spelling became regularized (roughly, with Johnson's *Dictionary* in 1755), compositors (typesetters) spelled many words according to their dialects and personal tastes, and they could also make spelling alterations to justify full lines of verse or prose. Thus compositors might set *do* or *doe*, *go* or *goe*, *catholic* or *catholick* or *catholique*. They might also differ in how they spaced around punctuation, displayed headings, and dealt with lines of verse too long for their composing sticks. In all these permitted and seemingly inconsequential ways compositors could produce yet one more version of the author's text. Compositors were also known to generate more striking alterations either because they thought their setting copy was wrong or because they could not make it out and were forced to guess. A probable instance is the famous textual crux in the First Folio (1623) edition of

Shakespeare's *Henry V* where the Hostesse, describing Falstaff's death, says, "for his Nose was as sharpe as a Pen, and a Table of greene fields" (lines 838–39). It is commonly thought today that the compositor at this point could not read the manuscript, which probably read "a babld [babbled] of greene fields," and produced a version of the text that is not what Shakespeare wrote and that makes little or no sense.

Since the standardization of spelling, compositors have not been allowed the luxury of varying the author's spelling of common words (unless the author spells unconventionally) but have managed to perpetrate various sins of omission and commission on the texts they have set in type. Anyone who has ever spent time reading proofs will have countless examples of the transpositions, omissions, repetitions, and the like produced by compositors. The sorts of errors may change as technology changes. Hand setting in the nineteenth century produced different missettings than does computer composing in the late twentieth. But the dicta of W. W. Greg in *The Calculus of Variants* that "the process of transcription is characterized by variation" and that "such variation may be assumed to be universal, every transcription introducing some variants [. . .] in all but the shortest texts," hold true no matter by what means a text passes from one form to another (8).

Authors—and authors' agents (copyeditors, correctors for the press who check or are supposed to check proofs against copy, secretaries, spouses, friends, and literary executors)—have regularly been given the opportunity to correct texts in proof or in subsequent editions. Charlton Hinman has demonstrated that as early as 1623, Shakespeare's works in the First Folio were rather carelessly proofed in places, probably by Jaggard, the printer. And since the late eighteenth century it has been a regular part of the publication process to supply the author with proofs. However, not only has bibliographical study shown that reading proofs does not remove all the variants introduced by the printing process, but it has also demonstrated that the very process of proofreading, revising by the author during proofreading, and making the proof corrections in the type or plates introduces further errors and thus creates other forms of the text.

Clearly, a doctrine of textual original sin could be one of the creedal statements of literary scholars. Not only do all texts have lives, but these lives tend to go from bad to worse. But what from one perspective may appear sinful may appear from another as the legitimate and legitimating accommodations of a text to its readership over time or as a natural process like that producing a fine patina on a Chinese bronze. It is not simply a matter of reading texts suspiciously to find the "correct" text. The study of texts' composition, revision, physical embodiments, process of transmission, and manner of reception are central to a historical understanding of literature. Even those who do not directly engage in bibliographical and textual scholarship will benefit from its products—bibliographies, histories of printing and publishing, scholarly editions, and so forth. The use of these will be enhanced by an acquaintance with the assumptions, aims, vocabulary, and methods that lie behind them.

Reference Bibliography

To the general public, the most familiar product of bibliography is a list compiled according to some set of conventions such as those given in the *MLA Handbook* or *The Chicago Manual of Style*. The art of compiling such lists (and sometimes such a list itself) is called reference bibliography or systematic bibliography. Its primary focus is less on books (or periodicals or whatever) as physical objects than on the works contained in them. A reference bibliography that is merely a list is an enumerative bibliography; one that includes abstracts, summaries, or descriptions of the works is an annotated bibliography. Annotated or enumerative, such a bibliography is the product of a principle of discovery and selection, a method of citation, and a system of organization that require careful thought and difficult decisions (see Harner). Many reference bibliographies are among the standard tools of scholarship—for example, the *New Cambridge Bibliography of English Literature* and the *MLA International Bibliography*. The subject of reference bibliography is beyond the scope of this work and will not be discussed further.

Historical Bibliography

As its name implies, this branch of bibliography concerns itself with the history of the book. Usually it treats either printing history (including the economics and technology of book production) or book-trade history (including the methods of sale and distribution and the organization of the book trade). Historical bibliographers may concentrate their efforts on a particular publisher, printer, bookseller, binder, or typefounder, or they may devote themselves to the study of paper, type, presses of a particular kind or period, bindings, book illustration, and similar matters. Some work in this field, however, takes larger concerns for its subject and may discuss such matters as the impact of printing on Western culture, the cultural impact of the transition from manuscript to print, the effect of a mass literary market on literary standards, or, more recently, the effect of electronic data processing on language and literature. The linking of bibliographical study to "big questions in history," is evident, for example, in Robert Darnton's study of French popular fiction of the late eighteenth century. He asks, "What causes revolutions? Why do value systems change? How does public opinion influence events?" But then says that he will approach such questions by asking one "of a different order, one that can be answered: What did the French read in the eighteenth century?" And that question leads him to intend "a bibliography of the entire corpus of forbidden books in pre-Revolutionary France, with information about their geographical distribution and relative strength of demand for each of them" (*Forbidden Best-Sellers* xvii, xxi–xxii). This broader view of historical bibliography, often termed *l'histoire du livre*, may also be seen in Lucien Febvre and Henri-Jean Martin's influential *L'apparition du Livre* (1958; available in English as *The Coming of the Book*), a study not merely of printing history but primarily of the impact of the book on civilization through the end of the eighteenth century, in Elizabeth L. Eisenstein's *The Printing Press as an Agent of Change*, and in the multivolume series History of the Book in Britain, commissioned by Cambridge University Press in 1989. (For another important study of the history of the book, see Darnton, *Business*.) This movement has led to the establishment of many centers or projects for the book at research institutions around the world, and it has been summarized in Peter D. McDonald's "Implicit Structure and Explicit Interactions: Pierre Bourdieu and the History of the Book" and in the collection *The Book Encompassed*, edited by Peter Davison. The current growth of bibliography as almost a social science is reflected in this advertisement in the 31 March 1998 *Times Literary Supplement* for a master of arts course at the University of London's School of Advanced Study:

> An interdisciplinary MA providing an unparalleled opportunity to study [. . .] the history of the book and its influence on cultural and intellectual change. [. . .] Students with a good honours degree in English, History, Cultural Studies, or any relevant subject are eligible. [. . .] Seminars will consider books not only as material objects but their interaction with society, emphasising publication, manufacture, distribution, reception, and survival.

Analytical Bibliography

This branch of bibliographical investigation considers books (and other embodiments of texts) as witnesses to the processes that brought them into being. Analytical bibliographers examine books as physical objects, in much the same way that, say, geologists examine rocks or botanists plants. Through analysis, they try to determine the date and method of composition, the source and nature of the compositors' copy, the identity and proclivities of the compositors, and the kind and quantity of type or the kind of machine used in composition. In the period of hand printing (approximately before 1800) they will want to know when and in what order the pages of type were imposed, sent to the press, and then washed, rinsed, and distributed back into the type cases. In the period after 1800 they will want to know whether stereotype or other kinds of plates were made and how these plates were subsequently corrected and used. They will want to know how the book was exposed to the public (whether it was sold or given away, how many copies from what sources were issued at a specific time). In the modern era they will study the book's binding and dust jacket as well as the book itself. Finally, they will usually want to ask these questions about all books by a particular author or printer or publisher, about all books with a particular title, or about a particular kind of book. Thus they may examine copies of all books by Fielding, all of *Tom Jones*, or all novels issued by the same publisher in the 1740s. Their primary concern, while practicing analytical bibliography, is not with what any of the books say but with how their physical features reveal the history of their production.

It is this branch of bibliography that has taken most of the abuse from the tongues and pens of fellow scholars and critics. This opposition reflects the attackers' failure to see—and the bibliographers' failure to demonstrate—the necessity of such investigation. The objective and disinterested examination of books as physical objects feeds the other branches of bibliography and, in turn, helps produce the raw material for the study of literature. The analytical studies of just one book, the First Folio of Shakespeare's works, by Charlton Hinman, Trevor Howard-Hill, Andrew Cairncross, W. W. Greg, and many others have produced often startling results, the implications of which extend not only to the text of Shakespeare's works but also to any work printed during the same era. All this information, with obvious applications to other sorts of bibliography and to literary studies generally, was uncovered by analytical bibliographers, who came on it by considering books only as physical objects. It is unlikely that investigators who treated the First Folio in any other way would have found it, as they would not have been looking for physical evidence. The First Folio regarded as a literary treasure of the English language, which it certainly is, will not yield the same evidence as does the First Folio studied as a book produced according to certain physical processes, just like those used to produce an almanac for 1623 or an herbal, that can be analyzed by anyone with a clear understanding of how type gets impressed into paper.

Descriptive Bibliography

Descriptive bibliography differs from analytical bibliography only because its aim is different. Though both are concerned with the book as physical object (and thus can be lumped together under the term *physical bibliography*), analytical bibliography attempts to anatomize the process that brought the book into being, while descriptive bibliography seeks to describe accurately the object produced by the process and all the variations caused by alterations in the process. In methodology and terminology the two fields are nearly identical. Not all bibliographies concerned with the books as physical objects are necessarily descriptive in the full sense of the term. Some may be enumerative, based on more or less physical analysis but presenting lists with minimal descriptive detail. Some of these are among the most outstanding accomplishments of descriptive bibliography, such as A. W. Pollard and G. R. Redgrave's *A Short-Title Catalogue of Books Printed in England, Scotland, and Ireland, and of English Books Printed Abroad, 1475–1640*, first published in 1926 and then in an extensively augmented and revised second edition that was begun by W. A. Jackson and F. S. Ferguson, brought to completion by Katharine F. Pantzer, and presented in three volumes (1976, 1986, and 1991).

A full descriptive bibliography presents an orderly, usually chronological description of the physical embodiments of texts. Normally it physically describes all the books containing works by a single author or publisher, perhaps within a given time span, or all the books of a particular type. From an examination of particular copies, it produces an ideal description of a book—a historical reconstruction of the book as the publisher exposed it to the public—and it records all the variants from this ideal form. Bibliographical description of a book or part of a book may also be employed in a historical or critical essay that considers the material forms in which texts have appeared.

The purpose of descriptive bibliography is twofold. First, through examination where possible of multiple copies, it tries to provide a history of the forms in which a particular book or group of books was issued. Second, it provides descriptions that serve as a standard for the identification and evaluation of additional copies of these books. The surviving copies of a novel published in 1936 are so numerous that it is not usually possible to examine all copies, and one copy in a library in a remote corner of Wyoming or New York City may contain a significant variant in physical form. For the books of earlier periods, unrecorded copies are constantly being unearthed, and they too may contain variants.

Textual Criticism

Sometimes considered a subdivision of bibliography but perhaps more properly regarded as a distinct discipline that nonetheless employs bibliographical investigation, textual criticism is the study of the transmission of texts. Its aim is to trace the history of texts and to establish (that is, to edit) texts according to certain principles and using certain methods, which have varied from period to period of history and even within periods. The focus here is the text—roughly, the wording—rather than its physical embodiments, but obviously texts are intimately related to their physical embodiments. Hence, textual criticism uses many of the findings of analytical and descriptive bibliography. For example, if analytical and descriptive bibliography discover that the gatherings of a Jacobean play quarto were set in series ("seriatim"), this information indicates to the textual critic a range of possible explanations for textual variations that occur early or late in a particular gathering. More obviously, the evidence of analytical and descriptive bibliography assists the textual critic in determining the sequence and correctness of textual alterations made during the printing of a book. Such direct application of analytical bibliography to textual questions is sometimes called textual bibliography.

Textual criticism must also deal with the relations between different states and versions of a text produced over a period of time—normally, successive editions in the period of printing. Analytical and descriptive bibliography can help here as well. For example, these two fields have solved the question of the supposed first edition of Sir John Davies's *Nosce Teipsum* (1599) by demonstrating from physical evidence that before the first quarto had been completed and sold, a line-for-line resetting of the work had begun and that early on copies appeared containing mixed sheets from these two settings. As would be expected, the resetting introduced textual variation (for studies of the text see Krueger; Taylor). Textual critics, without the aid of analytical and descriptive bibliography, might not have uncovered this bit of bibliographical history that illuminates the textual history of Davies's work and that provides evidence for the editorial evaluation and treatment of the resulting textual variants. However, although modern textual criticism is notable for its reliance, wherever possible, on physical evidence, bibliography alone is not sufficient for solving textual problems. Textual critics have also resorted to paleography (the study of ancient writing or, more generally, of handwriting), lexical rules (authors cannot use a word that did not exist at the time they were writing), metrical rules (in works with regular metrical patterns, nonmetrical readings are judged inferior), genetic relationships of texts (as in stemmatics, the diagramming of a group of texts in patterns resembling family trees), and quasi-mathematical ordering of texts (a calculuslike arrangement of variant patterns in texts such as the systems devised by W. W. Greg and Vinton Dearing). Furthermore, it should be remembered that textual criticism is critical, requiring the exercise of judgment in both the gathering and interpretation of evidence.

There are, it seems, two poles in textual criticism. At one is the tendency to restrict judgment and to be limited by documentary evidence; at the other is the tendency to give rather free rein to judgment. These poles can be seen in a small hubbub that arose in the *Times Literary Supplement*, where a reviewer of Roger Sale's *Modern Heroism* pointed out that William Empson had "mutilated" a passage from Pope's *Moral Epistle IV* when he quoted it in *Seven Types of Ambiguity* thus:

> Another age shall see the golden ear
> Embrown the slope, and nod on the parterre,
> Deep harvest [sic] bury all his pride has planned,
> And laughing Ceres reassume the land.

Empson responded by saying that the *s* had been dropped from "harvests" in the Courthope and Everyman editions (1881 and 1924 respectively) and so in this case it was the sensitive Victorians, and not I, who had divined the true text. There can be little doubt that Pope first wrote our version, and only printed the prosy one out of timidity.

The reviewer, however, would have none of that:

> I am sorry that Professor Empson has been misled by inferior texts. F. W. Bateson's Twickenham Edition (which is based on the 1744 "death-bed" edition and takes into account the nine previous editions or reprints) gives "harvests" in the plural and lists no singular variant in its *apparatus criticus*. I cannot see any reason to add a "sensitive" emendation which depends on the doubtful editorial procedure of divination. I have no such way of being certain about [. . .] the working of his [Pope's] mind. Neither has Professor Empson—but what Pope actually wrote seems the safest indication.

Both Empson and the reviewer at least pretend to resort to Pope as the basis of authority for the text of the poem. But the reviewer, at one pole, takes the surviving documentary texts as evidence of what Pope wrote. And Empson, playfully at the other pole, accepts divination as a better guide to what Pope "first wrote." Most textual criticism, of course, is situated somewhere in between.

Scholarly editing may take a number of forms, ranging from the faithful transcription of a particular state of a text (that found in a particular document) to a historical reconstruction of a text on a basis such as authorial intention. This latter form, critical editing, has dominated contemporary textual criticism. It involves the textual critic in several matters, some bibliographical and some critical. Textual critics must be textually acute, possessing a full knowledge of analytical, descriptive, historical, and textual bibliography and their applications; but they must also be critically acute, with a full knowledge of literary history, philology, poetic or prosaic stylistics, the structure of given works in a given period, and the characteristics of the author in question.

ANALYTICAL
BIBLIOGRAPHY

Not as ours the books of old—
Things that steam can stamp and fold;
Not as ours the books of yore—
Rows of type, and nothing more.

—*Austin Dobson,* At the Sign of the Lyre *(1885)*

Analytical bibliography attempts to determine the printing history of books by examining their physical features. (Physical examination of manuscripts, including manuscript books, is part of the field known as codicology.) Like detective work—indeed, it has forensic applications—bibliographical analysis combines drudgery with excitement and can turn up bits of information that, though seemingly minor, may have considerable significance. As a discipline, analytical bibliography developed largely through the study of textual problems in English Renaissance drama. By 1958, although the field was still young (having flowered only in the twentieth century in work by such scholars as W. W. Greg, R. B. McKerrow, Alice Walker, Charlton Hinman, and Fredson Bowers), Bowers could justly advise "that when the evidence of analytical bibliography is available, critical judgment must be limited by bibliographical probabilities and must never run contrary to bibliographical findings" ("Bibliographical Way" 18). If Bowers demonstrates the importance of analytical bibliography, he also recognizes its limits. Bibliography may provide evidence and findings that the critic, textual or otherwise, cannot ignore. But it does not replace critical judgment, and, of course, bibliographers themselves employ judgment in the interpretation of evidence. Using watermarks, type batter, press variants, spelling habits, running titles, and the like, the bibliographer may establish the date of a book, identify the compositors who set its pages, and determine the sequence of variant states of the parts. The textual critic must take these findings into account, but they do not themselves constitute the editorial function.

A focus on editorial applications has both helped and hindered analytical bibliography. It has provided justification for what some might otherwise label as mere pedantry and has forced bibliographers to see their endeavors in relation to other areas, literary and historical. Yet the focus also has tended to obscure the independence of bibliography as a discipline that can illuminate not only the printing of a particular literary work but also the larger history of printing and of the book as an instrument and product of human culture. In recent years analytical bibliography (or at least the physical features that are its concern) has gained increasing literary critical attention. Critics are reading not just texts but books. Thus, for example, in *Repression and Recovery* Cary Nelson argues that "the first step in reconstituting the history" of American poetry from the first half of the twentieth century is "to get as close as possible to the actual publications of the period" (181). Nelson himself provides readings that get close, taking into account typeface, type size, page size, layout, dust jacket design, and so forth.

Evidence and Analysis

The primary evidence in analytical bibliography is that of the books themselves. While this evidence may be certain, the conclusions based on it—or hypotheses constructed to explain it—are often uncertain. As Bowers has pointed out, they range from the demonstrable to the probable to the merely possible. Insufficient evidence and ignorance of conflicting evidence plague bibliography just as they do any field. And as D. F. McKenzie has demonstrated, bibliographers at times have based conclusions on questionable assumptions about the normality and regularity of printing-house practices (see esp. Bowers, *Bibliography*; McKenzie, "Printers"). Bibliographical analysis both relies on and contributes to our knowledge of these practices, and it seeks corroborative evidence from a variety of sources.

Books themselves are one source of secondary evidence, for they contain statements about themselves. Title pages and copyright pages, for example, often list dates, printers, publishers, and the like, but it should be remembered that this secondary evidence is not always reliable. The earliest date in an English printed book, M. CCCC. LXVIII (1468), is now recognized as a misprint for M. CCCC. LXXVIII (1478). The first edition of Pope's *Dunciad* (1728) appeared, anonymously, with a title page falsely claiming that it was a reprinting of an earlier Dublin edition. E. B. Browning's *The Runaway Slave at Pilgrim's Point*, despite its title page, was not published by Chapman and Hall in 1849; the book is a forgery by T. J. Wise and was probably printed in 1888. The Warner paperback of Carl Bernstein and Bob Woodward's *All the President's Men* claiming to be the "First Printing: February, 1975" was available from retail bookstores at least as early as 17 December 1974.

Other secondary evidence derives from a wide variety of sources. The records and archives of printers and publishers, for example, are invaluable, and some have been deposited in research libraries or made more widely available in microform. Records of copyright often contain information on the date, authorship, and manufacture of books. Many of these are available in print: *A Transcript of the Registers of the Company of Stationers* (i.e., of the guild that controlled the English book trade) has been edited for the years 1554–1640 by Edward Arber and for 1640–1708 by George E. B. Eyre, and a record of American copyrights since 1891 appears in the *Catalog of Copyright Entries*. Similarly useful are the publishing industry's trade lists, such as the *Term Catalogues, 1668–1709*, edited by Edward Arber, and the well-known *Publishers' Trade List Annual* (1874–) and *Books in Print* (1948–). For an understanding of printing methods used during various periods, analytical bibliographers consult contemporary printers' manuals, such as Joseph Moxon's *Mechanick Exercises on the Whole Art of Printing* (1683–84) and W. Savage's *A Dictionary of the Art of Printing* (1841). And they consult retrospective studies of book production and trade, such as R. B. McKerrow's *A Dictionary of Printers and Booksellers in England, Scotland, and Ireland, and of Foreign Printers of English Books, 1557–1640*, Daniel B. Updike's *Printing Types: Their History, Forms, and Use*, James Moran's *Printing Presses: History and Development from the Fifteenth Century to Modern Times*, Rollo Silver's *The American Printer, 1787–1825*, and Marjorie Plant's *The English Book Trade: An Economic History of the Making and Sale of Books*. In other words, the vast body of material for the study of the history of books—their materials, manufacture, and sale—has obvious relevance for analytical bibliography.

Among the sources of physical evidence are the ingredients and form of paper. The manufacture of book paper requires some type of fiber and a sizing to stiffen the fiber and prevent the feathering of wet ink. Coatings, pigments, and fillers of various types may also be added. Microscopy can sometimes identify the kinds of fibers or fillers used in a particular sample of paper, and relatively simple chemical tests can reveal these and other constituents as well. For example, a solution of phloroglucinol dropped on a piece of paper reveals the presence of mechanically pulped wood fibers by reacting with their lignin and turning red or magenta, the deepness of the color serving as a rough indication of the amount present. Similar tests can detect alum, rosin, starch, animal glue, and casein. In addition to differentiating between two stocks of paper, these tests may establish the earliest date a paper, and thus a book, could have been manufactured, because it is known when certain ingredients were introduced in papermaking: for instance, soda wood pulp in 1845, mechanical wood pulp in 1869, esparto grass in 1861, chemically pulped wood in 1874, rosin in 1835, clay filler in 1870 (Browning 335–36).

Such qualitative analysis of paper served John Carter and Graham Pollard in their well-known exposure of the forgeries of T. J. Wise (see also Barker and Collins). Among the activities, respectable and not, to which Wise devoted his skill was the forgery of more than fifty pamphlets containing works by Ruskin, Swinburne, Tennyson, Kipling, the Brownings, and others. Dated earlier than previous publications of the works and appearing in limited editions, these pamphlets fetched handsome prices in the rare-book trade and made their way into standard bibliographies of these authors' works, some of the bibliographies compiled by Wise himself. Carter and Pollard discovered that though esparto grass was not used in book papers before 1861 and chemical wood pulp not before 1874, some of the pamphlets bearing earlier dates had been printed on paper containing these ingredients. E. B. Browning's *Runaway Slave*, for example, could not have been printed in 1849, as its title page claimed, for its paper could not have been manufactured until some time after 1874.

Papermaking processes also leave their traces. Until the early nineteenth century, book paper was handmade, produced with sievelike molds dipped into vats of pulped rags. The molds were rectangular frames with closely spaced wires running lengthwise and larger wires ("chains") running across at intervals of about twenty-five millimeters. One can see this pattern of wires if one holds such paper (called "laid" paper) up to the light. Usually also visible are watermarks, which were created when designs were fixed with wire into the center of one half of the mold. (Beginning in the sixteenth century, extra marks, called "countermarks," were sometimes placed in the other half of the mold.) In the early nineteenth century, "wove" paper became common. It was first made by hand, with molds that used a woven wire mesh. Shortly thereafter, wove paper was made by machine, to which was sometimes attached a dandy roll that imposed watermarks and even what look like wire and chain lines.

Because watermarks and countermarks were used variously (at various times) to indicate the papermill, size of sheet, quality of paper, and date of manufacture, they are obvious bits of bibliographical evidence and are recoverable even from heavily printed sheets by a beta-radiographic process (for a description of the process, see Simmons, "Delft" and "Leningrad"; Barnes). In the early years of the New Bibliography, for example, investigations by Pollard, Greg ("On Certain False Dates"), and William Neidig proved that a number of Shakespeare's quartos bore false dates. The presence of identical watermarks in quartos dated 1600, 1608, and 1619, when combined with other physical evidence, indicated that the suspect quartos had all been printed in 1619 by Pavier. Until the revelation, some of the misdated quartos had been regarded as first editions or as editions derived from rival manuscripts.

A more complex use of watermark evidence is found in A. H. Stevenson's *The Problem of the Missale Speciale*. A missal, often called the Constance Missal, had been the subject of great controversy since the first description of a copy in 1898. Many scholars thought it to predate the Psalter of 1457 and even the Gutenberg Bible of 1455, making it possibly the earliest extant book printed from movable type. Others, using typographical or liturgical evidence, offered dates ranging up to the 1480s. Although there had been some mention of paper evidence, it was not used with thoroughness and understanding until

Stevenson's investigation. Examining the four extant copies of the missal, Stevenson identified its paper molds through the watermarks and the sewing dots that showed where the watermarks had been attached to the wires and chains of the molds. Finding paper from the same molds in eleven other books, all from the 1470s, Stevenson narrowed the possible range of dates. Then, tracing the variant states of the watermarks in the missal and other books—states resulting from deterioration of the marks—and joining this evidence with that of colophons, rubrication dates, type styles, bindings, and liturgical history, he arrived at the date of 1473.

The other principal kind of physical evidence is that of type—or, more accurately, the inked impressions made by type or plates. Ink itself has been little used in analytical bibliography. Its potential, though, can be seen in recent attempts to employ cyclotron analysis to determine the chemical "fingerprints" of ink in early books. Similar analysis of the so-called Vinland map of 1400 has produced mixed results. Initial analysis of the ink on this map, which was for some time thought to prove that the Norse had reached North America before Columbus did, suggested that it was a forgery, containing titanium-based pigments not manufactured until after 1920 (McCrone). Further analysis found only traces of titanium, not enough for it to be a pigment base (Cahill). Thus the matter of date remains unsettled.

It has been the image, not the ink, that has chiefly concerned bibliographers. It is, for example, a clue to the printing process used in a book. Under a hand lens, an image printed by type or relief plates has edges containing a ring of ink; by gravure, edges that are serrated; and by offset, edges that are smooth and evenly inked. The image is also, so to speak, the fingerprint of the type used to create it: it identifies the type and ornaments. Records of various fonts and styles of type used in particular times and places sometimes appear in type-specimen books, in studies of type and typefounders, and indirectly, of course, in other books using the same kind of type. Especially in the early handpress period, printers' woodcut ornaments and to some extent even their stocks of type tended to be unique, thus serving to identify their work or, since printers sometimes lent ornaments to other printers, serving to indicate relationships within the book trade. Identification of both a type font and a printer's unique stock assisted Carter and Pollard in exposing the Wise forgeries. Some sixteen suspect pamphlets employed a kernless type—that is, a type in which the ascending or descending portions of letters like *f* and *j* do not extend beyond the body of the type. Though bearing dates of 1842 through 1873, the pamphlets must have been printed after 1883, when such kernless type came into use. Carter and Pollard also noticed that the type used in some pamphlets, such as E. B. Browning's *Sonnets* ("1847"), came from a mixed font: to the kernless type had been added a peculiar question mark from another font. This mixed font probably belonged only to one printer. Finding it also present in a reprint of Matthew Arnold's *Alaric at Rome* (1893), Carter and Pollard concluded that its printer, Richard Clay and Sons Ltd., had also printed the spurious pamphlets. The kind of work done by Carter and Pollard is now being facilitated by digitalization of type and other graphic features of books.

The other major source of primary evidence, in addition to the materials of the book, is that left by the processes of composition (setting the type), imposition (arranging the pages of type for the printing of sheets), proofing (finding and correcting errors of composition), and presswork (printing of the sheets). Some of the traces left by these processes may be inadvertent, but they are nonetheless useful. A "new edition" of Byron's *Don Juan*, cantos 1 and 2, bears the date 1822 and the imprint of John Murray. But on the verso of the title page in at least one copy, there is faintly printed another title page—one from an 1824 edition of cantos 15 and 16 and with the imprint of John Hunt (Poe A27c.2). How did this happen? We know that after printing one side of a sheet (or stack of sheets) and before printing the other side, a printer would have to let the ink set or use additional sheets to protect the press; otherwise, the printed image would be transferred to the tympan (a parchment-backed frame used to hold the sheet when printing) and then be set off onto the next sheet printed. Setoff might also result from contact of two sheets. Such setoff evidently occurred when the supposed 1822 edition and the 1824 edition were being printed concurrently. Unable to publish legally the first five cantos because Murray held the copyright, Hunt resorted to piracy. The 1822 edition is actually an 1824 edition, and it is Hunt's, not Murray's. Thus it is often not the regularities but the irregularities of books that serve as evidence as to their production. A further example is provided by William B. Todd (*Gutenberg*), who sees certain anomalies of the Gutenberg Bible as indicating compositional fidelity to the manuscript used as printer's copy. (See also Needham, who uses a wide range of bibliographical evidence to dispute Todd's hypothesis.) Todd observed that one copy of this first book to be printed from movable type had on one page two pairs of reversed lines. Indeed, the pairs were in identical positions in the two columns on the page. This coincidence suggested to him that composition must have proceeded not down one column and then the other but rather across the two columns. For that to be true, the compositors would have had to be following their manuscript copy quite closely, line by line and page by page. The Gutenberg Bible, like other early printed books, would in a sense be an imitation manuscript, even a type facsimile of a specific manuscript. If so, Todd has argued, then its much-discussed variation in numbers of lines per page, previously accounted for by postulating a laborious process of twice filing down thousands of individual pieces of type, may well be instead an artifact of the manuscript it reproduces.

Using the evidence left by the processes of production requires a knowledge of when, where, and how the processes were employed and of the possible significance of deviations from "normal" practice. Certain habits or practices of composition, for example, are peculiar to particular times and places. Even the bibliographically uninitiated recognize the long *s* (*ſ*) as uncharacteristic of modern printing, since it died out in the late eighteenth and early nineteenth centuries. It is used occasionally nowadays, to provide a cultivated quaintness, but it is likely to reveal itself as modern. Several years ago, a restaurant called the Fyfe and Drum sought to enhance its Revolutionary War atmosphere by sporting long *s* in its menus. The prices alone served to date the menu, of course, but the long *s* was fishy too. The modern compositor had used it throughout, unaware that earlier printers used short s at the ends of words and generally before the letters *b, k,* and *f.* Another obvious example of differences in compositorial (or editorial) practice is that between British and American style. A recent book with the spellings *honour, arse,* and *connexion,* with single quotation marks enclosing simple quotations, and with periods and commas occurring outside the closing quotation mark (at least when not part of the quotation) was probably set into type in England rather than in the United States. Similarly but somewhat less obviously, as R. A. Sayce has shown, compositors' practices in setting catchwords, signatures, page numbers, and dates can identify the locality and period in which a book was printed. For example, a handpress book with page numbers enclosed in square brackets is almost certainly English and probably of the eighteenth century, while one with numbers enclosed in ornaments is almost certainly German.

Another kind of compositor study seeks to identify the compositor or compositors who set the type for some book or books. Until spelling began to be standardized in the mid-eighteenth century, compositors spelled according to their tastes and felt no great need to preserve the spelling of their copy. While one compositor in a printshop might prefer such spellings as *sweete, young, traytor, mistresse,* and *suddenly,* another might prefer *sweet, yong, traitor, mistris,* and *sodainely.* Compositors' habits could also differ in the abbreviation of dramatic speech prefixes, in the punctuation of abbreviations, in the use of italic (e.g., for names in a roman text), in spacing before and after punctuation, in the lineation of verse, in capitalization, and in the placement of signatures on pages. Compositor study is greatly aided—and its textual applications become clearer—when compositors' work can be compared to the copy that they followed. Such comparison reveals the compositors' level and kind of accuracy—the extent to which they were prone to substitution, omission, transposition, and "correction." This knowledge is of obvious use to the textual critic who must decide whether and how to emend a text set by a particular compositor.

Composition cannot be isolated from imposition or for that matter from the other processes of book production. If we assume, for example, that efficient production would require a balance between composition and presswork, then the method of doing one would directly affect the other. Otherwise, the press and its operators would stand idle while the compositors worked, and vice versa. To some extent, then, imposition mediates between composition and presswork. As such it reflects backward to reveal how, by whom, and in what order the pages of type were composed, and it reflects forward to reveal the order in which the formes (or assembled type pages) were printed, the possibility of delays in printing, and the extent and method of proofing. Imposition is the arrangement of pages of set type within a rectangular frame called a chase so that a sheet printed from the arrangement could be folded to produce a gathering (or part of a gathering) with its pages in the correct order. We discuss various schemes of imposition in our chapter on descriptive bibliography. Here, though, we can use the example of one scheme for imposing sheets in quarto. Since a sheet of paper has two sides, our scheme requires two formes, the "outer" forme for pages 1, 4, 5, and 8 and the "inner" forme for pages 2, 3, 6, and 7 (see fig. 1). Around each set of type pages would be fixed a "skeleton" forme—that is, the chase in which the type pages were locked up for printing, the wooden "furniture" used to hold the type, the wedges ("quoins") used to tighten the fit, and the typographical matter used in the headlines, including running titles and page numbers.

Although our quarto would require two formes for printing, it would not necessarily require two chases or two sets of headlines and wooden furniture—or, in the printer's jargon, two skeletons. For after printing from one forme, the printer could rinse the skeleton and then use it to enclose the other. An examination of headlines indicates that some books were printed with but one skeleton, others with two or more. The clue to the number of skeletons used in printing a book, then, is the number of sets of headlines, since a set of headlines would migrate with the skeleton as it was used in a sequence of formes.

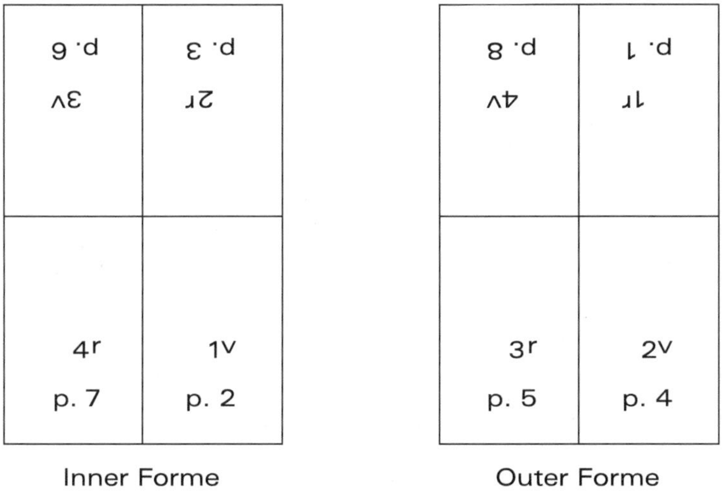

| | Inner Forme | | Outer Forme |

FIG. 1. *Imposition for a sheet in quarto.*

The individual headlines, at least in pre-nineteenth-century books, can often be identified—and their recurrence throughout the sheets of the book traced—by their spelling, capitalization, punctuation, spacing, type font, or broken or otherwise unique pieces of type. A headline used in page 2 of an inner forme might reappear on page 4 of the outer forme of the same sheet if the book was printed with one skeleton. Of course, using but one skeleton would cause delay. Unless some other book was being printed concurrently, the press would be idle while the skeleton was rinsed and transferred to the next forme. To avoid delay, the printer might use two skeletons (and thus two sets of headlines), one for each forme of a sheet. These two sets can also be traced through a book. The skeleton used for the inner forme might appear again on the inner forme of the next sheet, and so on. Analytical bibliography attempts to determine the pattern in which headlines occur, to detect deviations from the pattern—deviations of headline position within successive formes, of the whole set in the sequence, and within individual headlines—and to draw various conclusions from the pattern and deviations.

If, for example, the pattern of headline recurrence in a book indicates two skeletons, the bibliographer can make tentative conclusions about the proofing that the book may have undergone (and thus about the accuracy of the text and the kinds of emendations that an editor may or may not have to make). Collating multiple copies of such a book may reveal that, in every sheet, one forme (i.e., one side of the sheet) contains textual variants indicating proof correction, while the other forme is invariant. This pattern of variant and invariant formes, coinciding with the pattern of two-skeleton printing, may be quite regular, as when all inner formes bear textual variants and all outer formes lack them. This pattern might seem to suggest that, for some reason, the outer formes did not undergo proof correction. But more likely they did. In "Elizabethan Proofing," Fredson Bowers outlines the printing and proofing sequence that produced sheets made up of variant and invariant formes in two-skeleton printing. After imposition, the first sheet printed from the inner forme would be used for proofing, but printing continued until the proofing was completed. At that time, the forme would be removed from the press and corrected. Meanwhile, the outer forme, which was being imposed while the inner forme was being printed, was placed on the press and a sheet printed for proofing. It was removed from the press for correction and replaced by the corrected inner forme for further printing. The outer forme was corrected and returned to the press after the printing of the inner forme. Thus the presence of invariant formes does not rule out proofing. In our example, both formes were proofed, but only one (the inner) would show proof correction because only it was at one stage printed in an uncorrected state.

The analysis of headlines has further applications. Suppose that a particular headline appears in gatherings A through D with a misprint and then in gatherings E through M with the misprint corrected. It would seem that gatherings A through D were composed, imposed, and printed before the others. Compositors working from manuscript generally set the preliminaries (title page, preface, etc.) after the rest of the book; since in this book the first gathering (A), containing the preliminaries, was evidently set before gatherings E–M, the book may well be a reprint of an earlier edition and not a direct descendant of a manuscript. Bibliographers may also infer the order of composition from headline variation, such as that seen in the progressive deterioration of or damage to type used in a headline or that caused by the failure to alter running titles to reflect changes in the contents of a book. And the presence of a headline unique to a particular leaf (or leaves) may indicate that the leaf is a cancel—that a leaf has been excised and replaced by another. Similarly, a whole gathering with headlines unrepeated in any other may be a cancel, the work of another compositor, or a sheet from an earlier edition. These inferences from headline analysis are often tentative, but they can be strengthened by corroborative evidence from paper, typography, compositorial habits, and other sources.

Because of its painstaking use of bibliographical analysis, Charlton Hinman's *The Printing and Proof-reading of the First Folio of Shakespeare* can serve as a textbook in method. Studies of the Folio have been of two kinds. One, largely textual though employing bibliography, has sought to identify the setting copy used for each of the thirty-six plays, whether it is "good" quarto, "bad" quarto, corrected quarto, scribal fair copy, Shakespeare's foul papers, or some combination of these. The other is more strictly bibliographical, attempting to enter the printing shop of Isaac Jaggard to observe the processes that produced the book. This kind of study also has textual applications, of course, for it may reveal the nature and extent of modifications the copy received during printing.

Hinman addressed himself to this second kind of study. Using a device of his own design (the Hinman collator), he compared multiple copies of the Folio and uncovered a great body of useful evidence, consisting mostly of textual variants and identifiable, recurrent pieces of type. Joined with other evidence and with reasonable assumptions about printing-shop practices, the results of his machine collation became the basis for conclusions about the number of copies printed, the number of presses used, the number of compositors and the parts set by each, the order in which parts were set, the type cases used by each compositor, the time taken in printing, the delays in printing, and the way the book was proofread and corrected. If Hinman did not get through the door of Jaggard's shop, he certainly achieved a good view from a window.

A central finding of Hinman's was that Jaggard set the book by formes rather than by successive pages. The Folio is so called because of its imposition format: pages of type were arranged so that each printed sheet was folded once to create two leaves, a total of four pages. Beyond that, the 1623 folio is in sixes—that is, each gathering consists of three quired folio sheets (see fig. 2).

One might expect that the compositors would begin setting type with the first page and then progress to the twelfth; they did not. Hinman identified about six hundred pieces of distinctively damaged type that recurred in the Folio, some over one hundred times (for a total of 13,000 or so appearances). He found certain pieces not only in various six-leaf gatherings but also within one gathering, even within the first seven pages of a gathering. If a type appears on, say, page 1 and then again on page 5 of the same gathering, then the pages of the gathering could not have been set successively. For page 1 would be printed with page 12, its pair in the outer forme of the sheet. The type would then have to be returned to the case (i.e., distributed) before it could be used for setting and printing page 5. Thus, Hinman concluded, the Folio was set by formes. Page 1 was not set before page 5, though. Since a particular piece of type cannot occur in two consecutive formes (one being on the press while the other was being set), the pattern of recurrence indicated that most of the gatherings were set from the inside out: the inner forme of sheet 3 (pp. 6, 7), then the outer (pp. 5, 8), then the inner forme of sheet 2 (pp. 4, 9), and so on to the outer forme of sheet 1 (pp. 1, 12). Needless to say, this procedure required some calculation if the text were to fit into the pages. Faulty casting off, as the calculations are called, could result in either too much or too little text for the space available—a problem solved in some instances by altering the text by setting prose as verse to take up extra space, deleting spaces between words to

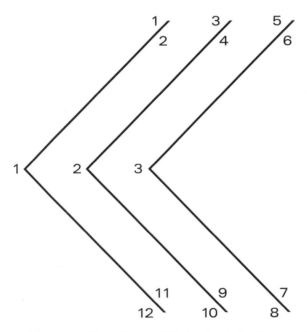

F I G . 2 . *Folio in sixes. Three sheets are folded and quired to form a gathering of six leaves, or twelve pages.*

force text into a smaller space while relineating verse (as in the hypermetrical line "Will fate it felfe in a Celeftialbed,& prey on garbage" in *Hamlet*), and omitting words and perhaps lines. (For an application of Hinman's findings, see Prosser.)

Although Hinman's identification of the Folio's compositors and the portions set by each has been subject to argument and revision, his method is exemplary. He identified five compositors. The two who set most of the Folio were Compositor A (who preferred the spellings *doe, goe,* and *here*) and Compositor B (who preferred *do, go, heere*). Combining spelling evidence with that of types revealed that three type cases (each actually a complex of four cases) were used and that the cases could be assigned to compositors—for example, Case Y to Compositor B. Thus when spelling alone did not identify the compositor of a particular forme, the case might. If we know which compositor set what and if we know the habits of the compositors (e.g., that Compositor B made more errors than A and "took frequent and various liberties with his copy" [1: 10]), then we can better recover what Shakespeare actually wrote. What might appear to be an authorial alteration may in fact be a compositor's characteristic and perhaps ingenious misreading.

Hinman also found hundreds of textual variants that resulted from proof corrections (which occurred simultaneously with the printing). For two formes the press was stopped three times for correction. Most proofreading, he discovered, was "confined to some six or eight plays in one section" and largely to the work of one compositor, E, who may have been an apprentice (1: 227). Moreover, the proofing, generally late and careless, was concerned more with typographical appearance than with accuracy of text. The corrector, who may have been Jaggard himself, sometimes consulted copy, sometimes not.

One of the important features of Hinman's work was the notice it took of concurrent printing (what other books Jaggard was printing just before, during, and just after the Folio). Following Hinman's example, Peter W. M. Blayney is engaged in a study of the texts of *King Lear*, especially the Quarto edition. The first volume of Blayney's *The Texts of* King Lear *and Their Origins* is *Nicholas Okes and the First Quarto*. Blayney's study of the printer Nicholas Okes and the work he undertook in the years 1604–09, including the Quarto of *Lear* in 1608, is far too detailed to elaborate here, for there are over 350 pages of appendixes concerned with a checklist of Okes's books, original documents, illustrations, recurrent type in Lear, recurrent type in other Okes books, and other matters. But Blayney's work, like Hinman's, clearly demonstrates two things about analytical bibliography. First, it shows how detailed bibliographic analysis is inevitably tied to historical bibliography, with each discipline informing and supporting the other. Second, it shows how these disciplines provide information of use to both textual and literary critics. For more than 250 years editors have presented the text of *Lear* in a version that took readings from both the

Quarto and the Folio and that became the basis for literary criticism. Starting in 1980, however, there has been much debate about whether the Quarto and the Folio of *Lear* contain two texts of the same play or whether they contain two versions of it—in effect, two plays on the same subject by the same author. Much of the textual and critical evidence is set forth in *The Division of the Kingdoms: Shakespeare's Two Versions of* King Lear, a collection of essays edited by Gary Taylor and Michael Warren. Although most of the essays are obvious examples of textual criticism informed by analytical bibliography (e.g., Paul Werstine's "Folio Editors, Folio Compositors, and the Folio Text of *King Lear*"), others are the sort of revisionist literary criticism that has become more prevalent and will probably change following generations' critical thinking about the play or plays (e.g., Warren's "The Diminution of Kent"). Indeed, because of the confluence of bibliographical, textual, and critical arguments, the Oxford Shakespeare edited by Taylor and Stanley Wells (1986) prints two texts of *Lear*, one based on the Quarto and one on the Folio, and the *Norton Shakespeare* (1997), edited by Stephen Greenblatt and others, follows the Oxford edition in printing the Folio and Quarto texts but prints a conflated text as well.[1]

Taxonomy

Hinman and Blayney analyzed only single editions, but many of their methods, as well as those discussed earlier, can also be used in identifying and organizing the multiple editions and other forms that constitute a printing history. Again, the aim may be textual: to discover the relations between a text and its physical embodiments. It may be literary historical: to investigate, for example, the popularity of a work by determining the number of its editions. It may be bibliophilic: to aid the collector in acquiring all forms of a book. Or it may be purely bibliographical: to provide a basis of organization for a descriptive bibliography. Regardless of aim, the problem is to determine what the forms of a book are and how they are related. This task requires analytical bibliography, since the concepts used—edition, impression, state, and issue—are defined according to printing processes and are detectable through examination of physical evidence.

An edition, in the strict bibliographical sense, consists of all copies of a book that are printed from one setting of type, whether directly from the type or indirectly through plates made from it. (Modern phototypesetting creates an image without actually setting any metal type. All copies that reproduce the same image, though it may be photographically enlarged or reduced, belong to the same edition.) Since the act of typesetting defines an edition, identifying different editions requires the detection of different settings of type. However, an edition may—and often does—consist of copies not entirely identical to one another. During and between pressruns, for example, the type or plates used for the edition may be damaged. There may also be changes in the text, as when type or plates are corrected or revised. Such changes do not create a new edition unless they are so extensive as to result in a substantially new typesetting. Evidence that a new typesetting has taken place and thus that a new edition has been created includes alterations in typefaces, type size, and distribution of text on the pages. Even when one edition is a line-for-line resetting of another, it will contain variations, at least in the spacing of letters and words.

Within an edition there may be several impressions (also called printings and pressruns), each consisting of all copies of an edition that are printed at any one time. Often, detecting different impressions is difficult, since the type may be unchanged. But if the set type has been considerably revised, one is probably dealing with a new impression. If some copies of an edition are printed on a stock of paper different from that used in others (different in watermark, distance between chain lines, thickness, color, ingredients, etc.), they may be a different impression, but this evidence is suggestive rather than conclusive, since two or more stocks may be used within a single impression. If, however, the first impression was known to be printed in 1850 and if some copies of the book are found with paper dated after that, then those copies obviously belong to another impression. A change in scheme of imposition is also evidence of a new impression. One impression may have its pages imposed to form gatherings of eight leaves, while another has its pages arranged for gatherings of sixteen. Even without such a change in imposition format, there are likely to be measurable differences in the impositions of two impressions, especially in the "gutter" margins (the sum of the inner margins of two conjugate pages).

Until the development of stereotype plating in the early nineteenth century, editions generally consisted of but one impression. (Type for most books was too scarce and expensive to be kept standing; if, after printing one impression, publishers needed more copies of a book, type would have to be set again.) Plating is often detectable. As Peter Shillingsburg has shown, for example, plates cast in plaster produce a type page slightly smaller than the type itself, since both the molds and the metal cast in them tend to shrink, and twentieth-century photo-offset plates may reduce or enlarge the type-page image photographically ("Detecting"). Distinguishing between multiple impressions printed from one set of plates requires the same evidence as distinguishing between impressions printed from type. And because plates, like type, were subject to damage and because the greatest damage would occur in handling and storage between impressions, the presence of damage also suggests a new impression, as does resetting to repair the damage.

Within an impression there may be two or more states. These may result from alterations in the type or plates during the printing of an impression, often through stop-press corrections. Or they may result later from a number of other causes, such as the insertion of an errata slip or the removal, or cancellation, of a leaf (which may be replaced by another). Often it is more accurate to assign states to sheets or even formes, since a particular copy of an impression may contain any of several combinations of corrected or uncorrected parts. An impression may also consist of more than one issue, an issue being all copies of an impression that are identifiable as a separate unit of sale. Unit of sale, of course, implies publishing rather than printing history, but for such a unit to be identifiable, it must contain some physical feature derived from its production. Often this feature is a variant title page, listing perhaps a different publisher or date, or it may be a cheaper or more expensive paper. Sometimes publishers take a certain number of copies of an impression, insert an extra page stating that the book is a "limited edition" and bearing the author's signature, and then sell these copies to collectors. Thus they create two issues—a limited issue and a trade issue—of one impression.

Our taxonomy of editions, impressions, issues, and states reflects printing and publishing history only if we also know the chronological sequence of these forms. A time-honored rule for determining the order of editions is that the handsomest is the first. The first edition establishes the reputation of the book. Subsequent editions can rely more on that reputation and less on appearance to gain buyers, and less handsome and therefore cheaper editions will appeal to another sector of the market. Thus today an edition bound in cloth and enclosed in a colorful jacket generally precedes the cheaper, smaller-sized paperback edition. So too in, say, the seventeenth century the first edition might have been printed in a large format (e.g., folio), while later editions might have appeared in quarto, octavo, or sixteenmo. The first might have a two-color title page and blank pages between textual divisions, while later editions would have one-color title pages and few blank pages.

The care taken over the appearance of the first edition tends also to extend to the composition and printing. Later editions often have more misprints, and thus textual readings can aid in the determination of sequence. The kind of misprints may also be significant. Ronald B. McKerrow's *Introduction to Bibliography for Literary Students*, published in the 1920s but still a good introduction to analytical bibliography, presents an example from Nashe's *Pierce Penilesse*, three editions of which were published in 1592.

> Edition A: 'frantick'
> Edition B: 'fran- / tick'
> Edition C: 'fran-tick'   (196)

Edition A, known on other evidence to be first, prints the word midway in a line. It was followed by edition B, which broke the word between two lines. The compositor of edition C evidently used edition B as copy, setting the word midway in a line but incorrectly retaining the hypen.

Caution is required, however, in analyzing textual variants to determine the order of editions. Bibliographical taxonomy does not necessarily coincide with the textual stemma. The compositor or compositors setting type for a second edition could not use a third edition for their copy, but they might not have used the first edition either; they could have used the same manuscript that served as a copy for the first edition. Likewise, a fifth edition could have been set from any of four previous editions, from several editions, or from various manuscripts.

Naturally, a compositor would prefer to set from printed matter rather than from manuscript. Especially in the handpress period, it is sometimes possible to determine whether a book has been set from manuscript or is a "reprint" (not to be confused with reimpression) of a previously printed book. Again, McKerrow provides some general rules. Setting from a manuscript, a compositor generally began with the text itself rather than with the preliminaries (title page, preface, and the like), and thus would begin by setting the second gathering of the book. Whether the compositor began with the text or with the preliminaries can sometimes be inferred from the way the book is "signed"—that is, from the sequence of letters, numbers, or other symbols that the compositor placed at the foot of the initial leaves of gatherings to ensure their proper arrangement in binding. If an edition has signatures "all of one alphabet, beginning with A and proceeding regularly," according to McKerrow, it is "likely to be later than an edition in which the preliminary leaves have a separate signature" (190). Likewise, if the text of an edition starts on a leaf other than the first of a gathering, the edition is likely a reprint, for the compositor probably began setting with the preliminaries. A somewhat different application of McKerrow's observations can be made to these two editions of a book:

> Edition X. Consists of 18 gatherings, each with 4 leaves. The first gathering is signed A, the second, a, the rest B through S. The preliminaries end on leaf a4 (the fourth leaf of the gathering signed a); the text begins on leaf B1.
>
> Edition Y. It too consists of 18 gatherings of 4 leaves each. The first gathering is signed A, the second, B, and the rest, C through T. The text begins on leaf C1.   (Adapted from McKerrow 190)

Edition X may well have been set from manuscript. The compositor perhaps began setting the text with gathering B, leaving A for the preliminaries, which turned out to be longer than expected and so required the additional gathering a. Edition Y is likely a reprint; otherwise, the compositor may not have known that the text would begin in gathering C. Such conclusions can often be supported by further evidence. Suppose, for example, that in edition Y the second leaf of gathering E bears the incorrect signature D2 and that editions X and Y contain, page for page, the same distribution of printed matter. It is likely that, forgetting the new system of signatures (which eliminated the minuscule a signature), the compositor missigned the leaf while reprinting edition Y from edition X.

General rules have specific exceptions and must be used cautiously. They are not substitutes for thorough bibliographical analysis. It might appear, for example, that the 1594 quarto of Christopher Marlowe's *Edward II* is a reprint of a now lost edition. It has a collation formula of A–M^4 (twelve gatherings of four leaves each), with the text beginning on leaf A2. But, as Fredson Bowers has shown, it probably is an original edition, set from manuscript rather than from any earlier edition (see "Was There" and his introd. to *Edward II*). Although the text begins in sheet A, setting began in sheet B. Thus, as was usual with editions set from manuscript, the preliminaries were set last. One bit of evidence for this conclusion comes from the skeleton formes. Through the distinctive appearance of running titles, Bowers identified two skeleton formes in this quarto, one skeleton used for the inner forme of every sheet (the side containing pages 2, 3, 6, and 7) and the other for the outer forme. But a peculiar dislocation of the running titles in sheet A suggests that A was printed after M, since the dislocation resulted from three blank pages in sheet M. This evidence coincides with the pattern of recurrence of identifiable pieces of type. Types distributed from sheet B reappear in sheet D, types from C reappear in E, and so on to the end; then types from L reappear in A; but no sheet seems to have been set from distributed types of sheet A. Thus the preliminaries and the text of sheet A were set last. Further corroboration comes from the text and depends on the identification of the compositors. There were two. In addition to having different spelling habits, they differed in their practice of using signatures. Compositor X regularly supplied signatures for the first three leaves of his sheets (sigs. A–E), and Compositor Y regularly supplied them for the first two leaves of his (sigs. F–M). This information can then be applied to the question of whether the quarto is a reprint. There is considerable disparity between the two compositors' abilities to lineate the verse of Marlowe's play, Compositor Y mislining much more frequently than X. If the 1594 quarto were a reprint, the compositors would probably have followed the earlier edition's lineation and thus would not have produced the disparity (except in the unlikely event that the prior edition also had two compositors who set the same shares as X and Y did in 1594). On the basis of this bibliographical evidence, Bowers concludes that the 1594 quarto is a first edition set from manuscript and not a reprint of a lost earlier edition.

In recovering the sequence in which several editions were printed, the bibliographer can also use the evidence provided by progressive deterioration, or batter, of type and ornaments (just as Hinman used type batter within Shakespeare's First Folio to determine the order in which its parts were printed). A woodcut ornament, for example, may be in pristine condition in a first edition, slightly damaged in a second, and greatly damaged in a third. Such damage may also serve to date an edition, if the dates of other books using the ornament are known and if there is a clear progression of deterioration. Similarly, the progressive batter (and repair) of plates may both differentiate impressions and establish their sequence.

This sort of evidence from analytical bibliography, corroborated with publisher's records and other secondary evidence, reveals the history of the three 1850 editions of *The Scarlet Letter* published by Ticknor and Fields (see Bowers's introd. to *Centenary Edition*; Clark). The first edition consists of one impression, printed from type. It exists in two states, because gathering 21 was set in duplicate, presumably for more economical handling of this short final gathering. After the type for all gatherings through 13 and for part of gatherings 14 and 15 had been distributed, the publisher required additional copies of the novel. Resetting the portion already distributed and joining it with the undistributed type from gatherings 14 through 21, the printer manufactured more copies—a second edition, since the type was substantially reset. After the printing of these copies, the second-edition type was distributed. Later the same year, still more copies were wanted. Again type was set, creating a third edition, but this time stereotype plates were made from the type. One impression was printed from the plates in 1850 (followed by many more over the following years).

Bibliographically, it is not an especially remarkable or complex history. Yet it was unavailable until discovered by the bibliographical analysis undertaken for the *Centenary Edition* of Hawthorne. Textual critics have benefited from the demonstration that resetting and thus opportunities for textual variation occurred. There are sixty-nine variant readings between the first and second editions, for example. Literary historians now have some indication that, whatever enthusiasm James T. Fields may have expressed for the novel as a literary work, he must have harbored doubts about its prospective sales; otherwise he would have had plates made right from the start and would not have waited until the third setting of the type (Bowers, "Bibliography" 176). Collectors will be interested to know that the variously dated advertisements bound with the first-edition copies do not reflect the dates of the sheets. In short, all those who study materials transmitted through the medium of print can use the findings of analytical bibliography, even if only indirectly through its applications in descriptive bibliography and textual criticism.

Reading Books

Although in analytical bibliography researchers "read" the physical features of books primarily for evidence on the immediate production of the books and although the impetus for much bibliographical analysis has been its editorial application, these same physical features may also be read in wider critical and historical contexts. We may not be aware of it, but we read that way all the time, judging books by their covers. And publishers consciously design books for such reading. The 1925 edition of the Chicago *Manual of Style*, aimed at "those who are concerned with matters of typographical style," begins with this reminder: "A book, on its material side, is the visible embodiment of the subject it presents" (3). The materials and design of books and other documents convey meaning that should be relevant to studies of such subjects as authorship, genre, publishing, reading, and reception.

The link between book production and genre is, in fact, embedded in our language. We speak of "pulp fiction" (sensational, melodramatic tales of love and crime) because many such works were printed on cheap paper made from wood pulp. Similarly, the term "steam fiction" arose in the nineteenth century as steam-powered presses began to mass-produce books for an expanding market. Triple-deckers, three-volume novels much in vogue from the 1830s to the 1880s, also demonstrate the link between literary production and book production. Triple-deckers were expensive but well suited to subscription lending libraries. Most readers could not afford to buy them outright, the price being roughly equivalent to a skilled worker's weekly wage. But lending libraries, whose income from subscriptions depended on the number of volumes lent, could guarantee publishers a fairly stable, predictable market for triple-deckers. Publication in three volumes would, of course, have some influence on both writing and reading, implying a three-part structure of the novel to match that of the physical volumes. Furthermore, the economy of publishing would favor some uniformity of product, creating expectations for the length of the text. So an authors' manual of 1839 notes that for a triple-decker, each volume properly consists of 300 pages, each page containing 22 lines and these lines averaging 8 words.[2]

The relation of book materials and design to literary content may also be seen in a recent study of *The Yellow Book*, a quarterly series founded by Aubrey Beardsley and Henry Harland and published by John Lane from 1894 to 1897. This study, by Edward Bishop, argues that *The Yellow Book* was a commercial success in selling the decadent movement to the middle class by combining the risqué with the respectable and by appearing to be noncommercial. Bishop observes that the volumes appeared in yellow covers that visually associated them with contemporary editions of French novels and Continental decadence. And, of course, they were books, with all the authoritative heft of books as compared to magazines. While keeping the price low (5 shillings rather than the 6 shillings typical then for one-volume novels), the publisher sought respectability through the materials and design of the volumes. The paper, though cheap, had some rag content and the books were issued with their leaves uncut and unopened. The typesetting was produced by Linotype, which had just been developed the previous decade and was used more for newspapers than for books at the time. Yet the pages were supplied with catchwords, which had faded from use in the late eighteenth century. In both content and appearance, then, *The Yellow Book* was, in Bishop's words, "somewhat schizophrenic" (290)—Linotype cheek by jowl with catchwords, Beardsley's art jowl by cheek with Sir Frederick Leighton's attack on naturalism and decadence. The volumes, ostensibly aimed at aesthetes, sought its real readers among the mildly daring members of the middle class.

The significance of what has been called "bibliographical environment" has led some critics to call for a broadening of the concept of text to include the materials and design of documents.[3] One need not accept this broadened definition to admit two obvious facts: that even linguistically identical texts, when embodied in differing bibliographical forms, will be read differently and that the study of texts, even texts in a narrow sense, cannot be separated from the study of the material forms that have brought these texts to readers.

Notes

[1] For a judicious survey of the editorial treatment of Shakespeare, including the controversy attending the publication of the Oxford Shakespeare, see Werstine.

[2] [F. Saunders], *The Author's Printing and Publishing Assistant*, 2nd ed. (London, 1839) 9–10, cit. in Gaskell, *New Introduction* 301.

[3] See, e.g., McGann, *Beauty* and *Textual Condition*. For a useful reminder that reading bibliographical features requires knowledge of printing practices and of the methods of analytical bibliography, see Shef. Insufficiently informed by analytical bibliography but nonetheless useful is Levenston.

DESCRIPTIVE BIBLIOGRAPHY

*Now this is what I call workmanship. There is nothing on earth
more exquisite than a bonny book, with well-placed columns of
rich black writing in beautiful borders, and illuminated pictures
cunningly inset. But nowadays, instead of looking at books,
people read them.*

—*George Bernard Shaw,* Saint Joan *(1923)*

A conventional entry in an enumerative bibliography looks like this:

Styron, William. *The Confessions of Nat Turner.* New York: Random, 1967.

The entry makes no distinction between the first impression, the second impression (the text of which differs from that of the first in twelve readings), the third impression (with two more variant readings), the fourth impression (with twelve more), and the fifth (with another twelve) (West 94–106). It could refer to any or all. Scholars therefore need a more precise record of the forms in which the novel has been presented to the public. Such a record of books as books is provided by descriptive bibliography, the aim of which is to produce a thorough account of the physical characteristics of books (and other printed forms, such as periodicals) and of their history of production. Such accounts, called descriptive bibliographies, serve (1) to enable textual and literary critics to locate the physical forms containing the texts they study, (2) to provide a source of identification, a standard against which a particular copy of a book can be compared, (3) to classify the books according to bibliographical taxonomy and to present the evidence on which taxonomy is based, and (4) to contribute to the larger history of printing and publishing by investigating a portion of it.

If identification were the only purpose, much of the detail found in descriptive bibliographies could be dispensed with. Often, a few points will serve to differentiate multiple editions, impressions, issues, and states. The presence of these points (a misprint, a particular watermark, the position of a signature, etc.) in the copy at hand would identify the book. But this assumes that the bibliographer has managed to examine and record every possible form of the book. And even if the bibliographer has done that, a description consisting of mere points of identification would fail to provide a printing, publishing, and textual history of use to literary critics and historians, textual critics, and other bibliographers. In a descriptive bibliography one could learn, for example, that the second edition of Louis Untermeyer's *Modern American Poetry* (1921) appeared in a size and in a grayish-green binding that make it seem, in looks as well as in contents, an imitation of *The New Poetry* (1917), a successful anthology edited by Harriet Monroe and Alice Corbin Henderson.

A descriptive bibliography would indicate that Marianne Moore's poem "Sun" (or poems, since there are several revisions) first appeared in the little magazine *Contemporary Verse* in January 1916; was omitted from her first collection, *Poems* (1921); appeared in the second edition of Monroe and Henderson's *The New Poetry* (1923); appeared the following year in Moore's second collection, *Observations* (1924), but with the title "Fear Is Hope"; did not appear in Moore's *Selected Poems* (1935) or *Collected Poems* (1951); reappeared in *The Mentor Book of Religious Verse* (1957); appeared with poems of more recent composition in *A Marianne Moore Reader* (1961); appeared as the final poem in Moore's *Tell Me, Tell Me* (1966), which is described by the dust jacket as containing "NEW POEMS AND PROSE" and where the poem is noted as having first appeared in *The Mentor Book of Religious Verse*; was collected again, as one of Moore's in a section titled "Later Poems," in Moore's incomplete *Complete Poems* (1967); and then appeared as the final poem in a new *Selected Poems* (1969). A descriptive bibliography would show that the first English impression of Styron's *The Confessions of Nat Turner* was printed from offset plates that were made by combining pages of two Random House impressions, thereby producing a bastard impression with both early and late stages of the text (which was further complicated by the English publisher's introducing other textual variants) (West 109–14). And such a bibliography would demonstrate, by identifying five different types used in the running titles, that Dekker's *Magnificent Entertainment* (1604), a quarto of thirty-six leaves, was evidently printed in five sections by as many different presses.

The kinds and amount of detail presented in a descriptive bibliography are determined, then, by its multiple purposes and by the materials dealt with. In general, whatever physical features may be useful in analytical bibliography are those given most attention in descriptive bibliography, both as evidence for the conclusions presented and as material for further analysis. Thus one finds collation formulas, records of running titles, and descriptions of paper and typography, for example.

How descriptions should be accommodated to the materials has been a matter of controversy, focused in discussions of the "degressive principle." This

phrase was used by Falconer Madan, who was writing before the flowering of
the New Bibliography. (For discussions of the principle, see Bowers, "Purposes"
and "Bibliography"; Tanselle, "Tolerances.") He meant by it that description
should vary according to the period or importance of the books being treated.
The principle is sound, the application difficult. For Madan it meant that incunables (books printed before 1501) required detailed descriptions and modern books almost none. In author bibliographies, the principle has been used as
a rationale for limiting the treatment given editions appearing after the author's
lifetime or containing nonauthoritative texts, though this practice has been crit-
icized for neglecting printing and publishing history. Not controversial, though,
is the principle that the kind of detail must vary with changes in the production processes. In modern printing, for example, there has been an increased
standardization and uniformity of product. Minute differences—often all that
distinguish multiple impressions—may be detected by machine collation (using
the Hinman collator or Lindstrand comparator), measurements of gutter margins, or other forms of analysis, and thus definitive descriptions of these books
must include such detail. So too must the specificity of detail suit the objects
described. Since variations of one to three millimeters in type-page size may indicate plating in nineteenth-century books, it does no good to report their
measurements merely to the nearest centimeter.

The degree of specificity, however, must not be so high as to make every
copy of a book (or every sheet or forme) a variant state. In bibliographical taxonomy as in biological, there are the "lumpers" and "splitters." Where lumpers
may see one state, splitters may see four. Yet both agree that descriptions should
give the range of variation and that states should be significant points within
the range—significant in that they reflect alterations (intended or not) in the
methods, materials, or circumstances of printing. Every copy of an edition is
unique in some way, however slight, but descriptive bibliographers do not describe particular copies: they describe the editions, impressions, issues, and
states, after examining as many particular copies as feasible. In doing so, they
are producing generalizations based on particular copies. These generalizations
are historical reconstructions of what is sometimes termed "ideal copy," which
has been defined thus by G. Thomas Tanselle:

> The *standard* or *"ideal"* copy [. . .] is a historical reconstruction of the form or
> forms of the copies of an impression or issue as they were released to the public
> by their producer. Such a reconstruction thus encompasses all states of an im-
> pression or issue, whether they result from design or accident; and it excludes
> alterations that occurred in individual copies after the time when those copies
> ceased to be under the control of the printer or publisher.   ("Concept" 46)

Fredson Bowers, on the other hand, referred to ideal copy as "the most perfect
state of the book as the printer or publisher finally intended to issue it" (*Princi-*

ples 113). Both definitions involve historical reconstruction—either of what was actually produced or of what was intended—and the recording of significant deviations of actual copies from ideal copy.

A full bibliographical description answers seven questions that more or less correspond to the divisions within it: (1) What is the book—what edition, for example? This question is answered in the heading of the description. (2) What does the book say about itself in the title page, colophon, copyright page, and other imprints? (3) How was the book put together? Considered here are the imposition format, collation formula, and pagination. (4) What does the book contain? (5) What is the book made of? What sort of type and paper were used? (6) How was the book packaged in a binding and dust jacket? (7) What is known, from bibliographical analysis and other sources, about the printing and publishing of the book, its variant states, and the irregularities of particular copies?

The descriptive methods that answer these questions have been standardized in Bowers's *Principles of Bibliographical Description*. There have also been recent elaborations and refinements, notably in a number of articles by G. Thomas Tanselle (listed in the reference bibliography). But it should be added that descriptive bibliographies have varied widely in the way they present information and in what information they present. Because of these variations, users of descriptive bibliographies should consult whatever introductory and explanatory matter these works contain. Our purpose here, as we consider the parts of bibliographical description corresponding to each of these questions, is to furnish not instruction in how to describe books but rather an introduction to some of the methods for those who may use descriptive bibliographies and for those who want an overview before reading further in the area. We should also point out that bibliographical descriptions appear not simply in descriptive bibliogaphies but also in a variety of bibliographical and textual studies, including scholarly editions.

Identification

Each entry in a descriptive bibliography begins with a heading that identifies the item and assigns it a number that indicates its position in the bibliography and serves as a means of precise reference in book catalogs, scholarly studies, and the bibliography itself. A typical author bibliography consists of several lettered sections within which chronology and bibliographical taxonomy serve as the bases of organization. The number and identifying nomenclature reflect that organization. Thus section A (separately published works) of C. E. Frazer Clark's Hawthorne bibliography gives the following headings for some entries described under A16, Hawthorne's sixteenth book:

A 16 THE SCARLET LETTER
A 16.1 First edition, only printing 1850
A 16.2 Second edition, only printing 1850
A 16.3.a Third edition, first printing (first plated edition) 1850
A 16.3.b Third edition, second printing 1851
A 16.3.c Third edition, third printing 1851

. . . .

A 16.13.a1 Riverside Edition (trade), first printing, American issue 1883
A 16.13.a2 Riverside Edition (trade), first printing, English issue 1883
A 16.13.b Riverside edition (large paper), second printing 1883   (141–48)

Title Pages and Imprints

Title pages, copyright pages, and colophons present information, some-times inaccurate, about authors, titles, dates and places of publication, publish-ers, printers, and so forth. In both the information conveyed and the typographical means of conveying it, these parts of books often serve as identi-fication. The title page can also be viewed as the book's public face, which, through the arrangement, selection, and emphasis of its features, can imply how the book was to meet and court its potential readers. In design and word-ing, for example, early title pages of Swift's *Travels into Several Remote Nations of the World*, commonly known as *Gulliver's Travels*, closely resembled those of authentic travel narratives enjoying great popularity in the early eighteenth cen-tury. For these reasons, title pages are often reproduced photographically, ren-dered in quasi facsimile, or presented in both ways.

The advantage of photographic reproduction is also its disadvantage. It pro-vides more information than quasi-facsimile transcription does, showing layout, typography, heaviness of inking, and so on. Yet some of what it shows will be pe-culiar to the individual copy photographed, and some will be an artifact of the reproductive method. Unlike quasi facsimile, it is not a description of ideal copy.

Quasi-facsimile transcription attempts to give a sense of the title page or other matter without reproducing it photographically. It transcribes the precise wording, including spelling, punctuation, and capitalization (though large and small capitals are differentiated only if they occur in the same line); reduces styles of type to three (roman, *italic*, and 𝔟𝔩𝔞𝔠𝔨 𝔩𝔢𝔱𝔱𝔢𝔯); and indicates line endings with a vertical stroke (ignoring variations in the spacing of lines). Especially in pre-eighteenth-century books, certain typographical features cause difficulty, in part because modern type fonts do not contain some types that were then com-mon. Thus some bibliographies ignore the distinction between long *s* ($\int$) and short *s* and do not reproduce ligatures (such as *ff* and *ſt*), though the digraphs *æ* and *œ* are usually reproduced. Swash (or scriptlike) letters, especially swash italic capitals *J* and *V*, are usually indicated, as are tailed italic letters (*n* and *m*). Even if lacking in modern fonts, such typographical features can be recorded by bracketed comments within the transcription, by description following it, or by special symbols (a tailed *m*, for example, may be indicated as *m*[.]). Within a transcription, the printing is assumed to be black unless otherwise noted. Such features as ornaments, rules, drawings, and devices are noted or described. Many title pages are enclosed in borders—either compartments (enclosures of single design and made up of an engraving or woodcut to form a single piece, even if later cut into more than one) or frames (enclosures of separate type ornaments, woodcuts, or rules pieced together). These borders are described and, if possible, identified in such standard references as R. B. McKerrow and F. S. Ferguson's *Title-Page Borders Used in England and Scotland, 1485–1640*. Whenever transcriptions cannot reproduce a required item, it is described in square brackets. These descriptions will vary according to the level of accuracy used in the bibliographies. One might describe a printer's rule merely as '[rule]', while another might write '[short rule]' and yet another write '[rule, 21 mm.]'. (Note that quotations of quasi facsimile are enclosed in single quotation marks to distinguish them from ordinary quotations.) Figure 4 shows Fredson Bowers's transcription of the title page in figure 3:

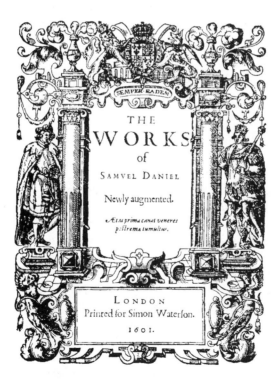

FIG. 3. *Title page.*

> [within a sected compartment: McK. & F. 229] THE |
> WORKS | of | SAMVEL DANIEL | Newly augmented. | *Ætas*
> *prima canat veneres | postrema tumultus.* | [within a slot] LON-
> DON | Printed for Simon Waterſon. | 1601. [WORKS *with*
> W *from filed* VV, *the first with shortened limb*]

FIG. 4. *Quasi-facsimile transcription of title page in fig. 3.*

Had a portion of the title page been in a color other than black, that fact would
be noted within brackets:

> THE | [red] WORKS | of | SAMVEL DANIEL |
> [black] Newly augmented. [. . .]

The color indicator applies to all items that follow it until a change is noted; in
the example, the second, third, and fourth lines are in red. (An alternative is to
begin the transcription with the notation '[in black and <u>red</u>]' and then under-
score the red portions.) Bibliographers sometimes indicate colors more precisely
by including a reference to the numbered color samples in the National Bureau
of Standards' color-name charts: '[dark red (16)]'. The same techniques of
quasi-facsimile transcription are applied to colophons (notes located at the ends
of books and giving information about their printing and publishing) and to
any other items, such as those on the copyright pages of modern books, that
give similar information.

Collation

To indicate how the leaves of a book were imposed and assembled, a bibliographical description presents a formula of its format and collation, which reflects how pages of type were arranged for printing sheets of paper and how,
after printing, these sheets were folded to make leaves and arranged within the
book. During the handpress period, the most common formats for the imposition of type pages were folio (2°), quarto (4°), octavo (8°), and duodecimo
(12°). (For these and other formats, see Gaskell, *New Introduction* 78–117.) If
we recall what paper from this period looks like, it is clear that the direction of
chain lines and position of the watermark are clues to imposition. As figure 5
shows, the chain lines of a folio run vertically on the leaves, and the watermark
is centered in one leaf (the countermark, if any, in the other).

In a quarto the sheet is folded twice to make four leaves (eight pages), with
the chain lines horizontal and the watermark in the middle of the spine fold

F IG. 5.   *Sheet of paper, with watermark on the left, countermark on the right, and vertical chain lines.*

(i.e., the gutter). In an octavo, the sheet is folded three times to produce eight leaves, with the chain lines vertical and the watermark at the head of the spine fold. For a duodecimo, also called twelvemo, the sheet can be folded (and perhaps cut) in several ways. In one (common 12°), it is folded twice across the longer dimension and thrice across the shorter, making twelve leaves; its chain lines will be horizontal, and the watermarks will appear toward the top of leaves 7 and 8 (or 11 and 12). In another (long 12°), the sheet is folded once across the short side and five times across the longer, making 12 leaves; its chain lines will be vertical, and the watermark will appear at the top of the outer margin of leaves 5 and 6 (or 11 and 12). In the machine-press period, imposition format is difficult or impossible to ascertain, because wove paper robs us of chain lines and because books are printed from multiple impositions on very large sheets or on rolls of paper. In descriptions of these books, therefore, the measurement of a typical leaf sometimes replaces the format notation in the formula.

From the example of Shakespeare's First Folio, it will be recalled that one sheet could be inserted (quired) into another after folding and before binding. Thus the Folio was a folio in sixes, each section (called a gathering) consisting of three folio sheets and thus six leaves. So too could a quarto sheet be quired with another to form a quarto in eights. Or, after a process called half-sheet imposition, a sixteen could be cut in half to form two gatherings of eight leaves each. In other words, the imposition format does not necessarily coincide with the scheme of gathering (though, of course, the type pages would have to be imposed so that their sequence would be correct after any quiring or cutting).

To aid binders in arranging the printed sheets (and to provide a means of reference when pagination or foliation was absent), compositors included marks called signatures toward the foot of the rectos (right-hand pages) of some leaves. A folio in sixes, for example, might have signatures on the rectos of leaves 1, 2, and 3 of each gathering. In England, the usual practice was and is to use as signatures the letters of the twenty-three-letter Latin alphabet (which omits *J, U,* and *W*). In American books, one may find the Latin alphabet, the twenty-six-letter alphabet, or numbers. The arrangement of sheets in gatherings can thus be expressed in a formula that uses the signatures to designate the gatherings and adds superscript figures to indicate the number of leaves in each gathering:

> 2°: A–H^6; 48 leaves.

Translated, this collation formula means that twenty-four folio sheets were arranged in eight gatherings (A–H), each gathering consisting of three sheets and thus six leaves and the whole book consisting of forty-eight leaves. If the signatures had been set in lowercase type or in numbers, these characters would replace the capitals:

> 2°: a–h^6; 48 leaves.
> 2°: 1–8^6; 48 leaves.

In books containing more than twenty-three gatherings and thus exhausting the alphabet, compositors usually began the alphabet anew with doubled letters (e.g., Aa or AA) and, if that group was exhausted, with tripled letters, and so on. A book with sixty-nine gatherings would thus have this formula:

> 2°: A–3Z^6; 414 leaves.

Within all examples so far, the gatherings have contained the same number of leaves. Often, however, there may be unequal gatherings:

> 2°: A^2 B–2E^4 2F–2G^2; 114 leaves.

It is also common to find books in which some gatherings are not signed. Often a signing can be inferred from the sequence and is indicated in square brackets or in italic:

> 2°: [A]^2 B–K^4 [L]^4 M–2E^4 2F^2 [2G]^2; 114 leaves.

or

> 2°: *A*^{2} B–K^4 *L*^{4} M–2E^4 2F^2 2*G*^{2}; 114 leaves.

If the unsigned gathering is preliminary and cannot be inferred, it is given as pi (π); if it appears elsewhere and cannot be inferred, it is given as chi (χ):

> 2°: π^2 A–G^4 χ^2 H–Z^4; 96 leaves.

The formula can even describe totally unsigned books or books in which the system of signing does not correspond to the actual folding. The bibliographer can identify the gatherings by knowing what sizes of gatherings are likely for the particular format and by locating the two conjugate leaves (and stitching) at the center of each gathering. In such a case the formula might look like this:

4°: [A]^2 [B–H]^4; 30 leaves.

or

4°: *A*^{2} *B–H*^{4}; 30 leaves.

The formula also takes account of leaves that have been added, removed, or removed and replaced by a cancel:

4°: A^8 (–A3) B–D^8 (±D7) E–F^8 (F6+1.2); 49 leaves.

In this example, leaf 3 of gathering A has been excised; leaf 7 of gathering D has been cancelled and a new leaf inserted in its place; and two conjugate leaves in gathering F have been added after leaf 6 (if the two added leaves were disjunct, a comma would replace the period, as in F6+1,2). The final item in the formula is a statement of where the signatures actually appear in each gathering:

4°: A–F^4; 24 leaves; $3 signed.

The dollar sign is simply a convenient notation for all gatherings. The number that follows it indicates the leaves that bear signatures. In this example, then, the first three leaves of each gathering are signed. Any irregularities in signing are also noted:

4°: A–F^4; 24 leaves; $3 signed (–A1, B3; +A4; F2 missigned 'G2').

The first three leaves in each gathering are signed, with the exception of leaves A1 and B3 and with the addition of leaf A4, and leaf F2 bears the wrong signature 'G2'.

Though not strictly part of the collation formula, a statement of pagination (or of foliation if leaves rather than pages are numbered) generally appears with it. Like the formula, this statement accounts for every leaf in the book. If every page were numbered, a pagination formula might look like this: pp. i–iv, 1–88. Often, however, some pages lack page numbers. If the numbers can be inferred, they are placed in square brackets or in italic; otherwise, the total number of adjacent numberless pages is reported by an italic figure in square brackets: [*2*] i–ii, [1–4] 5–88 pp. or [*2*] i–ii, *1–4* 5–88 pp. Misnumberings or misprintings of numbers are noted after the record of pagination.

Finally, for certain books, a record is made of press figures and catchwords. Press figures, in use from the late seventeenth through the early nineteenth centuries, appeared at the bottom of a page within a forme and marked that forme as the work of particular press or press operator. They are useful, therefore, in analyzing the presswork of a book; moreover, because the figures would be altered from impression to impression, they are useful for identification. How the figures are recorded varies from one bibliography to another, depending on what sort of chart, table, or list best exposes whatever pattern they make.[1] One method, not as revealing as a table, simply lists the figures and then the pages on which they appear:

> 1: A5r A7v C5r C7v
> 2: B3r B6r
> 3: D2v

Another procedure, recording the entries seriatim as page and figure (7–6, 14–2, etc.), quickly discloses any variation as one checks through the book, revealing at once, for example, three concealed impressions of Samuel Johnson's *The False Alarm*, "Second Edition," 1770.

Catchwords, in general use from the mid-sixteenth century through the eighteenth, helped printers arrange the type pages in the proper order for printing. (A catchword appears at the bottom of a page and anticipates the first word on the following page.) In addition to noting any miscatchings and absent catchwords, a bibliography may record all catchwords, a sample, or just those on the last page of each gathering.

Contents

In addition to its obvious literary purpose, a list of a book's contents serves a bibliographical one. The arrangement of matter within the gatherings, as we saw in chapter 2, may suggest whether the book is an original edition or a reprint. It also serves as a further means of identification. The list of contents accounts for every page, from first to last, including blank pages. References to pages of handpress books take the form of signature and leaf number plus the notations *r* and *v* (some bibliographers use *a* and *b*), which designate rectos (the fronts of leaves) and versos (the backs of leaves). References to pages of machine-press books generally use page numbers. The content of the pages is described, quoted (usually without quotation marks), or rendered in quasi facsimile (within single quotation marks). The contents of a simple book from the seventeenth century might be described as follows:

> $\pi 1^{r-v}$ blank, followed by engraved title page; $\pi 2^r$ printed title page; $\pi 2^v$ blank; $\pi 3^r$ dedication 'To | THE MOST NOBLE | John Doe | [rule, 5 mm.]'; $\pi 3^v$ blank; $\pi 4^{r-v}$ prefatory poem; A1–R4^r text; R4^v blank.

Because running titles label the sections of a book and thus can be an identifying feature and because in early books they may be evidence as to the setting of the formes, they are often recorded after the contents listing or elsewhere. For one method of recording them, see the sample description in figure 6.

Typography and Paper

To answer the question of what the book is made of, bibliographers describe the type and paper. A description of type (or, more accurately, its inked image) may include all or some of this information: the number of lines on a typical page, the size of the type page (height before width), the height of twenty (ten in modern books) lines of type, the type-face size and x height in millimeters, the actual point size of the type body and leading if it can be determined, and the style of type. Type style may be denoted with varying levels of specificity—as one of several large divisions (e.g., Renaissance, Baroque, Neo-Classical, Free Roman), as a group within these divisions (e.g., Early Renaissance, English Baroque, Modern Neo-Classical), as a subgroup (in Late Renaissance, e.g., are Caslon, Garamond, etc.), or as a specific font identified in a specimen book (e.g., Lanstom Monotype 268). Note may also be made of such features as particular broken types, identifiable ornaments, the positions of page numbers, the use of rules to frame the text, and gutter-margin measurements. The description of paper may include the size of the sheets, size of leaves, color, kind of paper (laid or wove), direction of chain lines (horizontal or vertical), distance between chain lines, watermarks (their size, location, and description), thickness of a single leaf, and the thickness of all leaves taken together.

Binding

Before the 1820s, the binding of books generally had little or no connection with their printing and publishing. Retail booksellers would sell books that were unbound, that they themselves had bound, or that specialist bookbinders had bound for them. The bindings of this period, therefore, do not constitute part of ideal copy; like owners' bookplates or coffee stains, they are features of individual copies. This is not to say that bindings lack significance. They were products of an art and craft and are studied as such. They also are valuable clues to the provenance of the particular copies that they contain. But, except insofar as they are secondary evidence, the bindings of this period are not treated in descriptive bibliographies. In the 1820s, however, with the development of new materials and mechanization and of new marketing patterns, edition binding became common. Large numbers of copies were bound uniformly in prefabricated cases before delivery to booksellers. The binding thus became part of ideal copy. These bindings sometimes serve to identify separate editions or impressions, and as a sort of packaging they suggest how books were sold and the markets they were intended to reach. Still, the connection between binding and sheets, even after the 1820s, can be tenuous. Old sheets may appear in a late binding, for example, and books may even appear in wrong bindings.

For bibliographers, a binding consists of more than covers. It includes the endpapers—sheets folded once into two halves, one half being pasted to the inside of a cover and the other allowed to stand free as protection of the leaves of the book—and whatever blank leaves or advertisements were bound up with the book, if they are not integral to the printed sheets.

In describing a binding, bibliographers note first the cloth or other materials of its cover. Especially in the nineteenth century, a wide variety of patterns were embossed on binding cloth: ripples, waves, checkerboards, dots and lines, hexagons, and the like. If reference is made to a standard system of nomenclature and classification, these patterns may be described quite accurately, as can their colors by reference to the NBS color-sample charts: "Diagonal wave-cloth (Tanselle 106ae), brownish black (65)." Next, in summary or quasi facsimile, is reported the printed, stamped, or blind-stamped matter on the front, spine, and back. Binding usually affects the actual sheets of the book; their edges may be sprinkled, gilded, stained, trimmed, cut, or left unopened. Endpapers, binder's leaves, and nonintegral advertisements are described both as material (i.e., as paper) and for whatever decoration or printed matter they may contain.

Dust jackets, in common use since the 1880s, are also described with the binding. Attention is given to the kind of paper and to the contents of the front, spine, back, and flaps. Aside from their strictly bibliographical significance, dust jackets are of interest because they suggest how the book was marketed, often contain illustrations by important artists, include blurbs in which authors puff their own work, and print criticism by other authors who were asked for statements to promote the work.

Bibliographical History

Either as an introductory narrative or as a terminal note or series of notes, a detailed discussion of the book's history often accompanies the bibliographical description. This discussion is based on bibliographical and textual analysis and on such secondary evidence as copyright records, the publisher's and printer's ledgers, and the correspondence between the author and publisher. Among the topics deserving mention are the variant states of the book, the peculiarities of individual copies, the relation of the book's text to that of other editions, the number of copies printed, the identity of the printer and compositors, the precise date of publication, the prices at which copies were sold, the date of copyright, references to the book in contemporary advertisements and trade records (e.g., the *Stationers' Register, Term Catalogues, Publishers Weekly*), the contemporary reception of the book in reviews and elsewhere, and the arrangements (financial and otherwise) between the author and publisher. Finally, the bibliographical entry lists the locations of the specific copies that were consulted in preparing the description and explains what is known about their provenance.

In addition to describing books, a typical descriptive bibliography contains descriptions or at least lists of all other relevant forms of publication for its subject: periodicals, recordings, motion pictures, musical scores, drawings, and so forth. Descriptive bibliographies devoted to individual authors may also list manuscripts of their works and may include a reference list of works about the authors, though these are not, strictly speaking, matters of descriptive bibliography. As histories of the physical forms in which texts have met the public, descriptive bibliographies are an essential means of understanding and gaining access to the raw materials of literary study.

Two Sample Descriptions

The first example (fig. 6, p. 48) is taken from W. W. Greg's *A Bibliography of the English Printed Drama to the Restoration*, volume 2 (London: Oxford UP, 1951), 641–42. The description generally employs the methods we have outlined. A few of Greg's abbreviations and conventions may require explanation: "HT" refers to the half title; "RT" refers to the running title; "*SR*" refers to entry in the *Stationers' Register*; and the double vertical line after "1634" in the title-page transcription indicates a rule that extends entirely or almost entirely across the type page. The second example (fig. 7, pp. 49–53) comes from a bibliography in process of John Crowe Ransom (Abbott). Within the introductory narrative, "TxU" indicates that the letter cited is in the collection at the Harry Ransom Humanities Research Center, University of Texas; "STW" that the item cited is from the collection of Stuart T. Wright; and "*SL*" that the letter appears in Ransom's *Selected Letters*.[2]

Notes

[1] A review of methods and recommendations appears in Tanselle, "Recording." The varying register in Samuel Johnson's works is noted in Todd.

[2] For an additional sample, nicely annotated with explanations of descriptive methods and accompanied by a "core listing of the theoretical literature of descriptive bibliography" since Bowers's *Principles*, see Tanselle, "A Sample Bibliographic Description."

497 The Temple of Love (10 Feb.–24 Mar. 1635) 1634

(*a**) THE | TEMPLE | *OF* | LOVE. | A Mafque. | Prefented by the QVEENES Ma-|jefty,
1634 and her Ladies, at *White-hall* on | Shrove-Tuefday, 1634. ‖ By *Inigo Iones*,
Surveyour of his Majefties | Workes; and *William Davenant*, her Ma-[jefties
Servant. | [double rule] | *LONDON* : | Printed for *Thomas Walkley*, and are to
be fold at his | Shop neare *White-hall*. 1634. [*OF* (*F* possibly a broken *E*)]

†) *variant title*] [as above except] By *Inigo Iones*, Surveyor of his Maties. Workes, |
and *William Davenant*, her Ma^tien. Servant. [&c. as above]

HT] THE TEMPLE | OF LOVE.

RT] *The Temple of Love*. [semi-colon on C4^v]

Collation: 4°, A⁴ B⁴(−B4) C⁴ D², 13 leaves unnumbered.
Title, A1 (verso blank). 'The Argument', A2. Text with HT, A3. 'The Masquers Names'
(headed by 'The Queenes Majesty') and those of 'The Lords and others that presented the Noble
Persian Youths' on D2 (verso blank).
Catchwords: A–B, D. Poefie.   B3–C, 3. *and* [B4^v, Barque,]   C–D, Thelema.   *FꞲ NꞲS.*
The speeches are in verse, with prose argument.

Notes—1. The type of the title was altered in the course of printing, and the abnormally wide space
above the double rule in (*a*†) shows this to be the later. The object of the change was apparently to
give greater prominence to Davenant's name, which in the original setting was in smaller type
than Jones's.
2. The leaf B4 was evidently meant to be cancelled though it appears to be present in the majority
of copies. The sheet had already been printed off when it was discovered that the entry of a Persian
Page had been omitted on B4. The composition of sheet C was therefore begun so as to connect
with B3^v and the matter originally filling the two pages of B4 was reset with the addition and
a slight consequential alteration.
3. The performance was on 10 Feb. 1635, and the dates on the title therefore follow the legal
reckoning.

Copies: (*a**)   BM (C. 34. i. 37, + B4)   Bodl. (D2 def., + B4)   Wise   Boston   Hunt.
Yale
(*a*†)   BM (1073. i. 5/4, wants B1)   Dyce (+ B4)   Chapin   Folger   Hunt.

SR 1658 Mar. 6. *Tr. T. Walkley to H. Moseley: The Temple of Love, a Masque at Whitehall
on Shrove Tuesday 1634, by Sir William Davenant.*

Adv. 1660. 'The Temple of Love, a Masque at White-Hall on Shrove-Tuesday, 1634. by Sir
W. Davenant, Knight' is advertised among 'Comedies and Tragedies' ' Printed for Humphrey
Moseley' as no. 242 in his separate List VI".

SR 1667 Aug. 19 (*see* Collection). *Temple of Love.*

F I G . 6 . *W. W. Greg's description of* The Temple of Love *(1634).*

Fig. 7.   *Excerpt from a bibliography of John Crowe Ransom.*

A2   Chills and Fever   1924

In a letter to Allen Tate on 17 December 1922, Ransom said that he had sent a manuscript of poetry to Henry Holt, who had rejected it early the previous summer; and now, he said, impatient in "waiting for the English proposition" (that is, for publication of *Grace after Meat*), he had recently sent "a better MS." to Alfred Harcourt, who in mid-1919 had left Holt to form his own publishing house (*SL* 116). By the time he wrote to Christopher Morley on 31 December 1922, however, Harcourt had already rejected the manuscript, which Ransom enclosed for Morley's examination. He asked Morley to send the manuscript to a "gullible" publisher or to send him a list of such publishers (TxU). Ransom himself later submitted the manuscript, revised, to Macmillan and received a vaguely worded rejection. Unless Morley objected, he wrote on 17 July 1923, he would now submit it to Alfred A. Knopf (TxU). He finally did so on 9 October, admitting that his *Poems about God* had "rather undistinguished sales" and now calling the manuscript *Philomela* (TxU). A month later, on 7 November, Blanche Knopf wrote Ransom to accept the manuscript but asked for reversion to the earlier title *Chills and Fever* (TxU), a phrase from his poem "Here Lies a Lady." In a 12 November letter to Louis Untermeyer, Ransom shared the good news, telling him of Harcourt's earlier rejection of the manuscript ("Harcourt was unable to 'see' my poems; an incapacity which most readers share"). But, Ransom added, "I am able since yesterday to say that Alfred A. Knopf is 'extremely enthusiastic' about my volume and offers to publish it; no earlier than 'early autumn of 1924,' however" (*SL* 123). The next day he thanked Morley for his "seasonable word" on the manuscript's behalf (TxU). The book contract, dated 16 November, was emended in Ransom's hand to allow for the publication of "a volume in England, through Hogarth Press" (STW). Knopf's acceptance of the book was announced in the December 1923 issue of the *Fugitive*: "John Crowe Ransom's second volume of poems is to be published by Alfred A. Knopf in early autumn of next year, under the title, 'Chills and Fever'" (163). In securing Knopf as publisher for *Chills*, Ransom was adding to what was already a distinguished list, one that included Ezra Pound's *Lustra* (1917), T. S. Eliot's *Poems* (1920), and Wallace Stevens's *Harmonium* (1923). For a listing of Knopf books from that period, see *The Borzoi: Being a Sort of Record of Ten Years of Publishing* (Knopf, 1925).

The manuscript first seen by Knopf must have differed considerably from that finally sent to the printer. Ransom continued to add new poems, most of which were appearing in the *Fugitive*, and to revise earlier ones. When Blanche Knopf sent the book contract to him on 15 November 1923, she asked Ransom to consult with Morley on the poems that had been added and omitted since Morley had last seen the manuscript, and she said that the final version must be delivered to the printer by 1 June 1924 for fall publication (TxU). Ransom continued to send Morley new poems and revisions of old ones. Thus, for example, on 12 February 1924, he sent three poems, including "*Agitato ma non troppo*," which he described as "a sort of confession of aesthetic faith" (TxU). On 27 February, he told Morley that Knopf would agree to whatever revisions Morley approved (TxU). The manuscript was due at Knopf by mid-May, and so on 1 May Ransom sent it to Morley for his final inspection. Enclosing 50 poems plus 2 or 3 extras in case Morley deleted any, Ransom explained that he had revised and arranged the poems carefully: the arrangement was "somewhat chronological" but also progressed from the more simple and romantic to the more philosophical. He began, he said, with the italicized "*Agitato*" as a kind of "key-note speech" and ended with his favorite poem, "Philomela" (TxU). By early July, Ransom was already reading proof (*SL* 139). Incomplete correction at this point may account for two discrepancies between the contents page and text: the contents page lists a foreword but there is none (aside from a brief note of acknowledgment); and the contents page gives the title "In Process of the Nuptials of the Duke" for the poem appearing as "In Process of a Noble Alliance" in the text.

FIG. 7   (*cont.*).

The book was published on 29 August 1924. It was considered for that year's Pulitzer Prize for poetry. Writing to Robert Graves on 12 June 1925, Ransom passed on some news that, he said, he would not "publish to the general": "I barely missed winning the Pulitzer Prize ($1,000) for 1924, being defeated in favor of Robinson (who had already won it in 1922) because my work was offensive to one elderly committeeman who wouldn't budge to suit the others' wish, and who had his way because the decision had to be unanimous" (*SL* 143). According to John Hohenberg's history of the Pulitzer Prizes, the judges for 1924 were Richard Burton, Wilbur Cross, and Ferris Greenslet. Setting aside E. A. Robinson's *The Man Who Died Twice* because Robinson had won previously, Cross and Greenslet voted for Ransom's *Chills and Fever*; Burton, however, argued in the committee report that Ransom's poetry was "a very mannered, freaky, morbid affair, representative of the introspective Freudian tendencies in our contemporary verse and literature" (quoted in Hohenberg 120). Faced with a divided committee, the Pulitzer advisory board decided on Robinson.

There was but one Knopf impression (perhaps of 1,500 copies, the number reported for Knopf's first edition of Wallace Stevens's *Harmonium*). It was issued over time in a series of bindings. The original typesetting was used in 1972 for a photo-offset reprinting by Folcroft Library Editions.

A2.a Knopf impression (1924)

Chills and Fever | *Poems* | *by* | *John Crowe Ransom* | [Borzoi device] | *New York Alfred* • *A* • *Knopf Mcmxxiv*

Copyright page (4): 'COPYRIGHT, 1924, BY ALFRED A. KNOPF, INC. • | PUBLISHED, AUGUST, 1924 • SET UP, AND | PRINTED BY THE VAIL-BALLOU PRESS, INC., | BINGHAMTON, N.Y. • PAPER FURNISHED BY | W. F. ETHERINGTON & CO., NEW YORK. • | BOUND BY THE H. WOLFF ESTATE, NEW YORK. | MANUFACTURED IN THE UNITED STATES OF AMERICA'.

206 × 138 mm. *1–6* ^{8}; 48 leaves. *1–12* 13–95 *96* pp.

1 half title '*Chills and Fever*'; 2 list of 8 other Borzoi poetry titles (from *Come Hither*, edited by Walter de la Mare, to *Ulug Beg* by Autolycus); 3 title page; 4 copyright page; 5 '*These poems I dedicate to* | R. R. R. [i.e., Robb Reavill Ransom, his wife] | *and the summer of 1921,* | *when, if ever, came perfect* | *days.*'; 6 blank; 7 acknowledgement for poems previously published, in 11 lines and signed 'JOHN CROWE RANSOM.'; 8 blank; 9–11 'CONTENTS'; 12 blank; 13–95 text (ending 'THE END'); 96 blank. The table of contents lists, without page number, a foreword, but none appears in the book.

Of the 49 poems collected in this volume, 37 had first appeared in the *Fugitive*, 5 were published here for the first time (see titles preceded by an asterisk), and the rest had appeared in *Double Dealer, Literary Review of the New York Evening Post*, and *Armageddon*. The *Philadelphia Public Ledger* is also acknowledged, and it may be that "Miriam Tazewell" had appeared in it (see C105). Most of the poems underwent revision for publication here; none had appeared in *Poems about God*.

Poems:

Agitato ma non troppo	*Two Sonnets (I. Yea, II. Nay)
Spectral Lovers	Spring Posy
Bells for John Whitesides' [sic] Daughter	To a Lady Celebrating Her Birthday
Winter Remembered	Vaunting Oak
Triumph	In Process of a Noble Alliance

FIG. 7 (*cont.*).

Parting at Dawn	Epitaph
Miriam Tazewell	Judith of Bethulia
Here Lies a Lady	Conrad Sits in Twilight
The Tall Girl	Nocturne
Fall of Leaf	Blackberry Winter
Rapunzel Has Submitted Herself to Fashion	Lichas to Polydor
The Vagrant	Spiel of the Three Mountebanks
Boris of Britain	Night Voices
April Treason	Adventure This Side of Pluralism
First Travels of Max	On the Road to Wockensutter
Grandgousier	Prometheus in Straits
*Miss Euphemia	Plea in Mitigation
*Winter's Tale	Tom, Tom, the Piper's Son
Emily Hardcastle, Spinster	Old Man Playing with Children
Number Five	Captain Carpenter
Good Ships	*These Winters
Youngest Daughter	Old Mansion
Necrological	Inland City
Armageddon	Philomela

Type-page with variable number of lines, 136 (141) × 89 mm, 10 lines = 43 mm (e.g., p. 43); typeface Caslon with 3.2 mm face, 1.6 mm x-height. Poem titles (e.g., '*Spectral Lovers*') in italic and centered, each poem beginning on a new page. No running titles; pagination centered in the direction line. White wove paper, no watermark, sheets bulk 11 mm.

Four bindings seen. 1. Bound in paper over boards, the paper having vertical bands of moderate brown (58), dark orange-yellow (72), strong yellow (84), and light grayish olive (109). Those are the predominant colors, the bands shading into lighter and darker hues in a wash-like effect. Front and back otherwise blank. Pale yellow (89) paper label (60 × 17 mm) printed in black or dark reddish brown (44) on the spine: '[17 mm ornamented border resembling a thick-thin rule with a central scroll] | [swash C and F] *Chills* | & | *Fever* | ♦ | [swash P] *Poems by* | JOHN | CROWE | RANSOM | [same ornamented border, inverted]'. White wove endpapers. Top edge trimmed and stained strong yellow (84), in some copies the stain having been imperfectly applied or having partially faded. Other edges unopened.

2. Bound in paper over boards, the paper having vertical bands of very light green (143) alternating with bands of red shaded from predominantly dark red (16) to light grayish red (18); very dark red (17) calico around the spine. The CSA, ICU, and ICN copies appear to have labels printed in black rather than brown. Spine, endpapers, and edges are identical to those of binding 1.

3. Bound in rainbow-like colored calico cloth over boards, the color bands running vertically and consisting of a repeated sequence of the hues purple, bluish green, and orange (almost 3 such sequences on front). Spine label, endpapers, and edges are the same as those of bindings 1 and 2.

4. Bound in pale purplish blue (203) paper over boards with grayish purplish red (262) calico cloth around the spine. Front and back blank. Spine label identical to that of other bindings except that the border consists of a series of diamond shapes, each containing a central dot, and except that the ornament after the title is a triangle resting on its hypotenuse, which is intersected centrally by a short vertical line. (The label paper appears to have been white rather than yellow, though discoloration or fading may have taken place). Endpapers and edges are the same as those of the other bindings.

FIG. 7 *(cont.)*.

One or more of the bindings of paper over boards appear to precede the cloth binding, since the volume was listed in the *Cumulative Book Index* (July 1924–June 1925) as issued in boards. Binding 1 is probably the earliest of these. It is the binding of a review copy dated 17 August 1924 and of the earliest inscribed copy seen, with a date of September 1924. And evidently referring to binding 1, the reviewer for the November *Bookman* described the binding as "variegated paper ranging from yellow to brown to grey and resembling spectroscopic records by some astronomer." The same binding was described in a January 1925 review in the *American Oxonian* as sporting "handsome feverish yellow stripes down the board covers" (this reviewer also notes the presence of "a yellow wrapper, upon which Christopher Morley has set down two paragraphs about Ransom"). There is no evidence that these bindings represent distinct impressions of the book. Similarly colorful paper-boards bindings, followed by a cloth remainder binding, had been used for successive bindings-up of Stevens's *Harmonium* (Edelstein A1.a).

Dust jacket (seen on each binding) of white paper coated moderate yellow (87) and printed in dark brown (59). Front: '[flower border extending across whole of jacket, including flaps] | *Chills and Fever* | [swash P and B] *Poems By* | [swash C and R] *John Crowe Ransom* | CHRISTOPHER MORLEY says: | [24-line blurb] | [capitals in swash] *Alfred A. Knopf* [Borzoi Books device] *Publisher, N.Y.* | [flower border as above]'. Spine: '[border] | *Chills* | *and* | *Fever* | [swash P] *Poems by* | *JOHN* | *CROWE* | *RANSOM* | [Borzoi Books device] | ALFRED | • A • | KNOPF | [border]'. Back: between the borders at head and foot and within a rule frame ornamented with fleurs-de-lis is an advertisement for '*New* BORZOI BOOKS *Fall, 1924*' (from Dale Collins's *Ordeal* to Mildred Cram's *The Tide*). Front flap: borders at head and foot, price ('$1.50 net'), and 13-line biographical note on Ransom. (The biographical note, with some rearrangement, was that supplied Knopf by Ransom on 26 February 1924.) Back flap: borders at head and foot, and an advertisement and subscription form for the *American Mercury*. One copy seen has an unprinted glassine cover around the jacket and may have been so issued (STW).

A later dust jacket, seen on binding 4, is of light yellowish brown (76) wove paper printed in dark brown (59). Front: '[border of centrally dotted diamond shapes] | *Chills and Fever* | [swash P and R] *Poems by* | *John Crowe Ransom* | [flourish] | ALFRED • A • KNOPF [borzoi] PUBLISHER • N•Y•'. Spine: '[border continued from the front] | [swash C and F] *Chills* | *&* | *Fever* | [ornament resembling a triangle resting on its hypotenuse and intersected by a short vertical line] | *Poems by* | *John* | *Crowe* | *Ransom* | [border] | [borzoi] | ALFRED • A • | KNOPF'. Back: advertisement for 16 Borzoi books, from George W. Fuller's *A History of the Pacific Northwest* to Charles E. Crane's *Winter in Vermont*. Front flap: price ('$1.50 | net'), biographical blurb substantively identical to that of the earlier jacket. Back flap: advertisement for war savings bonds and stamps and a request that readers send the book, once read, to the U.S.O.

Copies: CSA (bindings 1 and 2), ICN (binding 2), ICU (binding 2), IEN (binding 3, spine taped), IU (binding 3, spine label partially missing), InU-Lilly (binding 2, with jacket), InU (binding 4), OGK (2 copies, binding 1), STW (4 copies, including a copy in binding 1 with jacket, Robert Penn Warren's review copy in binding 1 and signed and dated by him on 17 August 1924, a copy in binding 3 with jacket, and a copy in binding 4 but with the early jacket), T (binding 1), TNV (7 copies, including a copy in binding 1 inscribed by Ransom to Walter Clyde Curry September 1924, a copy in binding 1 inscribed to Alfred Starr September 1924, a copy in binding 1 inscribed to Louis Untermeyer 10 October 1924, a copy in binding 1 dated by owner Roberta Dillon Lyne as December 1924 and inscribed to her 10 June 1937, a copy in binding 2 and without inscription, a copy in binding 3 without inscription, and a copy in binding 4 with Ransom's autograph annotations and revisions and with duplicate leaves laid in but the title page

F IG . 7   *(cont.)*.

missing), TxU-HRC (3 copies: one with binding 1 and jacket, one from the Knopf collection with binding 2 and jacket, another from Knopf with binding 4 and later jacket), WU (binding 1).

Published at $1.50 on 29 August 1924; copyright registration A801838 (copies deposited 15 September 1924). Forthcoming publication announced in *Fugitive* December 1923: 163 and August 1924: 98. Publication noted in "The Weekly Record," *Publishers' Weekly* 6 September 1924: 727 (with Ransom spelled "Ransome"); listed in "Latest Books," *New York Times Book Review* 7 September 1924: 30, and in "Some Interesting Fall Books," *Nation* 22 October 1924: 401. Advertised in *New York Times Book Review* 7 September 1924: 26 and 14 September 1924: 28; and in *Publishers' Weekly* 20 September 1924: 863. *Chills and Fever* was still in print as late as 31 October 1949, when Ransom's royalty statement for the previous six months shows the sale of 28 copies (TNV).

Reviewed in *Borzoi Broadside* July–August 1924: 34 (Christopher Morley); *Nashville Tennessean* 31 August 1924, Firing Line section: 9 (Donald Davidson); *Saturday Review of Literature* 13 September 1924: 120 (William Rose Benét); *New York Times Book Review* 14 September 1924: 14 (Herbert S. Gorman); *Literary Review* 27 September 1924: 15 (signed W.Y., probably William Yust, a regular contributor); *Nation* 22 October 1924: 446 (Mark Van Doren); *Bookman* November 1924: 345–46 (Bernice Lesbia Kenyon); *Guardian* November 1924: 25 (Allen Tate); *Voices* November 1924: 24–25 (Robert Penn Warren); *Independent* 1 November 1924: 347 (E. A. Niles); *Saturday Review of Literature* 27 December 1924: 412 (Robert Graves; for a response to Graves's review see a letter by Edwin Mims, 28 February 1925: 570); *Double Dealer* January-February 1925: 114–16 (William Alexander Percy, signed W.A.P.); *American Oxonian* January 1925: 29; *Sewanee Review* Janury 1925: 105–11; *Measure* March 1925: 15–17 (Rolfe Humphries); *Dial* April 1925: 337 (Marianne Moore, unsigned); *New Republic* 27 May 1925: 23–24 (Babette Deutsch); *Yale Review* July 1925: 791–97 (Louis Untermeyer).

A Text And Its Embodiments

The world's a printing-house; our words, our thoughts,
Our deeds are characters of sev'ral sizes:
Each soul is a compos'tor; of whose faults
The Levites are correctors; heav'n revises:
Death is the common press; from whence being driv'n,
We're gathered sheet by sheet, and bound for heav'n.

—*Anonymous,* The New Foundling Hospital for Wit *(1768)*

As we said earlier, the text is primary to literary studies. To make more concrete an understanding of how a text passes through its various embodiments, we would like to trace a complete history of two imaginary texts, one produced during the handpress period (1500–1800) and the other during the machine-press period (1801–1950). We constructed these examples to illustrate as many features as possible of the transmission of texts in each period; few actual texts would have survived in all these forms, and not every actual text would have passed through all these stages, whether they had been preserved down to our time or not.

The Life of a Text from the Handpress Period

Of course, any text begins life in the mind of the author. Fortunately, or unfortunately, this form of the text is never directly available for study. However, letters, diaries, commonplace books, and similar documents may give some indication of ideas the author had before he set pen to paper (e.g., Milton's list of possible subjects in the Trinity manuscript). After the idea for the work come notes of various sorts, from a rough outline of the entire work to rather full drafts of portions. Let us suppose that from these notes our hypothetical author attempts the first rough-draft manuscript (Rd 1). It is unlikely that he will get it just the way he wants it with the first effort, so he will probably produce a series of autograph manuscripts, each bearing successive alterations in the text (Rd 2–4). Were all these manuscripts to survive, we would see how the work evolved from its earliest rough form to something like the state the author desired.

Now several things might happen, but let us use a complex example. The author makes one fair copy in his own hand for his own use (Fc 1). From this copy he then produces, again in his own hand, another fair copy for presentation to a patron (Fc 2) and yet another fair copy to show to his colleagues for their judgment (Fc 3). (These people in turn might make additional copies.) Thus, at this stage we have three autograph fair-copy manuscripts by the author, but like most writers, as he makes each successive fair copy he alters the text. Although all three manuscripts are written by the author, each presents a slightly different version of the text. However, two manuscripts (Fc 2 and Fc 3) derive from the copy he keeps for himself, and it, in turn, derives from his working drafts. Although the first sets of notes and rough drafts were successive, the author later goes back and consults them and conflates his text as the work approaches maturity. Rough draft 3 is almost "it" but not quite; rough draft 4 is produced by consulting all previous drafts; and the first fair copy substantially duplicates rough draft 4 but also adds some things from rough draft 3.

Although his patron would probably not suggest any revisions, it is likely that his colleagues would do so, even marking on the manuscript circulated among them, and that the author would accept some of their suggestions while rejecting others. He might even revise his personal copy so as to adopt the suggestions he prefers.

The author might then think the work sufficiently advanced to employ a professional copyist to prepare a much more elaborate and careful copy, or several copies, for circulation to friends and possible patrons. This scribal copy (Sc) derives from the personal fair copy but conflates it with at least the fair copy sent to colleagues and includes alterations made, purposely or not, by the scribe or scribes (see fig. 8).

By this time the author has sought or attracted the interest of a printer-publisher. Although the range of copies that an author might supply to a publisher is almost limitless, in our hypothetical instance the author uses the scribal copy, with some minor revisions made in his own hand. From this the printer begins to prepare the work for printing. First, the printer-publisher decides on the size of the edition to be printed, the typography, the format, and other such technical matters. (Until the eighteenth century authors usually had little say about any step in the publication process.) The printer then decides whether to print the book by formes or seriatim, depending on the number of compositors employed, the amount of work under way, and the time allotted for production. To print by formes the printer must cast off the manuscript—that is, mark it into units closely approximating a type page in this particular typography—and pass it on to the compositors for setting. We currently do not know how much a master printer, or the printer's staff, might tinker with the text of the manuscript

before giving it to the compositors. But we do know that the compositors, simply by making another copy of the work, would introduce variations into the
text, by either accident or design, just as the author had done when he produced Fc 2 and Fc 3 or as the copyist had done when producing Sc.

Sometime between the completion of composition and the ending of the
pressrun, a member of the printing-house staff might look over printed sheets
of most formes to check for errors. (This practice varied widely from one printing house to another and from book to book within a given printing house.)
We know that those in the printing trade were much more likely to detect flaws
in layout (e.g., broken rules or ornaments) than to attempt to ensure the accuracy of the text. Until the middle of the seventeenth century, at the earliest, it
was not common to send out any sort of author's proofs, but the author was
often welcomed into the printing house to check sheets at an early stage in the
printing process. (The practice of regularly supplying proofs to authors stems,
to a great extent, from a reduction in the price and scarcity of paper and from
changes in copyright laws.) If the printer's proofreader or the author detected
errors, the press would be stopped and the errors corrected. But it evidently was
not normal, unless the problem was of considerable size and importance, to dispose of the sheets that had already been printed. The author or proofreader
could even check the sheet after the first stop-press correction had been made
and discover another needed change, producing yet another layer of stop-press
correction. Thus, any side of any leaf of a book from the handpress period may
present not only a new state of the text produced by the compositors, transfer-

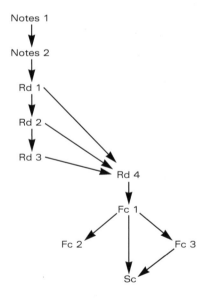

F I G . 8 .   *Textual transmission, from notes to scribal copy.*

ring the words of their manuscript copy into type, but also a second version of printed text produced by stop-press correction, and then a third layer produced by another stop-press correction. A further complication is that the sheets containing all the various versions of the text would have been gathered and bound indiscriminately in copies of the book eventually offered for sale.

The practice of sending out author's proofs before printing commenced certainly changed the amount of stop-press correction found in printed books, but even the works of twentieth-century novelists may contain such corrections. If our hypothetical author lived in the later portion of the handpress period, he probably would have corrected several sets of proofs (Edmund Burke once demanded nine), thus producing further versions of the text. And the published book, incorporating the changes indicated by the author's proofs, would yield yet another. Had the author lived in the earlier period there might not have been any marked author's proofs, and the only evidence of proofing would be found in the stop-press corrections, if any.

Having got out the first edition—in quarto, say—of our hypothetical work, let us expand our diagram to indicate how much longer our textual history has become (see fig. 9). (Historical variations, such as author's proofs, are shown in brackets.) The reader should bear in mind that each point on the diagram represents a distinct and unique version of the text and should note that the first quarto edition is not, textually, a single entity at all but rather an amalgam of versions of the text.

Let us suppose that the work turns out to be unexpectedly popular, so the printer-publisher does two rather common things: has the compositors set a new edition, this time using a copy of the printed quarto as setting copy, and has a new title page set and printed with a more current date and the words "Newly revised and augmented" printed on it. This title page is inserted in all remaining unsold copies of the first quarto edition, and the original title page is removed and discarded. The publisher then markets the remaining copies of the first quarto edition as though they were a revision, even though they are the same sheets printed some months before and have been neither "newly revised" nor "augmented" in any way save for the addition of a new title page. If the printer-publisher is lucky, the shop will have reset the work (probably line for line) and printed a new supply of copies by the time the stock of old sheets has been exhausted. This is then put on the market looking, to the untrained eye, just like more copies of the "doctored" remainder sheets of the first quarto edition.

Of the textual situation that now exists at least two aspects are worth remarking on. First, because the author has had nothing to do with the text of his work since the proofreading stage, the version produced by the line-for-line reprint based on some copy of the first quarto edition will have all the readings of the first setting, the first stop-press corrections, or the second stop-press corrections (depending on which particular version of a given forme happens to be

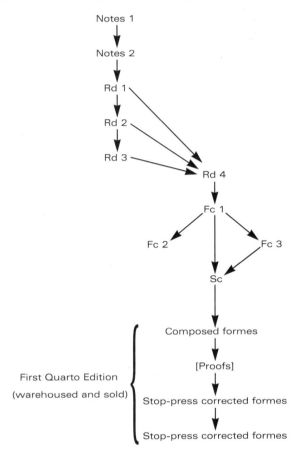

Notes 1

Notes 2

Rd 1

Rd 2

Rd 3

Rd 4

Fc 1

Fc 2   Fc 3

Sc

Composed formes

[Proofs]

First Quarto Edition
(warehoused and sold)

Stop-press corrected formes

Stop-press corrected formes

F I G . 9 . *Textual transmission, from notes to first edition.*

bound up in the copy used for setting the reprint), plus all those errors made by
the compositors while setting the reprint. The reprint can represent only a further decay of the author's text. Second, if the first edition stocks happen to survive a little longer than was expected and are thus in the warehouse when the
printed sheets from the reprint begin to arrive, then copies of the work could
exist with these permutations: cancel title page with sheets of first quarto edition, cancel title page with sheets of first quarto edition and reprint mixed,
reprint title page with sheets of the first quarto and reprint mixed, reprint title
page with sheets of the reprint. No copies will contain the original title page,
and it is unlikely that any will contain only reprint sheets headed by the cancel
title page, since the reprint title page would form an integral part of the preliminary reprint sheets. Our diagram can now be expanded (see fig. 10).

Let us now assume that this mixed batch of sheets in the warehouse continues to sell well and that in a few years another edition is required. This time the

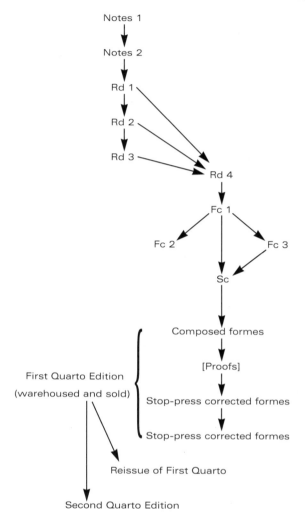

Notes 1

Notes 2

Rd 1

Rd 2

Rd 3

Rd 4

Fc 1

Fc 2

Fc 3

Sc

Composed formes

[Proofs]

First Quarto Edition

(warehoused and sold)

Stop-press corrected formes

Stop-press corrected formes

Reissue of First Quarto

Second Quarto Edition

FIG. 10. *Textual transmission, from notes to second edition.*

printer-publisher asks the author if he would like to revise his work. Normally, the author would take a copy of the printed edition and mark it up with his re-visions. Were he to use a copy with mixed sheets from the first and second quarto editions, the textual situation might be very confusing, though eventu-ally rather straightforward to explain. However, let us assume that the author decides to make rather sweeping changes and produces another manuscript, without consulting any of the printed editions, states, or issues. He would, of course, consult his own notes and fair copy, but essentially he creates a new ver-sion of the work. Naturally, there would be at least one rough draft followed by at least one fair copy for the compositors. From this new, though related, start

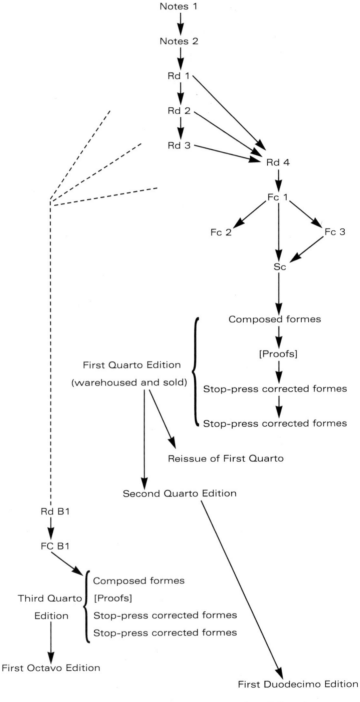

FIG. 11. *Textual transmission, from notes through five editions.*

another version of the text is born in the production of the fair copy and yet another when the compositor sets the manuscript into type. Then the same processes of proofing, stop-press corrections, and the like will occur.

The popularity of the work continues, and the printer-publisher now decides to produce, without consulting the author, a cheap octavo edition. The compositors simply set line for line from a single copy of the third quarto edition (page-for-page setting would not be feasible given the change in format), and the octavo is published without proofing or checking of any kind. Again, of course, any possible combination of corrected and uncorrected sheets might be present in the copy chosen for setting this edition.

Popularity now begins to wane, and many years pass before another edition is called for. The printer-publisher either dies or retires and transfers the copyrights to another printer-publisher, and the next published edition is a duodecimo, set from a copy of the second quarto edition. Again, no proofing or authorial intervention occurs, and the final form of the diagram is seen in figure 11.

Obviously, the life of a text can be complex, but textual criticism, assisted by the methods and evidence of analytical bibliography, can recover much of it from the surviving documents and from secondary evidence. It should be apparent that the history of the text is closely linked to that of the documents that contain it, though one should not assume that the chronology of the physical documents necessarily corresponds to that of the text itself. The text in a particular document may mix early and late readings, and late documents may contain early states of the text. It is also clear that at each stage of the transmission, the text is likely to undergo alterations—in this example by the author, colleagues, scribes, printers, and compositors. Some of the alterations are corrections and revisions in the eyes of their makers; others occur more or less by happenstance, as slips of author's, scribes', and compositors' eyes, pens, minds, or fingers. The transmission does not occur in isolation from its historical circumstances, for it has been affected by the author's popular reception, by the author's relations to several audiences (patron, colleagues, and wider public), and by the methods of printing and publishing at the time.

The Life of a Text from the Machine-Press Period

At the outset this hypothetical work also exists only as ideas and notes in the author's mind and hand, but eventually it will be placed in a more formal setting. For variety we will assume that our author lives after the invention and perfection of the typewriter, so the first version of this text is the author's rough-draft typescript (Rdt). The rough draft contains the inevitable typographical errors, which the author may or may not correct at the time or subsequently, as well as second thoughts, additions, deletions, and the like made by the author in pen or pencil. At the end of this draft our author has a very rough and dirty but more or less readable typescript. She produces neither a carbon nor any sort of photocopy of the typescript. Since her typing is not great she revises a little more by hand and by typing extra sheets and then sends the work off to a professional typist who produces a clean typescript (Pt) and a carbon (Ptc).

Perhaps for reasons explained only by the doctrine of original sin, the author then contrives to mix the carbon sheets with the ribbon sheets so that she has two complete copies of the professional typescript, each containing some of the carbon and some of the ribbon pages (Ptc 1 and Ptc 2). This situation is interesting because no matter how careful and professional the typist, some errors made and corrected in the ribbon copy will not be corrected in the carbon, so that Pt and Ptc will represent two different forms of the text rather than two identical copies.[1] The author has produced, by mixing carbon and ribbon copies, the same sort of situation that we observed in the mixing of sheets of the first and second quarto editions in our handpress-period example. The author now carefully revises one of the typescripts, Ptc 1, let us say, and submits it to a publisher. The publisher agrees to publish the work, and Ptc 1 is now subjected to the scrutiny of the publisher's editor; the result is another version of the text that carries the house styling and the wishes of the publisher and editorial staff (PubEd). Although four different versions of the text are involved (namely, ribbon copy, carbon copy, authorially revised mixed ribbon and carbon copy, and publisher-edited copy), there is only one physical object—Ptc 1. The four versions of the text exist as typewriter impressions, carbon images, author's handwriting, and editor's handwriting on the same sheets of paper.

The edited and revised typescript now is sent out for typesetting. The result, yet another version of the text because of the changes introduced by the compositor, is galley proofs (Gal). These are read by both the author and the publisher (RGal) and returned to the compositor for correction. After imposing the type into formes, the compositor produces another set of proofs—page proofs (PPro)—which are also read by the publisher and the author (RPPro) and returned for further correction.

Finally, the work is printed, bound, and put on sale. This is the first edition (1st ed) of the work and the first form in which the author's usual audience has seen it. Before printing started, however, the publisher had the printer make three sets of stereotype plates, putting two (Pl 1 and Pl 2) in storage and using the third to print this edition. Three different times the printer is asked to print copies of the work, so that the original typesetting, in plate form, is put on the press and printed at three distinct periods of time, creating three impressions of the first edition. Subsequently, the title page, dedication, and a few other parts of the printed book are altered for a variety of reasons, and the printer again mounts the plates on the press and prints a revised fourth impression of the first edition.

Later, the author takes a copy of this revised impression and marks it up extensively with changes, revisions, and corrections. The publisher uses this copy to have a second edition set and printed but does not request any proofs. Over the years plates of this setting of type are used at five different times to produce five impressions, until the plates become so worn that they will no longer print satisfactorily. At this point the publisher takes Pl 1 from storage, has the title page changed to reflect the later date and to state that this is the "Third Edition," and has copies of the book printed. But in truth this is the fifth impression of the first edition, not the third edition, and it represents a state of the text that has been supplanted by both the second edition and the revised fourth impression of the first edition.

Because damage occurs to Pl 1, the publisher brings Pl 2 out of storage and alters the title page to call this the "Fourth Edition," but it is really the sixth impression of the first edition. Several years later the work is reset from a copy of the "Fourth Edition," and this resetting is used to print an actual third edition. Even later, the new technique of photo-offset printing is used to produce more copies, which are, in effect, the second impression of the third edition.

Toward the end of her life the author so thoroughly changes her conception of her work that she writes an entirely new rough draft (NRdt) and has a typist produce a ribbon copy (NPt) and a carbon (NPtc). This time NPt goes directly from typist to publisher, is edited into compositor's copy by the publisher's staff (NPubEd), and is set into galleys (NGal). The publisher happily advertises the imminent publication of a completely revised edition. The author dies before she can read the galleys, but the publisher reads them and uses them as the basis for the fourth edition, called "Fifth Edition, newly revised" on the title page. All this can be represented diagrammatically (fig. 12).

This example, like that of the handpress period, indicates the potential complexity of textual transmission. We could easily have made it more complicated by adding serialization, adaptation for film, expurgation or other alteration for another audience (or market), simultaneous or later publication in another country, and selection by book clubs. It is a prevalent but mistaken notion that textual variation, common in the handpress period, is relatively rare in the machine-press period. Although individual impressions from the machine-press period tend to be uniform, there is often wide variation between impressions and between editions. Furthermore, an author's initial (if not final) notion of a text ready for publication may differ greatly from a publisher's. In the machine-press period, plating and photographic reproduction as well as altered forms of publication may add new wrinkles, but we still see generally the same face of textual transmission.

A few words should probably be said about electronic and desktop publishing since they too are now of importance to bibliographers and textual critics. One of the most radical aspects of the adoption of computers by authors and publishers is that, typically, newer forms of a text obliterate earlier forms; that is, when changes are made in a text, or file, the saving of them in the computer overwrites the earlier form of the text. Thus a large number of documents

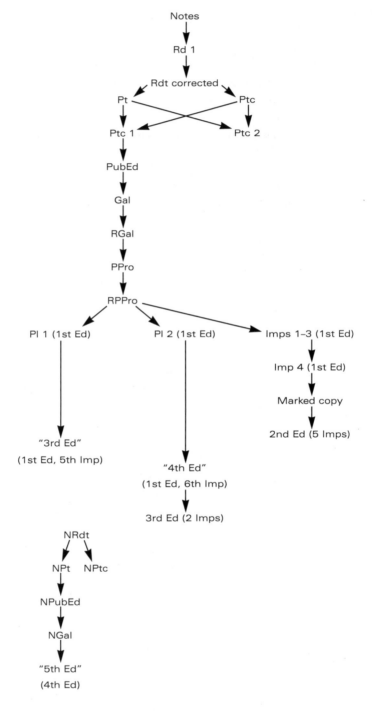

FIG. 12.   *Textual transmission, from notes through four editions.*

containing prepublication stages of textual development will not exist, except in the collections of authors who are inveterate savers of computer printouts and old backup disks, as one of the authors of the present volume must confess himself to be. But, no doubt, as subsequent generations become more accustomed to the use of computers, there will probably be fewer and fewer hoarders of old printouts and such. Still, because both computer hardware and software develop rapidly, obsolescence threatens the retrievability of electronically stored texts. This threat is not restricted to such texts. Think of the difficulty today in getting access to texts stored on the reels of wire used in wire recorders (precursors of tape recorders) or even in playing 78-rpm records. Or suppose an author used an IBM Magnetic Card Selectric Typewriter or even a 5.25-inch single-sided, single-density floppy disk. Unless texts thus stored are frequently transferred to new storage media, they become increasingly difficult to retrieve, and transfer brings with it the possibility of textual alteration.

Another change wrought by new technology has been greater control by authors over the layout of their published work and in general an extension of the author's role into functions previously associated with publishers and printers. Increasingly, publishers expect authors not only to provide the text on disk but also to insert the required typesetting codes into the file. Or publishers have authors prepare camera-ready copy from which printing plates are made. Although these functions may be performed to publishers' specifications, and we are not looking at a situation like that of Blake or Whitman, who strove for complete control over the preparation of some of their works for print, authors may gradually have more control over the printed embodiment of their work than they have had since Gutenberg.

So-called desktop publishing certainly offers that sort of control. Actually, it is not as new as we might think. Vachel Lindsay's hawking his rhymes on vagabonding trips through the United States is an early example of desktop publishing. But the appearance of relatively cheap microcomputers, good-quality printers, and computer programs that produce handsome layouts and typography introduces a new and bewildering element into sorting out the embodiments a text might have. Under these circumstances it is now possible for every copy of a given text to be different from every other copy. If an author, with such electronic gear, produces a collection of poems by this method and makes changes on the electronic file before printing each successive copy, none will be the same and only the last version will continue to exist electronically. Perhaps this simply takes us back to the period before printing, from which we assume every copy is unique.

That possibility also exists in electronic publishing. The text you read today on the Internet may not be the same one you find there tomorrow. In fact, it may not be there tomorrow, for cybertexts can be as ephemeral as they are mutable. Usenet newsgroups (that is, electronic discussion groups such as alt.prose, rec.arts.prose, and rec.arts.poems) allow authors easy, almost unrestricted self-publication, but what is published in them may disappear from most news servers within days. Tracing the forms and histories of electronic texts, then, presents considerable challenges.

Furthermore, electronic publishing tends to blur the distinction between authors and readers and, for that matter, between one author and another. Although the largely uncontrolled space of newsgroups and Web sites, free from editorial boards and market forces, offers authors control over what readers receive, the readers can easily manipulate texts, and the traces of these manipulations (and thus the forms of the text as they were actually received) may be impossible to recover. And much that appears on the Internet is collaboratively written, often without much indication of authorship, individual or collective. If the traditional notion of authorship faces annulment in cyberspace, so do textual boundaries and textual integrity. These seem to dissolve through hypertext links and through the loss of the redundant signs of identity and wholeness found in books, such as half titles, title pages, copyright pages, cataloging-in-publication data, dedications, forewords, prefaces, tables of contents, running titles, margins, signatures, page numbers, catchwords, chapter numbers, afterwords, indexes, colophons, endpapers, bindings, and dust jackets. There are still some voices today celebrating the liberation of texts—or, more likely, of "information"—from the prison house of the printed book. Yet there are still plenty of old books around, and there seems no end to the production of new ones. And regardless of the future of books, texts will still come to us through some form of technology and will have histories to be investigated.[2]

It is too early to know how bibliographers and textual critics will deal with such challenges, but they have dealt with the advent of printing, plating, typewriters, and photocomposition and will no doubt deal with this new technology as well. And the basic questions in the study of textual transmission will likely remain the same: What are the circumstances and stages of transmission represented by what documents or other records? What are the relations between the various stages? (For example, what state of a text descended from what other or others? What served as compositor's copy or as the source of a digitized image?) What alterations were made before and during reproduction (whether in a scriptorium, in a printing house, or at a computer workstation)? What or who caused alterations? How has the process and means of transmission affected the text and its reception by readers? These questions are central to textual criticism and thus to scholarly editing: before a text can be established, its history must be known.

Notes

[1] Since the advent of the photocopy machine this particular wrinkle is much less common, but even now an error may be changed in the ribbon copy after the sup-

posedly identical photocopy of the typescript has been made. Similar results occur when changes are made not to the most recent computer file but to an earlier one.

  [2] For discussions of the relation of new technology to such issues as the structure of texts and textual norms and the processes of reading and writing, see Nunberg.

TEXTUAL 5 CRITICISM

These days I stroll along,
casually turning corners where
someone in black collects

my lines on a white page,
then scurries off, long
scroll trailing. No idea
what he does with them.

—*Lucien Stryk, "Why I Write" (1979)*

Taking as its subject the transmission of texts, textual criticism lies midway between literary criticism, which focuses on works, and bibliography, which focuses on books as books. It seeks to identify the texts of a work and their various states, determine the relations between the texts, discover the sources of textual variation, and establish a text on a scholarly basis. Literary critics often use the term *text* as more or less synonymous with *work*. Textual critics, however, generally use the term in a narrower sense, to refer to a work's letters, words, capitalization, punctuation, and so forth. Employing the language of semiotics, perhaps we can say that the primary interest of textual critics is not the text as sign (consisting of signifier and signified) but the text as signifier.

Though its eye is on the text as wording, textual criticism cannot ignore literary criticism on the one hand and analytical bibliography on the other. As A. E. Housman said, "Because a man is not a born critic, he need not therefore act like a born fool; but when he engages in textual criticism, he often does" (1060). Generally, a critical rather than a purely textual or bibliographical concern motivates textual study in the first place. Moreover, criticism defines the text by identifying the work, for texts are of works. Are the variant versions of Marianne Moore's "Poetry" merely variant forms of the same text, or do they really represent distinct works? The question is critical, but it has textual implications; its answer may determine whether there is one text to edit or several. Moreover, evaluating textual variants requires critical judgment. In establishing the text of Melville's *Typee*, for instance, the editors sought to discern largely on a critical basis which variants in the American revised edition resulted from the publisher's demand for expurgation and which from Melville's efforts at more nearly realizing his own conception of the work.

Another example of the application of criticism can be manufactured out of a comment in Barbara Herrnstein Smith's *Poetic Closure*. Smith says that the final words of John Donne's epigram "Hero and Leander" are "so strongly determined by all that precedes them (including, of course, the title), that one could hardly imagine how the epigram might have been otherwise concluded" (204–05). Now suppose that the epigram came down to us with some tatter in its mortal dress—with a lacuna that denied us the "strongly determined" words.

> Both robd of ayre, we both ly in one ground,
> Both whom one fyre had burn'd, _____.

If we are good critics, we should be able to reconstruct Donne's text by filling the blank, relying on our knowledge of the epigrammatic conventions and of the linguistic usage and metrical conventions of the period and author and on our sensitivity to poetic form and language generally. Our experience in the classroom is that some students can indeed imagine how the epigram might have otherwise concluded ("the worms go round," "the gods confound," "are toasty brown"); but many arrive at the correct answer, and many others at least recognize its superiority: "one water dround." Completing the story of Hero and Leander, it also fits grammatically and metrically, supplies the expected rhyme, adds the missing element of water to the sequence of air, earth ("ground"), and fire, and in general satisfies formal and thematic expectations.

Of course, textual critics have sometimes gone to editorial extremes, not resisting the temptation to tinker and to try their hands at creation rather than emendation. In his 1732 edition of Milton's *Paradise Lost*, for example, Richard Bentley notes that in book 4,

> Ithuriel here finds a *Toad* in Adam's Bower; and so very presuming as to sit close at *Eve's* Ear, while she lay asleep! This alone might discover him to be *Satan*, before he touch'd him with his Spear. For we know, the Bower was sacred and sequestered to *Adam* and *Eve* only; IV.703.
> > *Other Creature there,*
> > *Beast, Bird, Insect or Worm, durst enter none.*
> This the Two Angels could not be ignorant of: and therefore why may not I add *one* Verse to *Milton*, as well as his Editor add so *many*: especially, since I do not do it clandestinely. [. . .]

So add he does, putting a real toad of a line into Milton's imaginary garden:

> Him thus intent Ithuriel with his spear
> Knowing no real Toad durst there intrude,

> Touch'd lightly: for no falshood can endure
> Touch of Celestial temper. [. . .] (Sig. T1r)

The second line is Bentley's.

Though, as Bowers says, "to disbar critical judgment from the editorial process would be an act of madness" (*Bibliography* 19), such judgment that defies or ignores bibliographical findings is madness too. Bibliography is especially useful in determining the temporal sequence of textual variation and often can reveal the likely source of or at least the occasion for textual variation. In Melville's *White-Jacket*, one might on critical grounds prefer a misprint ("soiled fish" for "coiled fish"), but it remains a misprint.[1] If bibliography cannot always make the judgment as to the source and authority of a text or textual variant, it can usually delimit the area in which judgment must be applied. Furthermore, bibliography takes on added importance if, as has been urged by D. F. McKenzie (e.g., *Bibliography*), Jerome McGann (e.g., *Textual Condition*), and others, the concept of text is expanded beyond wording to include nonlinguistic features of documents. McGann speaks of a text as consisting of both linguistic codes and bibliographical codes, or as linguistic text and bibliographical text. Whether or not one accepts the expansion of the term *text* in this way, there is no denying that such bibliographical features as typography, layout, format, and paper have signifying functions. Some authors, such as Lawrence Sterne, have quite obviously played with the conventions separating texts (in the linguistic sense) from their bibliographical presentation. Sterne's novel *The Life and Opinions of Tristram Shandy* (1759–67) makes use of blank pages, black pages, marbled pages, dots, odd dashes, and the like. Even when authors do not use bibliographical features so obviously, they often extend their interest beyond matters of wording. Elizabeth Bishop, writing to her publisher about her first book, *North & South* (1946), expressed her dislike of "modern unglazed linen bindings" and asked for a glazed binding, in dark gray with the spine title in gilt. She also had preferences in type: "It seems to me that the Baskerville monotype 169E, 11 point, would be perfect." Bishop got an unglazed dark blue binding with the title in silver, but she did get her eleven-point Baskerville (qtd. in MacMahon 7–8). While authors generally have had primary control over wording, printers and publishers have had primary control over bibliographical features.

Textual criticism in its broadest sense is not limited to its application in the editing of texts. Much of it takes the form of essays in textual history, addressing such questions as these: How did an author revise the text? Who else had a hand in the composition of the text? How has the process of scribal copying or of printing influenced the text? What texts were available to readers at a particular time—for example, when an author's reputation was being established? How have economic considerations affected texts? How did editors of various periods alter texts to satisfy their aesthetic, moral, or other principles? Thus, for example, R. G. Moyles's *The Text of* Paradise Lost: *A Study in Editorial Proce-*

dure traces the textual history of Milton's poem from the first edition in 1667 until the late twentieth century. As Moyles says, the poem "has been printed, in complete and distinct editions, at a rate equivalent to once every year, more often perhaps than any other work of literature in the English language" (ix). Moyles describes this transmission and the varying treatment of the text by such editors as Tickell (1720), Fenton (1725), Bentley (1732), Newton (1749), Darbishire (1931), and Wright (1956).

If, broadly considered, textual criticism is the study of the history of texts, its ultimate aim is still generally thought to be the production of scholarly editions. Not all editing, of course, is "scholarly." Publishing firms employ a variety of editors to alter texts for publication. Thus editors at Macmillan and then at Appleton-Century collaborated with Willard Motley to reduce his 600,000-word typescript of *Knock on Any Door* to 250,000 words, to eliminate parts of the novel they judged wooden, to soften the depiction of sexuality and political corruption, and to manufacture a book that they could market at three dollars a copy. Their main concern was not fidelity to Motley's wording but creation of a marketable product. Most such editors remain in the shadows though some, like Maxwell Perkins, become as well known as the authors whose works they midwife. Publishers also employ copy editors, who mark copy for printers and seek to eliminate authors' departures from clarity, sense, and consistency and from conventions of grammar, usage, punctuation, and the like. And then there are noted critics and scholars whose names are affixed as "editors" to what is often a mere reprinting of standard literary works. Many textbooks—or trade books used as textbooks—fit this category. The texts they contain are often corrupt and may not have had any attention from the critics commissioned to "edit" them (see, e.g., "Practical Editions"). Scholarly editing, however, is based on textual scholarship. It takes two major forms: documentary editing and critical editing.

Documentary Editing

Documentary (or diplomatic or noncritical) editing aims to reproduce a manuscript or printed text as a historical artifact. It presents a text as it was available at a particular time in a particular document. Such editing is noncritical in that it does not emend the text, even a text that may not accurately reproduce an author's words. The First Quarto of *Hamlet* is a "bad" quarto, probably based on a memorial reconstruction by one actor or more. Its text, though probably not authoritative, is of interest and can be made more widely available through a documentary edition. So too can the texts of an author's letters, journals, and other papers; in fact, documentary editing is often the method of choice for texts that their authors did not prepare or intend to prepare for publication. Scholarly editing, both documentary and critical, is not limited to literary works. In recent years historians have become more aware of their need for soundly edited texts, often in documentary editions. Previously, the letters, diaries, and other papers of historical (as well as literary) figures were often edited with more concern for their informational than for their evidentiary value and with the assumption that readers would demand textual tidiness in matters of spelling, punctuation, capitalization, and grammar. Since the founding of the Association for Documentary Editing in 1978, however, there has been a greatly increased attention to the principles and practices of editing such papers.

Documentary editing aims for exact fidelity to the text's wording, spelling, punctuation, and the like. To alter them is to tamper with the text as a historical artifact. If F. Scott Fitzgerald spelled poorly in his letters, we want to see it. If the First Quarto of *Hamlet* reads "sallied flesh" rather than "sullied flesh" or "solid flesh," then the text must read "sallied." One method of presenting a documentary text is through a "diplomatic reprint," which preserves only the text—the wording, spelling, punctuation, and so forth. Such a reprint may also be accompanied by notes or other kinds of apparatus that record textual variants from other documents. Variorum editions often take that form. For their three-volume textual variorum of Whitman's *Leaves of Grass*, Sculley Bradley and his fellow editors selected as a base text that of the final authorized impression of the 1881 edition, and they noted chronologically all variant readings from the previous editions. The variorum thereby allows a reader to see the complex thirty-year progress of *Leaves of Grass*—its development, additions, deletions, conflations, revisions, and groupings and regroupings of poems. Such an edition is documentary rather than critical; in other words, it does not emend the text, even a text known to contain errors (as in fact the *Leaves* base text does). Even critical variorum editions generally present a documentary, not critically edited, text. The word *critical* in their designation refers to the kind of annotation keyed to the base text—that is, annotation presenting a record of interpretive, philological, and other commentary on the text (including textual emendations proposed or made by previous editors). The volumes in the Modern Language Association's New Variorum Edition of Shakespeare series are examples of this kind of documentary editing.

Documentary editions may also present a text in facsimile, including photofacsimile, which preserves (if it is carefully made) much of the extratextual physical detail of the document, including typography, lineation of prose, and spacing. David L. Vander Meulen's photofacsimile edition of Pope's 1728 *Dunciad* is a good example. Vander Meulen had to choose for reproduction from among the three so-called 1728 editions and then from among the multiple copies of whichever edition he selected. That choice required bibliographical investigation. There were actually, he noted, four impressions. The so-called editions had been printed from standing type (roughly one gathering in each was reset). Choosing the first impression, Vander Meulen still had to choose between its two issues: one imposed in duodecimo ($12°$: A–E^6 F^2) and one in octavo (8°: a⁴ b² B–G⁴ H²). The book in both formats had been printed in the work-and-turn manner. On the bed of the press were all the type pages for a gathering, both inner and outer formes. Each sheet would have been printed on one side, turned 180°, printed on the other side, and then cut in half to produce two copies of each gathering. The subject of some debate, though, was which issue came first, the octavo (the deluxe issue, since it would have less type per sheet and thus wider margins) or the smaller duodecimo. To satisfy human curiosity but also because the question involved the priority of textual differences between the two issues, Vander Meulen resorted to headline analysis. He found that the printer first printed gatherings B and C of the duodecimo, then reimposed the type pages and printed them for gatherings B, C, and D of the octavo, and then followed the same procedure for the remaining gatherings. Vander Meulen's edition reproduces a copy of the duodecimo issue, a copy in which one of Pope's friends had recorded his collation of an early manuscript of the poem. The edition also supplies the histories and analyses of the work, the 1728 edition and its impressions, and the individual copy used. These are joined by appendixes providing, for example, full textual collations of the 1728 impressions, notes on the texts of unauthorized editions of 1728, and analysis of the variant states of the book's frontispiece.

Charlton Hinman, following his extensive bibliographical analysis of Shakespeare's First Folio, produced a photofacsimile edition that, unlike Vander Meulen's edition of the *Dunciad*, reproduced not a single copy of the book but one constructed from multiple copies of the Folio. Because of stop-press corrections (some 370 by Hinman's reckoning) and other factors, no two copies of the Folio are textually identical, and individual copies mix early and late stages of the text. From thirty copies, Hinman created an "ideal" one, made up of pages that represent what he judged to be the latest or most fully corrected state of the text and that are relatively well printed, with a minimum of ink-filled letters, underinked letters, and show-through from the other side of the leaf. His edition identifies the particular copies used for each portion of the facsimile and reports Folio variants that affect meaning.

Documentary editing may also make use of genetic or synoptic transcription, as when a single document contains several states of a text. Manuscripts, for example, often contain crossings out, interlineations, multiple readings, and the like. These states can be rendered in genetic transcription, which employs various symbols to record the textual variation and its chronology. An edition of Melville's *Billy Budd* provides an example. Unpublished in Melville's lifetime, the novel comes to us in a semifinal draft. There was no satisfactory edition until 1962, when the University of Chicago Press published both a "reading text" and a "genetic text" edited by Harrison Hayford and Merton M. Sealts, Jr. The reading text is a product of critical editing; the genetic text, of documentary editing. For the genetic text, Hayford and Sealts made a literal transcript of

the manuscript, leaf by leaf. The base for the transcription is the earliest version
of each of the 370 leaves. They reported the numerous revisions found on the
leaves as bracketed interruptions and identified each revision according to the
stage of revision it represents. The result, then, is not mere transcription, itself
an often difficult task in documentary editing, but transcription that reflects
painstaking analysis of how Melville went about developing his story. And just
as the editors of the variorum *Leaves of Grass* employed analytical bibliography
to untangle a complex printing history of multiple editions and impressions
and thus to identify correctly the documents that contained the evolving text,
so too did Hayford and Sealts resort to physical analysis of Melville's manuscript. By identifying the several stocks of paper, matching the edges of leaves
cut and torn from larger sheets, and tracing the various colors of Melville's ink,
crayon, and pencil, they were better able to establish the chronology of revision.

Although some textual critics would restrict the term *genetic* to refer to editions presenting a text and its alterations as found within one manuscript, the
term has also been used (along with *synoptic*) to refer to editions that present multiple documentary texts of a work. The presentation, like that of Hayford and
Sealts's *Billy Budd*, brings together in one sequence, not in notes or an appendic-
ular apparatus, the multiple stages of textual development, the various stages
being indicated by sometimes very complex schemes of brackets and diacritical
marks. Such genetic editing has gained impetus in France from what has been
called *critique génétique*, a movement influenced by French structuralism and interested not in a particular state of a work's text but rather with the various textual
states as a process or as a field of possibilities of selection and combination.

Other formats or combinations of formats for documentary editions include
photofacsimile and literal transcription on facing pages and transcription of variant states in parallel columns. And, of course, documentary editions of various
formats can be presented electronically on disks or over the Internet. Unfortunately, the desire to get texts into electronic form has not always been combined
with bibliographical and textual scholarship. The Gutenberg Project, for example, with its announced goal to "Give Away One Trillion Etext Files by December 30, 2001" (that is, ten thousand titles each to one hundred million readers)
("Information"), offers texts free of charge but also free of scholarship identifying
their sources and ensuring fidelity to the sources used. Doubtless it has its uses,
but its characterization as "a textual junkyard" does seem apt (Shillingsburg,
Scholarly Editing 161). But quite a few projects are more informed by the needs
and principles of scholarship. In addition to carefully transcribing texts and
identifying their documentary sources, such projects generally mark up the bibliographical, generic, linguistic, typographic, rhetorical, and formal features of
texts. Guidelines for such markup have been developed by the Text Encoding
Initiative (TEI), sponsored by the Association for Computers and the Humanities, Association for Computational Linguistics, and Association for Literary and

Linguistic Computing.[2] TEI codes conform to Standard Generalized Markup Language and thus are not dependent on particular hardware or software. The codes make possible databases that do not have file-format compatibility problems and that contain information needed for analysis, retrieval, browsing, and further processing (including typesetting). An exemplary project employing the TEI guidelines is the *Brown Women Writers Project*, which is creating a full-text database of pre-Victorian women's writing in English. (A description of the project appears at its Web site [http://www.wwp.brown.edu].) A similarly ambitious project, centered on a particular author (and artist), is *Complete Writings and Pictures of Dante Gabriel Rossetti: A Hypermedia Archive*. Still under development, it is intended to "hold a digital image of every textual and pictorial document relevant to the study of Rossetti," marked up for electronic search and analysis, supplied with scholarly annotations, and overlaid with a hypertext network linking the files.[3] Whatever the format—print, microform, electronic form, or some combination—documentary editions are all intended to report as accurately and clearly as possible the texts of documents as historical artifacts.

Critical Editing

Critical editing, the second major form of scholarly editing, does not reproduce the text of a particular surviving document or documents but constructs a text that may incorporate readings from several documentary texts and may include editorial emendations that establish readings not found in any document. It assumes that none of the documentary texts representing a work is, according to some standard or need, entirely satisfactory. In a small way, any reader who mentally corrects what he or she supposes to be a misprint is engaged in critical editing.

Until the twentieth century, critical editing was dominated by classical and biblical studies and was applied, at least in its sophisticated form, to classical and vernacular texts that had been transmitted over centuries through manuscripts. For Ovid's *Metamorphoses*, there are some five hundred manuscripts; for the New Testament, some five thousand. Scholars have developed various methods for such texts and to some extent have adapted them to texts transmitted through print. One of the earliest, the eclectic method, called for assembling the various states of a text, discovering their textual variants, and then selecting those readings that met some criterion. In another method, best-text editing, an editor would select an early "good" documentary text and then generally restrict emendation to the correction of its obvious errors. At least for some textual situations, an advance over these methods was the stemmatic or genealogical method, also called the Lachmannian method, after Karl Lachmann, one of its nineteenth-century practitioners. This method has three interrelated parts: (1) *recensio*, the study of the manuscript tradition so as to construct a family tree, or stemma, representing the relations of descent and derivation of the manuscript texts and to reconstruct an "archetype" to which the other texts are "witnesses"; (2) *examinatio*, the determination of the authority of the texts and their variant readings; (3) *divinatio*, the conjectural emendation to correct errors. Evidence for the stemma derives largely from common errors among manuscripts (common errors indicating common ancestry), striking agreements or disagreements among manuscripts, and the date and provenance of the manuscripts.

Also useful, both in arriving at a stemma and in evaluating variant readings, are certain principles based on knowledge of scribal practice. The principle *difficilior lectio potior* (the more difficult reading is to be preferred) recognizes scribes' tendency to "trivialize" a text by substituting an easy reading for one with which they have difficulty. The relevance of this principle is especially great, for example, in examining the work of scribes in the Middle Ages, whose knowledge of Latin was less than that of the authors whose texts they were copying. It also explains certain readings in the Greek manuscripts of the New Testament. In Greek, for example, the common word for *did* looks much like the less common word for *perplexed*. So, in some manuscripts (and in the Revised Standard Version), when Herod heard John, "he was much perplexed, and yet he heard him gladly"; in other manuscripts (and in the King James Version), "he did many things, and heard him gladly" (Mark 6.20; Colwell 76). But the principle of *difficilior lectio* has a fairly universal application, as when nowadays a medical transcriptionist produces "skinny lips" from the dictated phrase "skin ellipse" or when your word processor's spelling checker suggests "antiaircraft" for "undercroft," "steamy" for "stemma," "screwball" for "scribal," or "termites" for "Thersites." Another principle, *brevior lectio potior* (the shorter reading is to be preferred), recognizes the tendency of scribal copying to incorporate manuscript marginalia into the body of the text. In the twentieth century, aided by computers and statistical methods, some textual critics have employed a stemmatics based more on an analysis of textual variation (a calculus of variants) than on the genealogy of particular states of texts as embodied in particular manuscripts. And they have appropriated from biology the principles and methods of cladistics, the classification (or taxonomy) of organisms based on their evolutionary relationships.

The editors of classical texts face both an abundance and a dearth of evidence. There may be a great many manuscripts of a work, yet none authorial or even contemporary with the author, most being separated from any authorial document by at least seven hundred years and by many lost manuscripts. The editing of postclassical texts, our chief concern here, presents a different situation. No great chronological gulf separates surviving documents from the authorial; indeed, authors' notes, drafts, typescripts, and proofs may be available. Moreover, the texts have often been formally published and transmitted through print during the authors' lifetimes and with their direct involvement. Stemmatics remains important, but analytical bibliography is also crucial.

A critically edited text, when combined with an apparatus that presents the evidence used in the text's construction and that lists the variants of the authoritative states, is called a "critical edition." Critical editors, then, must have some principle of construction, some basis or standard on which to judge the authority of the variant readings and states of the text and on which to make emendations.[4] The standard may be aesthetic, leading to the construction of a text that satisfies some particular notion of literary excellence. Traces of this standard may be found in critical editions that regularize and normalize an author's metrics or word order, for example, often according to the conventions of the editor's time rather than the author's. But few scholarly editors adopt, at least overtly, such a standard as the primary basis for critical editing. (This is not to say, however, that aesthetic concerns do not figure in the selection of what texts to edit or even how to edit them.) Instead, they adopt a standard that involves them in editing as an act of historical reconstruction.

In documentary editing, the controlling standard or basis of authority is, as we have seen, the document itself: the aim is to present, as faithfully as facsimile or transcription allows, the text as it exists within a particular surviving document or documents. But critical editing may also have a primarily documentary concern: the reconstruction of a documentary text. Suppose, for example, that the texts of documents A, B, and C were all set or copied from an ancestral document X and thus are stemmatically equidistant from it. If document X were lost, it could be largely reconstructed, since where the other three agree they point to the text of X, and since where one of the other three is unique it probably deviates from X. Even in this simple example, though, there may be wrinkles. If two scribes or compositors altered the ancestor in the same way (for example, identically correcting the same error), tossing out the unique reading tosses out the ancestral reading. And if at an identical point each survivor presents a unique reading, mechanically tossing out all three readings leaves a hole. The point, however, is that by evaluating the evidence and exercising critical judgment, an editor can endeavor to reconstruct a lost documentary text. Whether that text is authorial or not is another matter altogether. Classical textual criticism provides a good example of this sort of reconstruction, although we should keep in mind that editors of classical texts have seen such reconstruction as a means of approaching an authorial text.

At least in the twentieth century and especially for postclassical texts most textual critics have appealed to authorial intention as the primary standard. They have sought to reconstruct texts as the texts were intended by the authors. Now, this is not quite the same thing as reconstructing texts as actually written by authors. That too is a legitimate goal, of course, and it leads to a particular application of the documentary reconstruction already discussed. But authorial action (what text did an author write in some document?) is not necessarily the same as authorial intention (what text did an author intend to write in that document or, more generally, intend to represent a work?). One obvious difference results from authors' slips of the pen or of fingers on the keyboard.

Accepting authorial intention as a basis for editing raises difficult theoretical and practical questions and especially in recent years has provoked much debate. How, for example, is intention to be determined? Should we infer it primarily from the text itself or from an author's statements about the text? For that matter, what do we mean by intention? In F. Scott Fitzgerald's *The Great Gatsby* appears a description of a billboard bearing a portrait of an oculist: "The eyes of Doctor T. J. Eckleburg are blue and gigantic—their retinas are one yard high" (qtd. in Bruccoli 49). There is no doubt that Fitzgerald wrote "retinas"; that was his linguistic intention and the text embodies it. But his semantic intention might well have been otherwise. He may have meant pupils or irises, which can be seen externally, and not retinas, the membranes lining the interior of the eyeballs. While some editors might retain "retinas," others might emend it. (Bruccoli offers an argument for "irises.")

Also complicating the matter of intention is that authors' intentions may change over time. Authorial revision may reflect an effort to achieve more satisfactorily an intended text of a work, or it may reflect a changed conception of the work. Critical editors may decide to reconstruct a text as it was intended at a particular historical moment. Often, when the revision is judged to reflect an author's progress toward a more satisfactory embodiment of the work, an editor may select to reconstruct a text as the author finally intended it. But especially when the revision is judged to create another version of the work or even a new work, editors may reconstruct multiple texts. In fact, authors may have intended multiple texts both over time and simultaneously. There may be, for example, a hieratic text that the author intended for circulation among friends and, at the same time, a demotic text intended for a wider public. There may be a theatrical text designed for performance and a reading text for sale in book form. (The title page of John Webster's *The Dutchesse of Malfy* [1623] tells its readers that the quarto contains "diuerse things Printed, that the length of the Play would not beare in the Presentment.") How to deal with textual multiplicity, especially that which suggests multiple versions of a work, remains controversial in critical editing.

Critical editions have commonly presented a single text, relegating textual variants to footnotes or appendixes. But works may be seen as represented not so much by a text or texts as by a textual history, as a process rather than as a discrete product. When Marianne Moore reduced "Poetry" to three lines for her 1967 *Complete Poems*, she knew that readers would recognize the reduction (and in fact included in her notes another text, which is earlier but not "original," as the note claims). Moore also called attention to the incompleteness of *Complete Poems*, prefacing the collection with the statement "Omissions are not accidents" (vii). Thus some of her poems are represented here by their absence, by zero texts. (For a discussion of Moore's substractive revision, see Kappel.) Revision and multiple texts make an interesting appearance also in John Crowe Ransom's 1969 *Selected Poems*, which includes sixteen pairings of "original" and "final" versions of poems. The so-called originals are not, for the most part, original, having been previously revised since their earliest publication. But they have been further revised for the 1969 publication, which thus presents some newly revised "originals," each paired with a "final" revision. In his preface to these pairings Ransom refers to them as "pairings or couplings of poems," not as pairings of variant texts or even of versions (109). Such examples do not so much challenge the enterprise of critical editing as they challenge textual critics to devise editions that clearly report textual histories and construct texts that better represent important moments in those histories.

Textual critics who adopt authorial final intention as the basis for editing do not necessarily accept an author's chronologically last alteration of a text. They are not likely, for example, to accept revision made under duress. Melville's *Ty-pee* provides an example of an author's intervening in his or her texts in a way considered corrupting. Melville struck certain passages from *Typee* for the revised American edition at his publisher's insistence, producing what Melville himself called an "expurgated" edition. The deletions seem not to represent his intention, final or otherwise, although certain other changes that he made in the edition do. Other instances may be less easily decided, such as one authorial alteration in Dickens's *David Copperfield*. In his manuscript, Dickens wrote this sentence in David's description of his life with the Murdstones: "I have been Tom Jones (a child's Tom Jones: a blameless creature), for a week together." Having had difficulty deciphering Dickens's cramped hand, especially in the portion of the sentence that appears in the manuscript as an interlinear insertion, the compositor set the sentence thus: "I have been Tom Jones (a child's Tom Jones), a brainless creature for a week together." Reading this missetting in proof but not consulting his manuscript, Dickens restored the closing parenthesis to its earlier position but changed the compositor's "brainless" to "harmless" rather than the manuscript's "blameless." And that is what saw publication. An editor might argue that Dickens would have been unlikely to replace "blameless" with "harmless" if there had been no error in typesetting and that, had he consulted the manuscript in proofing, he would not have introduced a new reading. The editor might therefore select the earlier manuscript reading. But it has also been suggested that either "blameless" or "harmless" be chosen "not because it was Dickens's first thought or his last, but because the editor prefers it on critical grounds" (Gaskell, *From Writer* 147). This suggestion does not abandon authorial intention as the basis for editing (it does not include the compositor's "brainless" among the choices), and the editor's choice presumably would be made not on the basis of personal critical preference (though that is possible, of course) but on the basis of the editor's judgment as to the author's preference.

One form of critical editing, called historical-critical editing by its mostly German practioners, uses authorial intention on a limited basis.[5] Its chief aim is to provide a complete textual history rather than to establish a text. Historical-critical editors see textual authority residing more in the states than in the individual readings of a text. To produce an eclectic text is, in their view, to violate this authority and create a contaminated text. Each documentary state of a text—that is, each combination of readings within a particular document—is a version. Not all versions, of course, have equal authority, since their authority varies according to whether the author commissioned, supervised, proofread, accepted, or was otherwise involved with them. A historical-critical editor selects one "authorized" version and then uses it as a base, presenting the remaining versions in an apparatus. (If no version is authorized, the editor selects the version nearest in line of transmission to a lost authority.) Yet this is not documentary editing, for it allows emendation. But the editor restricts emendation to the correction of "textual fault," which Hans Zeller defines as "an intermittent suspension of authorisation" (260). Textual faults exist only when the reading in question (1) violates sense and textual structure and (2) arises from a suspension of authorization demonstrated by analytical bibliography. (Thus, for editors like Zeller, not all misprints are textual faults, for some may be subsequently authorized.) Moreover, the method permits emendation only when the correction is unequivocal. This kind of editing, a form of best-text editing, supposedly avoids the problem of determining an author's intentions and of distinguishing between aesthetic and other intentions. Thus it is beside the point whether the expurgated version of Melville's *Typee* contains variants that fulfill his artistic conception of the work and variants that represent his reluctant acquiescence to his publisher's demand to soften or cut offensive passages. The expurgated version, like the earlier nonexpurgated version, is authorized. And in the view of historical-critical editing, to produce an edition that combines readings from the versions is to create a version without authority.

Authorial intention as an editorial standard has also been questioned. Jerome J. McGann has argued, for example, that modern editors' emphasis on "the autonomy of the isolated author" is "grounded in a Romantic conception of literary production" (*Critique* 8).[6] McGann does not reject authorial intention as one criterion for decisions in critical editing but denies that it should be the sole criterion. He calls for increased recognition that published texts are collaborative products involving the institutions of publishing as well as individual authors; thus he urges acceptance of "a socialized concept of authorship and textual authority" (8). According to McGann, textual authority should be expanded to include "the dynamic social relations which always exist in literary production" (81). McGann's expansion of textual authority accords with his expanded concept of textuality. If texts consist of both linguistic and bibliographic codes, then the collaboration inherent in textual production is readily apparent.

Authors produce the linguistic and printers-publishers the bibliographic, and each makes incursions on the other's domain. Further, the codes are not separate but exist in what McGann calls "a laced network" (*Textual Condition* 13). McGann's ideas have been widely influential, but primarily as the basis for essays in textual history, for critical readings that take into account bibliographical codes, and for further essays questioning critical editing. His views nonetheless have implications for editing. The signifying function of layout, typography, and other physical features of books (McGann's bibliographical codes) is a rationale for facsimile documentary editions and for the description, illustration, and interpretation of these features in nonfacsimile editions, including critical editions. And, accepting an expanded concept of textual authority, critical editors may decide to construct a text that adopts nonauthorial elements. It has long been recognized that friends, family members, scribes, publishers, printers, editors, and others alter authorial texts. Authors may welcome, accept, approve, regret, expect, depend on, or acquiesce in such alteration. Discovering that a printer's proofreader was tampering with his punctuation, Mark Twain said that he "telegraphed orders to have him shot without giving him time to pray." But many authors have relied on corrections or other alterations by copy editors, compositors, proofreaders, and others. Whatever the case, a critical editor could construct a text based on the intentions of more than the author. Moreover, authors are already socialized beings. And while they may create texts for personal reasons, they enter into a relation with the institutions of printing and publishing and, for that matter, with readers. The texts we read are products of these relationships. Recall the example of Willard Motley's 600,000-word typescript of *Knock on Any Door,* his first novel. Part of Motley's socialization (and his text's as well) came from his interaction with publishers, who taught Motley not only some points of conventional spelling and punctuation but also the lesson that publishing could not at the time accommodate a trade novel of that length or of such frankness in dealing with sexuality. Thus even editors whose primary basis for editing is authorial intention find themselves dealing with issues of socialization. Editors will differ as to whether and to what extent they broaden their concept of authorship and textual authority to include the nonauthorial. What is essential is that they hold a clear definition of the concept employed.

Because editors may adopt varying standards or concepts of textual authority in editing and because editors adopting an identical standard will nevertheless differ at times in their judgments, it should be remembered that critical editing does not so much establish the text as establish a text of a work (or, more accurate, it establishes a text and a textual history). Regardless of standard, the general method of critical editing is fairly uniform. It requires critical editors of whatever stripe (1) to discover the relevant documentary texts of the work; (2) to identify variant readings among the texts and the sources of that variation; (3) to construct a text consisting of readings judged to be authoritative according to the standard the editor has adopted; and (4) to detect erroneous readings and correct them by conjectural emendation based on the adopted standard.

One expedient that may be used in this process is what editors call copy-text. In a paper entitled "The Rationale of Copy-Text" (1949), W. W. Greg set forth an approach to editing Renaissance dramatic texts—an approach that was seen to have wider application and that was subsequently employed for a variety of texts from a variety of historical periods, including texts of nineteenth-century works edited under the auspices of the Center for Editions of American Authors (CEAA). Greg's argument was genealogical, or stemmatic. He suggested that editors select as the basis of an edition an early authoritative text (not, as some editors did, the last text published during an author's lifetime). Greg recognized that an early text would likely be more faithful to what an author wrote than a later one would be. Later texts would be likely to contain nonauthorial alterations, or "corruptions." Even a later text (that of, say, a third quarto rather than a first) that contains authorial revisions would be likely to retain some accumulated earlier corruptions and to introduce some new ones. Thus, employing Greg's concept of copy-text in constructing a critical text, an editor retains the readings of the copy-text unless there is evidence that variant readings of later states are authorial. The copy-text, in other words, is presumed to be authoritative except where the evidence indicates otherwise. Textual authority, as Greg pointed out, is often divided: authorial and nonauthorial readings can exist in the same state of a text. Adopting some readings from one state does not require uncritical adoption of its others. Editors are especially likely to find a division of authority between what Greg called, somewhat misleadingly, the "accidentals" (spelling, punctuation, capitalization, etc.) and the "substantives" (wording). Generally, later states of a text are likely to be less authoritative in accidentals than in substantives, because most authors pay less attention to accidentals and because compositors and others involved in printing and publishing or in the copying of manuscripts feel more free to alter them. Furthermore, it is especially in the matter of accidentals that clear evidence of authorial intention is lacking. Thus, unless there is evidence to the contrary, editors retain the accidentals of the copy-text, even if a later state of the text has the more authoritative substantive readings. If they could establish the authority of the accidentals and substantives of every state, editors would not need a copy-text: they would simply construct a text from all the authoritative readings. But seldom is there sufficient evidence to indicate the authority of every reading. Thus, faced with readings of indeterminate authority, editors rely on the copy-text to provide readings that are likely to be authoritative.

Greg did not intend his rationale as an inflexible rule for critical editing, but the perception that its application (especially in CEAA editions) was inflexible led to considerable debate about what was termed "copy-text editing" and "Greg-Bowers editing." When Greg's rationale was applied to texts for which authorial manuscripts survived, it tended to favor these manuscripts as copy-text. From a McGannian perspective, then, the retention of a manuscript's accidentals violated the collaborative relation between author and publisher. When it was applied to texts that had been so extensively revised as to create different versions of a work, it was seen as creating a textual hybrid that violated the integrity of the versions. When it distinguished as a practical matter between accidentals and substantives, it was making a false theoretical distinction since "accidentals" such as punctuation also convey meaning and thus are substantive. To some extent, such criticism was based on misunderstandings of Greg's position and intent and on an exaggerated sense of the intransigence of scholars who employed copy-text in critical editing. Bowers himself, an influential champion of Greg's rationale, allowed for sources other than an early manuscript or printed text for copy-text, as when a work existed in more than one version (as in Henry James), when an author engaged in extensive revision (as in Jonson), when an author took pains with accidentals in later texts (as in Whitman), and when a textual stemma revealed radiating rather than linear descent (as in Stephen Crane).

The concept of copy-text, if not in its usual sense, can be applied even when there is no single document containing a text of presumptive authority. In critically editing Joyce's *Ulysses* (1922), Hans Walter Gabler faced a situation in which printed editions of the text were unusually corrupt and in which there did not exist—and did not ever exist—a unified holograph, a manuscript in the author's hand. Gabler sought to recover the text as Joyce wrote it and repeatedly revised it during its progress through various drafts, fair copies, typescripts, and multiple proofs, with much of Joyce's composition taking place marginally and interlinearly on these documents. From the documents, Gabler assembled Joyce's autograph notations or inferred the notations from nonautograph text when such notation was lacking. Thus, in a sense, he created a continuous manuscript text to serve as a copy-text. He then emended the copy-text to incorporate later authorial corrections, as well as nonauthorial corrections that evidently received authorial sanction.

Obviously, the text of *Ulysses* edited according to, for example, "historical-critical editing" would little resemble that edited by Gabler, who himself observed that "an edition of *Ulysses* based on the first edition [or any other] would not in a full sense attain the quality or scope of a critical edition, but would remain essentially a corrected edition of the work's hitherto received text" (1894–95), a text that does not present the *Ulysses* Joyce wrote or intended to make public. Even editors adopting identical editorial principles and methods are likely to come to differing judgments at some points and thus to construct nonidentical critical texts.

One lesson, then, is that scholarly editions, of whatever type, should be used whole—as repositories not of a definitively established text but of a text produced according to particular editorial principles and accompanied by an apparatus that explains these principles, that provides a record of editorial decisions, and that accounts for the history of the text and its documents. If the various manuscripts of Chaucer's *Canterbury Tales* represent fragmentary stages in a developing but unfinished and not finally ordered work, readers who regard any one text of it as a definitive record of the whole work as Chaucer wrote it are letting their desire for an unequivocal text overrule the evidence of textual criticism. Perhaps, as Derek Pearsall has asserted, the *Tales* "should ideally be presented partly as a bound book (the first and last fragments are fixed) and partly as a set of fragments in a folder, with the fragmentary information as to their nature and placement fully displayed" (7). Similarly, perhaps partly with tongue in cheek, Lois Potter has suggested that an edition of Shakespeare could take the form of "a series of computer menus, each of which could in turn permutate to give versions of the text based on different editorial hypotheses and the different needs of each particular reader" (389).

Such proposals are in fact being implemented in electronic editions published online or on CD-ROM. While many electronic editions are documentary (reproducing the texts of particular documents), others are critical, and others, more commonly, combine documentary and critically constructed texts. An example of such combination is found in the *Piers Plowman* Electronic Archive that is now in progress.[7] William Langland's fourteenth-century poem survives in fifty-four more or less complete manuscripts and in three 1550 printings based on no longer surviving manuscripts. These texts appear to represent three authorial versions of the poem (conventionally designated A, B, and C). None of the manuscripts, however, is Langland's holograph (that is, a manuscript in his own hand); those who made the manuscript copies repeated errors from earlier manuscripts, introduced new errors and "corrections" of old ones, added words and lines to the texts, omitted lines, and "contaminated" their texts by combining readings from different versions. The editors of the archive plan for it to include not only digitized color images of the fifty-four manuscripts (with codicological and linguistic description of each) and TEI-conformant transcriptions of these manuscripts but also editorially constructed texts of the A, B, and C scribal archetypes and critical texts of the three authorial versions. These contents will be combined with software for the retrieval and manipulation of both texts and editorial annotation. Although the archive is to be published in CD-ROM (with periodic updatings), it may also be used to produce a printed critical edition (Duggan).

Computers have greatly increased readers' ability to gain access to transcriptions and digitized facsimiles of manuscript and printed texts and their ability to manipulate and analyze these texts. At the same time, at least for many works, there is still a need for critically edited texts that reflect the knowledge and judgment of editors. These too, of course, may be presented through (as well as prepared on) computers. Indeed, it seems likely that in the future most scholarly editions—documentary and critical—will appear in electronic form, probably accompanied by (or accompanying) printed texts published for general reading. It should be pointed out, however, that coding texts is a time-consuming, expensive process, as is suggested by the *partially* coded beginning sentence from Francis Bacon's essay on truth:[8]

> WH<f type="sc">>a<f type="r$quot;>t<f type="i"> is Truth <f type="r$quot;> ;
> |said ie{|lst}ing <f type="i$quot;>Pilate <f type="r$quot;> ; And would not
> {|st}ay for an An|swer . (Lancashire 4.1)

And coding itself is interpretive, not mechanical. Whether a coded text is presented as in a documentary or critical edition, it has inescapably been subjected to interpretation by the editor. Even digitized texts that reproduce the appearance of a document are, after all, abstractions from that document, which lack some of the "information" available to readers who have the original before them. While electronic texts have much to recommend them, they do not eliminate the need for access to originals nor the mediation of textual critics.

Notes

[1] The often-cited example of "soiled fish" occurs in Matthiessen's praise of a *discordia concors* in Melville's *White-Jacket*: "[. . .] hardly anyone but Melville could have created the shudder that results from calling this frightening vagueness some 'soiled fish of the sea'" (392). That "soiled" was a misprint for "coiled" was pointed out by Nichol.

[2] The TEI advisory board includes representatives from the American Historical Association, the Association for Documentary Editing, the Modern Language Association, and other organizations. For an introduction to the TEI, see Ide and Véronis.

[3] A demonstration model of *The Rossetti Archive* is available on the Internet in the University of Virginia's Institute for Advanced Technology in the Humanities, Research Reports, First Series 1993 (http://jefferson.village.virginia.edu/rossetti/rossetti.html). A description of the project appears in McGann, "Complete Writings."

[4] In *Scholarly Editing and the Computer Age* Shillingsburg identifies five "formal orientations" that each imply different bases for editing: documentary, aesthetic, authorial, sociological, and bibliographical (16–27). Greetham offers a scheme linking editorial approaches to literary theory and classifying editorial approaches as writer-based (W. W. Greg, Fredson Bowers, and G. Thomas Tanselle), text-based (Hans Gabler and Hans Zeller), and reader-based (Jerome McGann).

[5] Our description of this form is based primarily on Zeller, "New Approach." See also, however, Gabler, Bornstein, and Pierce.

[6] For a review of these and other issues raised by McGann, see Tanselle, "Historicism" and "Textual Criticism."

[7] The archive is being edited by Robert Adams, Hoyt N. Duggan, Eric Eliason, Ralph Hanna III, and Thorlac Turville-Petre. For a description of the editorial project and for links to materials within the archive, see Duggan.

[8] Here are the sections of the encoding guidelines for the Renaissance Electronic Texts Project, at the University of Toronto, edited by Ian Lancashire, as an example of the detail required in coding electronic texts: "1. INTRODUCTION, 2. GENERAL RULES FOR TRANSCRIPTION, 3.1 ENCODING: SGML Tags, 3.2 COCOA Tags, 3.3 The TEI Guidelines, 4.1 THE RENAISSANCE CHARACTER SET: Introduction, 4.2 Computer Representation, 4.3 Letter-numbers, 4.4 Punctuation, Delimiters, and Other Marks, 4.5 Graphics, 4.6 Abbreviations, 4.7 Delimiters, 5. RET Tags, 5.1 Global Tags, 5.2 Feature Tags, 5.3 Structural Tags, 5.4 Word-level Tags, 6. TAGGING EXAMPLES, 6.1 Abstracts, Arguments, and Summaries, 6.2 Acts, Scenes, and Classical Scenes, 6.3 Closings, Colophons, Epilogues, and Explicits, 6.4 Columns, 6.5 Comments, 6.6 Corrections, 6.7 Damaged Text, 6.8 Dedication, Epigraph, Epistle, Letter, Preface, and Prologue, 6.9 Dedicatory Poems, 6.10 Diacritics, 6.11 Dictionary Entries, 6.12 Divisions, 6.13 Dramatis Personae, 6.14 Errata, 6.15 Font, 6.16 Headings and Subheadings, 6.17 Language Shift, 6.18 Milestones, 6.19 Names, 6.20 Notes, End-, Foot-, and Marginal, 6.21 Ornaments, Leaves, and Lines, 6.22 Paragraphing, 6.23 Printer's Business, 6.24 Quotations, 6.25 Scribe's Business, 6.26 Speeches and Speech Prefixes, 6.27 Stage Directions, 6.28 Stanzas and Rhyme, 6.29 Table of Contents, 6.30 Title Pages, 6.31 Variants, Press and Textual, 6.32 Verse and Prose, 6.33 Words Cited as Objects, 6.34 Words, Hung and Split between Pages, 6.35 X-References and Hypertext, Bibliography, Appendix 1: The RET/TEI Header, Appendix 2: Document-Type Definitions."

EDITORIAL PROCEDURE

I have discharg'd the dull duty of an Editor,
to my best judgment, with more labour than I expect thanks.

—*Alexander Pope,* The Works of Shakespear *(1723)*

The duty of a collator is indeed dull, yet, like other tedious tasks,
is very necessary; but an emendatory critick would ill discharge
his duty, without qualities very different from dulness. [. . .]
Let us now be told no more of the dull duty of an editor.

—*Samuel Johnson,* The Plays of William Shakespeare *(1765)*

In the Anglo-American tradition of textual criticism, critical editing is most often used for texts that their authors intended for publication, whether in print or in manuscript. For this reason and because some of its methods (especially its study of textual transmission and variation) apply to other forms of textual study and scholarly editing, we will describe in some detail how critical editions are prepared.

Since the concern of an editor is the text in its various embodiments, as well as that form of the text considered authoritative according to whatever standard, such as authorial intention, adopted by the critic, the first task of the editor preparing a critical edition is to identify, locate, and assemble all the extant significant forms of the text. Although this task might at first appear straightforward, opinions vary widely on the necessity of obtaining and including certain types of material and on how to assemble the forms of the text. The financial support for textual studies in the humanities being what it is, most scholars these days find it more convenient to compile a master file of microfilm or xerographic copies of the relevant texts than to travel about the world spending as much time at a given library as it takes to collate all the texts located there. However, scholars should be aware that no matter how good a reproduction of a document may be, it is never a substitute for consulting the actual document and that editors will ultimately have to check any edition prepared from film or photocopies against the originals if they wish to avoid problems. For example,

George Walton Williams and Thomas L. Berger have pointed out, with the assistance of Neil Taylor, that several misreadings in T. H. Howard-Hill's *Oxford Shakespeare Concordance for* Henry IV, *Part II* derived from blots or stains on the originals that produced apparently different words when only a photographic facsimile was employed (111, 113, 115). It is also true that a fair amount of research must be devoted simply to discovering the locations of the desired copies and ascertaining that they have not been sold, moved, put on permanent loan, or lost. Although standard reference guides and bibliographies are of great assistance in such matters, the scholar may, or rather should, eventually write to likely libraries and use the free ads provided in the pages of many learned journals to request this kind of information. The editor will also want to gather other evidence relevant to the compositional and transmissional history of the work's text, such as letters, journals, printers' and publishers' records, and previous bibliographical and textual scholarship.

Assuming that the scholar has successfully compiled a complete list of forms of the text and locations of copies of the various forms, he or she must now decide how to deal with them. The editor will certainly want to use any forms of the text that are written or corrected in the author's own hand (manuscripts, typescripts, notebooks, proofs, and the like), as well as the printed forms of the text done within the author's life or over which the author's intended revisions may have had some control (the *Miscellaneous Poems* of Andrew Marvell or all the works of Sir Philip Sidney, save the *Defence of Poesy*, are good examples of the latter instance). For texts with an extensive manuscript tradition, the editor will want to consider not only manuscript material in the author's own hand but all the manuscripts dating from the author's lifetime—and in some cases well after it—to determine whether readings in this manuscript tradition derive from original authorial manuscripts and from revisions of such manuscripts by the author. Although this kind of problem most often dates from the first two centuries after the appearance of printing (the history of Donne's texts provides a good example), it can occur at any time, as the complex manuscript (and proof) situation surrounding the publication of James Joyce's *Ulysses* demonstrates.

Next, the question arises concerning how many copies of a given edition should be collated. For most editions produced before 1660 so few copies survive into our own times that the answer is usually simple: all the surviving copies. But for most works after 1660—and for some few before—so many copies survive that it becomes utterly impractical to collate all. Current discussion has settled on some number between twelve and twenty because the chances of discovering further press variants after collating this number diminishes to an insignificant statistical probability. One might choose to collate only ten copies of a particular edition but to check all obtainable copies at those spots where changes have been found or uncorrected errors observed, or one might select random samples in the edition and collate them against all, or nearly all, surviving copies. Or one might give over the remainder of a career and collate all the surviving copies of all the various editions of some text like Saul Bellow's *Herzog*. In any event, the textual scholar must decide at the outset, and the decision must be plausible. Next, the editor should secure the copies that must be consulted or arrange to visit all the locations of these copies, for he or she must now begin collating these texts, that is, comparing them symbol for symbol and recording any differences (see Appendix on Textual Notation).

Although the actual process of collation is uniform, it serves two distinct purposes, and thus we will speak as though there were two separate processes, one "horizontal" and the other "vertical." In the first, the horizontal comparison of texts, the editor collates with one another the copies produced from each individual typesetting (whether directly from type or indirectly through plates)—in other words, all those copies that are part of a single edition, as defined by analytical bibliography, whether or not they also form part of the subsets called impressions, issues, or states. The reason for undertaking this work is (1) to determine whether an edition contains stop-press corrections and if so to determine which of the readings produced by each correction is the "corrected" reading[1] or (2) to determine whether textual alterations were made between the various impressions of an edition and if possible to ascertain the source of the corrections. Since throughout the handpress period it was the normal practice not to dispose of the already printed sheets that contained uncorrected readings, surviving copies of the book are as likely to carry uncorrected readings as they are to carry corrected ones. Even in the modern era printers and publishers occasionally produce works that contain sheets with uncorrected readings, and since the advent of plating later impressions are often printed from plates that have been corrected to some degree. Thus, whether the alterations were done on the bed of the press during the actual printing process or done on plates or standing type between impressions, the importance of the evidence and the purpose and means for discovering it remain the same.

Collating procedures for a text transmitted through manuscript resemble those for multiple copies of a single printed edition. That is, the editor tries to determine which variants exist only because of the process of copying the manuscript and which are the result of the particular exemplar used to produce the manuscript. Such determinations allow the editor to group the various manuscripts into families, and the result is often similar to that for a printed book that has undergone several significant stop-press corrections.

Collation has always been a singularly dull and exacting practice, although several devices and computer programs have been perfected that greatly assist the process, in both ease and accuracy. At least at some point, most editors still follow the time-honored process of looking at two texts with the naked eye, symbol for symbol, to discover how they differ. This nonmechanical method, called sight collation, is prone to error, and the editor who employs it will usually want to repeat the process with any two texts several times to compensate for the collator's mental or visual errors. Certain minor sophistications are possible with this process: one might have a partner read the base text aloud while the other follows along in the second text (with world enough and money one might even have a large crew of such "followers" and one lector), or one might tape-record a spoken version of the base text and after correcting that tape use it as the lector while following along in subsequent copies of that text (this system at least reduces the potential for error caused by misspeaking). Beyond these refinements however, one must simply slog on with collations.

Editors can collate copies of a single setting of type (issues and states of an edition, impressions from the same standing type or plates, photographic reprints, and even xerographic copies) using either the Hinman collator or the Lindstrand comparator, or devices deriving from them. (See Dearing, "Poor Man's Mark IV," on constructing a rather peculiar device for collating microfilms.) The Hinman collator, developed by Charlton Hinman for the examination of multiple copies of Shakespeare's First Folio, superimposes reflected images of two copies and illuminates them with alternating light sources that cause variants—of even the smallest sort, such as broken letters—to appear to wave or blink. The Lindstrand comparator also uses reflected images but, through a central prismatic eyepiece, combines them in the user's nervous system, much as the old stereopticon did, so that variants appear to float off the page or are indecipherable blurs. In addition to facilitating textual collation, these two devices can aid bibliographical analysis by indicating the presence of type damage, shiftings of type within the chase, and areas of resetting that do not result in textual change. Machine collation, as the use of these devices is sometimes termed, does pose a certain logistical problem: editors must find copies of the work they intend to collate in places that possess collators or comparators, or they must obtain undistorted photocopies (Guffey). The chief limitation, though, is that the devices cannot be used for the collation of texts not of the same typesetting and thus are restricted to what we have called horizontal collation.

For many years it has been thought that the computer would bring an end to the drudgery of collating texts; but until very recently computer technology required the manual inputting of almost all texts—indeed, in most current applications it still does—and this creates yet one more point of possible textual error. However, optical scanning continues to improve, and it may soon be possible to have most books from the machine-press period put in machine-readable form without any, or much, human intervention. But problems with skewed lines, unusual type fonts, broken type, uneven inking, and the like mean that it will be a long time before books from the mid-eighteenth century and back can be made machine-readable by optical scanning. And of course, scanners will not handle manuscripts. There is the further practical problem of the costs of such advanced technology. Under current levels of financial support for editorial work in the humanities, it seems unlikely that any but the largest editing projects will be able to make a case for securing sufficient funds to use optical scanning. A more exciting, though more expensive and less accessible, method of transferring texts to the computer is digital imaging. This technology results not in the scanning of documents letter for letter, as in optical scanning, but in the transfer of the image of an entire page into digital form. It is the same technology that produces the satellite weather maps and space-flight pictures we see on television. Any document—or a photocopy, microfilm, photostat, or photographic print of it—can be digitized. As Paul R. Sternberg and John M. Brayer explained as early as 1983, the computer can reconstitute the digitized image to a specified size, typically on a television monitor, and can be instructed to superimpose the images for comparison, say, of two copies of the same edition. When the images from the same page of two copies are superimposed, shifts in type, textual variants, and other differences between them will appear to be shaded in a color, usually red or blue, that stands out from the black of the invariant portions of the two images. Aside from the advantage this system possesses for the sophisticated collation of documents, it also transfers texts into machine-readable form without human intervention and with less trouble than optical scanning now causes. Again, the cost of using such a system and the difficulty of gaining access to it may be prohibitive for some projects.

More practical for editors contemplating the application of computers to editing are microcomputers. Although the problems of getting the texts into machine-readable form still exist, the machines are within the financial range of even the most modest project, the editor is able to have a much closer control over the various operations, and there now exist a number of sophisticated collational programs—for example, those developed by the editors of the Donne variorum edition now in progress. Typically, such locally developed programs are available at very low cost. The Clark Library at the University of California, Los Angeles, has established a central depository of microcomputer programs, also available at low cost. Of course, the application of computers, particularly microcomputers, to any editorial task is a tricky business, and editors must engage in a good deal of preliminary thinking and consultation before they employ computers in their work. The advantages, though, are considerable, since in addition to facilitating collation, computer programs may also be used for analysis of variants, for construction of an edition's editorial apparatus, and eventually for computer typesetting (or presentation of an electronic edition). (See Shillingsburg, *Scholarly Editing*, for an excellent guide to the use of computers in editing.) At any rate, collation is essential, whether done on 3″ × 5″ cards, floppy disks, or mainframes.

Variants found among books belonging to the same edition generally fall into three categories: (1) variants created by mishaps in typesetting and printing,

(2) variants created by the proofreader without reference to copy, and (3) variants created either by the author in proofreading or revising or by the proofreader with reference to the author's copy. The first sort will obviously lack textual authority, but many variants created inadvertently may not appear, at first inspection, to be inadvertent. In texts printed before about 1800 damage to the crossbar of the letter *f* will produce the perfectly acceptable letter long *s*, turning such words as "funny," "fake," and "foil" into "sunny," "sake," and "soil." In books set with individual pieces of type, including modern books set by monotype, the loss of the letter *g* during either imposition or printing would produce a variant reading for the phrase "the Grecian grape." In modern books produced by compositional processes that deal with whole lines as physical units (linotype and certain kinds of photographic composition), lines can be reversed in ways that alter meaning without creating pure nonsense, as careful readers of newspaper picture captions can testify from their own experience. The advent of computer-generated typesetting, whether produced by a composing company alone or with the assistance of an author's encoded disks or tapes, is ushering in a new spectrum of variants, ranging from the expected errors produced in keyboarding (transpositions, eye skips, failures to space, and the like) to the obvious nonsense resulting from miscoding or even from the inclusion of the code into the text, so that, for example, "Pasiphaë" is printed as "Pasiphaeum" because the printing code for the umlaut, on one system, is "/um," the stroke not printing.

Of course, a knowledge of analytical and historical bibliography is necessary to untangle some variants of this first kind, though the great majority are transparently evident. However, two points about them must be stressed. First, such inadvertent variants will appear as "corrected" readings during collation since they are chronologically subsequent to the original, or "uncorrected," readings. Second, although they have no textual authority, they often induce the printer to attempt repairs during the printing process and thus may cause the second or third kind of variant to occur. Even more extreme forms of inadvertent variants may be found in cases where an accident in the printshop destroys a few plates or a page or more of set and printed type and the printer attempts to replace the lost material by replating or by resetting page for page or line for line. Such accidents will produce either anomalous readings in the variant record or deceptive "uncorrected" and "corrected" readings, and care must be exercised using the tools of analytical and historical bibliography to ensure an accurate understanding of the entire printing process.

The second kind of variant is much like the first except that it does involve human intervention with the conscious intention to correct the text, while the first kind is purely inadvertent. However, so long as the proofreaders do not refer to the setting copy, their corrections are no more authoritative than those produced by mishap and are much less authoritative than the modern critical editor's emendations, which are based on his or her study of all the bibliograph-ical facts and on critical judgment. Corrections made without reference to copy normally attempt to tidy up the printing, that is, to eliminate such things as turned letters, broken rules, faulty pagination or direction lines, and gross spelling errors. Experience has taught us that although such attempts may pro-ceed deep enough into the text to correct such an error as "John" for "George," they usually do not go so deep as to correct "can not" for "can." Furthermore, since this type of correction is a true stop-press correction and involves unlock-ing the chase or making other alterations in the imposed forms or plates, any accidents in making the correction will introduce variants of the first kind. But, as with the first kind, the very existence of such variants may generate the third kind, either at the same time or later.

The third kind of variant is, of course, what the textual critic is most inter-ested in. In this case the author, or a proofreader following the author's copy, has corrected a false reading in the text or replaced one authorial reading with another. However, as with the second kind of variant, correcting or revising the standing type or plates may introduce further unintended variants.

Separating these three kinds of variants from one another once the collation of the copies of a given edition is complete can be very complex. The editor must be constantly aware that the basic unit of press correction is the forme, that is, the type used to print one side of a sheet. Thus, if the outer forme of a gathering that shows only one instance of stop-press correction contains vari-ants clearly of type three (a change that can only have been made by the author or by reference to the author's copy) along with variants that could be either of that type or of type two, the editor is reasonably safe in assuming that these lat-ter variants were made at the same time and by the same agent as the former ones and thus have the same authority. Problems will certainly occur in dealing with variants produced by stop-press correction, and they require the applica-tion of critical judgment based on all the available evidence. In any event, the editor's aim is to construct an "ideal" text for each setting of the work. This ideal text, although it may be unlike any previous individual version, will em-body all the most authoritative readings found in all copies of that setting.

After producing an ideal text for each edition of the work done in the au-thor's lifetime or over which the author may have exercised any authority, the editor must collate these ideal versions and any manuscripts, corrected proofs, and the like. This set of collations, which we call the vertical comparison of texts, will reveal to the editor how the author or others may have altered the text from edition to edition, how the mere process of reproduction has intro-duced corruption, and how various earlier forms of the text, or completely new ones, were used as setting copy at a later time. For example, this sort of colla-tion will reveal that after a 1647 separate quarto edition of Jeremy Taylor's *The Liberty of Prophesying*, a second and a third issue of this quarto in a collected edition of various works (1648 and 1650), a second edition in a folio collection in 1657, and a third edition in another folio collection in 1674, finally a 1702 quarto edition set from a copy of the 1647 edition appeared with the designation "The Second Edition, Corrected" on its title page. However, major changes and additions made by Taylor in 1657 and repeated in 1674 are, of course, not in the 1702 edition, which is actually the fourth edition; and since the copy of 1647 used for setting copy was randomly selected and not compared with later editions, even some of the uncorrected readings of formes in 1647 were reproduced (Williams 39–77).

Now that all collations are complete the editor possesses a set of notes recording all variations, from whatever sources, along both the horizontal and the vertical axes of the text's history (see fig. 13). The record of textual variation, then, aids in the creation of a textual genealogy, represented in a stemma, and in establishing the chronology and taxonomy of the physical documents in which the text appears. For most texts, where external dating is clear and unambiguous, these tasks may be fairly easy, but the history of the study of the Shakespeare quartos before Pollard and Greg's work should warn all editors to be on their guard against false datings, forgeries, and other "machinations" of publishers out for gain above all else. The stemma should account for every major form of the text (in manuscripts, proofs, editions, and corrected states and impressions, though normally not variations within these forms such as stop-press corrections). The stemma allows the reader to see at a glance and in diagrammatic form the editor's view of the transmission of the text.

To construct the stemma the editor will have to make some crucial determinations based on an analysis of the variants found and recorded. For example, it will be important to decide, for each form of the text, what document or documents served as compositor's or scribe's copy. Although this copy will sometimes be easy to identify, as in the case of the 1702 *Liberty of Prophesying* mentioned above, it can be quite elusive, as in the cases of Shakespeare's *Othello, King Lear,* or *Henry IV, Part II.* As one moves forward in history, more and more of the documents used for setting have been preserved, making the editor's job clearer, if not easier; but even in so modern a work as D. H. Lawrence's *Women in Love,* two typescripts made up of mixed ribbon and carbon copies, some corrected by Lawrence himself and some by his wife, will certainly cause some editorial concern and deliberation.

For works from earlier periods the editor will attempt to determine compositorial practices and what portions of each edition were set by what compositors. This not only provides evidence about the order in which the edition was set and printed but also sheds light on how the compositors may have altered the author's text. Extensive research has been carried out on the compositors of the Shakespeare quartos and First Folio and of certain other sixteenth- and seventeenth-century works, and the study of this aspect of book production is

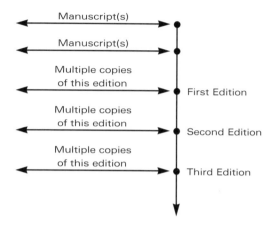

Fig. 13. *Horizontal and vertical collation.*

now taking in ever broader areas of the English book trade. Modern compositors have not been allowed the freedom of their colleagues of the earlier period, but the editor of modern works must still consider house style and copyediting.

The editor will also wish to investigate the proofreading of the printed editions. For early books evidence normally derives from an analysis of the stop-press corrections discovered during collation, and the work done with them is discussed above. (In addition to Bowers, "Elizabethan Proofing," and Hinman, *Printing*, see Simpson.) From the later seventeenth century the practice of providing authors with proofs before printing started became ever more common, and by the eighteenth century the editor may assume that this was normal practice for any serious work, though whether the author attended to them carefully is entirely another matter. Modern publishers frequently preserve an author's correspondence and several sets of marked proofs, and in such cases the editor will of course take care to evaluate such authorial changes as likely readings for the edited text. No matter what the circumstances, the editor must bend every effort to take full account of all the changes, errors, or failures to correct associated with setting, imposing, proofing, and printing. From these and other studies of the variants of the text, the editor will eventually be able to construct a life history of the text and to establish the relationships among the individual members of that family.

Stemmatic and bibliographical relationships of the texts will assist the editor in determining both the chronology and authority of textual variants. With sufficient evidence as to the authority of each state of the text and of any textual variation, an editor could then construct a critical text (or texts). When, as is usually the case, there is not sufficient evidence, the editor confronts what can be the most vexed question in critical editing and one that can save or damn the entire effort: selection of the copy-text for the edition. The editor using final authorial intention as the basis for editing will normally choose that text which lies closest to the author's manuscript. Thus, if no manuscripts or corrected proofs in the author's hand survive and if all printed editions are in ancestral relationship with one another, then the editor will choose the earliest printed edition as the copy-text, in part because it is more likely than any subsequent edition to preserve the accidentals of the text. If the author made substantive changes in subsequent editions, the editor will emend the copy-text accordingly, but such changes of words will have almost no effect on the accidentals of the text and will certainly not cause the editor to choose a different copy-text.

However, other considerations may enter in. For example, if the author in question can be demonstrated to have paid considerable attention to the accidentals—as well as, or even instead of, the substantives—of the text in every edition down to the last printed in his or her lifetime, then the editor will choose the latest edition as the copy-text, for this embodies the author's final intention in both substantives and accidentals. Or, if the author produced an entirely new manuscript or typescript from which a later edition was printed, then that later edition could contain the author's final intention and might be selected as copy-text. Another situation, common in the early drama but possible with any text, arises when the earliest edition is set from a document not produced by the author (in the drama, from a theater promptbook or a memorial transcription by a member of the theatrical company) and a later edition is then set from the author's manuscript. In such a case the later edition is obviously the choice for copy-text, but things are often not this straightforward.

A copy of the unauthoritative earlier edition, for example, will often be conflated with the author's manuscript, and the marked-up printed edition will serve as setting copy for the later edition. In such an instance neither the early nor the later edition will embody the author's intentions regarding the accidentals, except possibly in those passages of some length that are written into the printed copy from the author's manuscript. If the author exercises any control over the production of the later edition, selection of copy-text becomes rather arbitrary, but the editor would probably choose the later edition since it may contain authorial accidentals while the earlier edition would contain none. In any of these situations, however, the substantives would be adopted into the copy-text according to their authoritativeness no matter how the editions were produced.

In certain circumstances the editor may not be able to or may not choose to select a single copy-text at all. The two texts of Marlowe's *Doctor Faustus* or the early-edition and New York–edition texts of Henry James's novels represent different versions of these works—or perhaps different works altogether—and thus would be edited separately, each with its own copy-text.

Having selected the copy-text, the editor must now engage in emendation. In emending the copy-text, the editor relies on physical evidence and bibliographical inference, along with knowledge of the author's life and work and of the linguistic, literary, and publishing context of the time. Bringing to bear such knowledge, the editor emends the copy-text where it is judged to be in error and where its readings are judged less authoritative than those from other states of the text. For an edition based on final authorial intention, the editor emends the copy-text with later, more authoritative readings from other printed and manuscript documents when the vertical collation of texts and the analysis of the recorded variants indicate that the author intervened in the transmission of the text. Practice has shown us that such authorial intervention most often concerns substantive readings rather than accidentals, but editors must always be alert for either sort of authorial intervention. Thus, when the results of collation clearly show that the author has introduced certain changes in the text, the editor will probably adopt these readings and emend the copy-text. For example, as Arthur Colby Sprague has shown, Samuel Daniel became convinced that proper poetic style demanded lines with masculine rather than feminine endings (i.e., lines ending with stressed rather than unstressed syllables). He revised his sonnet sequence *Delia* according to this conviction and also tinkered with other features of the work, eventually revising it four times (xxxi). Faced with such a textual history and seeking to construct a text as Daniel finally intended it, an editor will adopt the substantive changes that Daniel made in the four revisions but retain the accidentals of the earliest text containing a given sonnet. The editor thus attempts to produce a text that embodies, at every point, Daniel's final intention, and the masculine endings and other substantive revisions were certainly Daniel's final intention. In some cases, however, authorial intervention may not represent authorial intention, as when Melville expurgated *Typee* at his publisher's insistence. An editor basing an edition on final authorial intention would then reject late readings produced by such intervention.

Although the editor may choose to incorporate an author's intended substantive changes into the copy-text, other textual concerns are not so clear-cut. Historical bibliography will provide the editor with much information about the operation of the publishing and printing industry during the period in question, and analytical bibliography will supply a model and a method for determining precisely how each printed version of the text was affected by the master printers, compositors, copy editors, censors, and others concerned with the production of books. Thus the editor may be in a position to emend the copy-text at various disputed points because of the detection of compositorial spelling habits, house styles, or the exigencies of having to fit a fixed amount of copy into a fixed amount of space in the printed book. It may be that the text has even been influenced by the typography. As Randall McLeod has noted, some spelling oddities in Renaissance books could be caused by kerning, the extension of the face of one piece of type over the body of another piece of type. With kerned type a compositor might, for example, set an author's "amongst" as "amongest" so that the back-kerning portion of the long *s* would rest on the body of the added *e* and thus not become fouled with the face of *g*. Shakespearean textual studies have devoted so much time to identifying compositors over the last decades that editors can isolate those accidentals and, in some cases, substantives in a text caused not by the intervention of authority but by compositorial preference or necessity. Or, for nineteenth- and twentieth-century American authors published first in Britain, the editor will wish to determine whether the American or the British spelling of such words as "colour" and "centre" has authority.

Naturally, the nature and source of the copy from which the book is set (or the manuscript is copied) are of great importance to the editor. Was the first edition set from the author's manuscript? Did the author read proofs? Was the copy a transcript at some number of removes from the author's manuscript, or was it an annotated copy of an earlier printed edition? The editor must also have a clear understanding of how the printer disposed of that setting copy. Was the copy cast off? If so, it will produce different composing, imposing, and formatting problems for the printers than will a book set serially. In books composed in the latter way, compositors will run short of space only at the ends of gatherings or the end of the book, and unauthorized changes in the text to fit the copy into the space available will occur only at these points. However, books cast off and set by formes, as was done in early printing to cut down on the amount of standing type, will have such changes at places other than the end, depending on the format of the book. Evidence supplied by analytical bibliography about the order of imposition and printing of the formes will allow the editor to avoid retaining unauthorized readings in the copy-text or, if no better reading is possible, to explain the likelihood of such readings being authorial.

Having now constructed a critical text, probably by choosing a copy-text and emending it according to the evidence and best judgment, the editor must decide how to present the text and its apparatus. For texts from the period of early modern English and before (approximately 1750 and back), a basic question must be answered. Will the critical text be old-spelling, regularized, or modernized? (Actually, the editor should make this decision at the beginning of the editing process, but it is more convenient to discuss it at this point.) This subject has produced a great amount of heat, and some light, in the twentieth century. Previously it was not given much consideration. For any edition, except some few intended for an exclusively antiquarian audience, most editors assumed that they should modernize everything—spelling, punctuation, paragraphing, and grammar. The rise of serious academic study of the vernacular literatures in the late nineteenth century reinforced bibliographical studies by demonstrating how much editorial practice, instead of advancing literary studies, actually impeded them. For example, many seventeenth-century prose writers had been subjected to full modernization by nineteenth-century editors, and the alteration of the punctuation had stripped their texts of what Morris Croll has called the "signposts" of their rhetoric (230–33). As one might expect, the reaction swung as far in the opposite direction as the practices being reacted against, and for a while diplomatic editing, verging on facsimile reprinting, was the common method used. As scholarship has regained its equilibrium, however, it has produced a scale of textual presentation that ranges from the most severe diplomatic editing through a graduated series of steps to the most free-wheeling modernized editing, which is closer to adaptation than to editing.

The major forms of presentation are old-spelling, regularized, and modernized. Old-spelling editors normally present their text as faithfully as is technically possible, preserving all spelling, capitalization, italics, and the like found in the copy-text and in the texts used to emend it. This method is but one step removed from true diplomatic editing, since it allows only for emendation of the "diploma" selected as copy-text. The first step on the graduated series is usually the reduction of *f* to *s*, almost always dictated by the practical consideration that the former letter is unavailable in most modern compositors' type fonts. At the next step *i, j, u, v,* and *w* are converted to modern usage. (In the older usage, *i* and *j* were the "same" letter, with *i* generally being used for both *i* and *j* and with *j* being used finally in combinations such as *ij*. Similarly, the use of *v* and *u* depended on position within a word and not on pronunciation, with *v* used initially, as in *vnder* [under] and *u* used medially, as in *euent* [event]. And *w* was often rendered as *uu* and *vv*.) Since these letters all exist in modern type fonts one always has the sinking feeling that this conversion results from the inability of typists, compositors, and the proofreading editors themselves to follow the older usage accurately. At this point the true old-spelling editor normally stops and will make no other silent changes in the text, although the editors of dramatic texts allow themselves further silent emendations in the dramatic paraphernalia of the text, such as speech headings and stage directions.

On the next step of the scale are the regularizing editors. They will certainly adopt all the silent changes made by the most liberal old-spelling editors and will, at least, make some silent adjustments in punctuation, capitalization, and spelling that, although not fully modernizing the text, will give it a greater internal consistency and bring it closer to modern usage. Thus regularizing editors may leave in the text old forms of words if they believe these forms might have a significance that their regularized forms would not. Obviously, this sort of editing calls for many critical judgments, none of them bibliographical. Regularized editions may be more completely altered, to the point of being what one might call "semimodernized" or "conservative modernized" editions. Such editorial work is even more critically demanding but can be very effective, as is the case with G. Blakemore Evans's *The Riverside Shakespeare*.

The final level is a fully modernized text. In these texts editors silently modernize almost everything—spelling, punctuation, and capitalization—changing to modern form just about all the accidentals of the text. Badly done, such modernization requires almost no critical judgment and might be performed by a competent copy editor in the publishing firm bringing out the edition; but well done, it requires critical sensitivity that may cause the editors to preserve important elements in the text that full modernization might obscure.[2]

The mode of presentation may depend on the intended audience for the edition. Scholarly editions for scholarly audiences will, of course, always be in old spelling. One assumes that regularized and modernized editions are intended for the classroom or for that largely mythical figure, the general reader. However, little evidence has ever been brought forward to prove that the general reader will be more inclined to read Sir Thomas Wyatt or Michael Drayton or Fulke Greville if he is given a modernized edition. The general reader's inclination to read these authors will bring with it a willingness, if not a desire, to read them as they wrote. A special plea is often made for modernization of such major authors as Shakespeare, Donne, and Dryden, but here again the general reader is probably up to the task of reading unmodernized texts. In the classroom we seldom have students read Chaucer in modernized adaptations but insist on having him read in Middle English; and the question must arise, if Chaucer, in original spelling, has not disappeared from the curriculum, is it likely that authors from the early modern period will vanish if they are offered in their own spelling? However, the world is wide and authors are resilient. There is room no doubt for editions of all sorts, as long as the economic dictum "bad money drives out good" does not cause modernized editions to close the market for scholarly old-spelling ones. In any case, no matter what form of textual presentation the editor chooses, the textual work lying behind the edition must be rigorous and thorough. A text must be established before it can be modernized.

Another major consideration is whether to present the edition in annotated or in clear-text form. Here the question is practical as well as academic. Sound critical editions presented in clear text—that is, with the text pages containing no annotation of any kind—are easily and practically reproducible by publishers in cheaper editions for the general reader and the classroom, and the annotations can be confined to the back of the scholarly edition. Such an arrangement allows the scholarly edition to present all the evidence and also provides for accurate cheaper editions, since in clear-text formats the publisher need not reset the text pages, thus avoiding the risk of introducing transmissional errors. However, the editor and publisher must carefully assess the potential for such cheaper publication, for many scholars have objected, and perhaps justly, to clear-text editions because their use requires flipping back and forth from the text to the textual notes at the end of the book and because they foreground a single, fixed text and thus obscure or subordinate the full textual history of a work.

Another method is to place all textual notes at the foot of the page to which they refer. With modern photo-offset printing, such an edition might still be reproducible in cheaper editions so long as no note numbers appeared in the text itself, but this method would be difficult and expensive. A middle ground adopted by some publishers is to place notes of emendation at the foot of the page and the rest of the apparatus at the end of the book. It is also possible to incorporate textual notes within the text, as they are in genetic and synoptic documentary editions. Here too there are may be objections, like those expressed by Lewis Mumford in 1968 when he reviewed the Harvard edition of Emerson's journals. Emerson's editors, Mumford said, have "performed current American scholarship's ultimate homage to a writer of genius: they have made him unreadable." They have presented him behind "a barbed wire entanglement of diacritical marks" (4). Although they too may not satisfy everyone and although their full potential is still being explored, computerized editions can easily offer multiple methods of presentation of both text—or, more likely, texts—and apparatus. They can include a clear text with links to variants, variants with links to texts, windows for viewing multiple texts, and programs allowing the reader to construct texts according to multiple standards of textual authority.

No matter what form of presentation is adopted, any true scholarly edition must include somewhere a full textual apparatus that presents a textual history, the editorial decisions made, and the evidence on which they were made. Although publication costs and audience will enter into these decisions, a critical text not accompanied by an apparatus, no matter how carefully edited, does not constitute a critical edition. Some methods of getting around costs appear below.

A critical edition will have an introduction (or appendix or annotation) that places the work and author in their historical setting and that fully describes the forms of the text and the method of editing employed. All editorial conventions and silent emendations should be explained here. The introductions of scholarly editions generally do not engage in evaluative, interpretive, or polemical criticism.

Ideally, an apparatus should allow a user to reconstruct any form of the text, and thus it should record the history of the variants. Such a record requires the presentation of two types of evidence. The first is the historical collation, a complete record of the vertical variants of all collated forms of the text, including the present edition's. The second is a record of the stop-press corrections, the horizontal variants, in the copy-text and in any other forms that the editor deems it necessary to present. These two items allow a user of the edition to fulfill the aim of reconstructing any form of the text. In practice, however, economic considerations often cause some compromise of the ideal. Thus many critical apparatuses record the accidentals and substantives of the copy-text but only the substantives of other authoritative texts. Also essential to the apparatus is a record of all emendations of the copy-text, both in accidentals and substantives. Typically, it may be joined with textual notes that discuss the reasons for emendation or for refusing to emend what may appear to be errors.

Editors of prose texts generally also include in their apparatus a list of ambiguous line-end hyphenations. The lineation of one typesetting of the text may not match the lineation of another. Thus, for example, the word *windowpane* may have been hyphenated (as *window-pane*) between two lines in the copy-text but may occur unhyphenated within a line of the edited text, or vice versa. The record of such end-of-line hyphenations allows reconstruction of the copy-text and indicates whether in quoting the edited text a person should retain its particular hyphenations.

Almost any edition will contain at least one other class of information that the editor will think it important to include—a table of a particular pattern of wrong-font settings demonstrating the work of a particular compositor, repro-ductions of ornaments that identify an unnamed printer, or similar informa-tion. How much additional information should be included depends on how much information scholars need to use the edition properly and on the limits the publisher sets for additions to the apparatus. One way around the latter constraints is to announce in the edition that supplemental apparatus material has been deposited, in typescript, microfilm, or digital form, in major research libraries or at a location on the Internet and that consultation is freely available and copies may be made at cost.

Finally, depending usually on the publisher's format for the series in which the edition appears and on the supposed audience for the edition, the apparatus may include explanatory notes in which the editors gloss words, trace allusions and sources, and supply historical references.

Four Examples

Since textual apparatuses are packaged in several ways, we believe that the brief examples on the following pages may be of use. The first (figs. 14A–14E) is from volume 3 of *The Dramatic Works of Thomas Dekker*, edited by Fredson Bowers (Cambridge: Cambridge UP, 1958); the second (figs. 15A–15D) is from volumes 1 and 4 of *The Plays and Poems of Philip Massinger*, edited by Philip Edwards and Colin Gibson (Oxford: Clarendon, 1976); the third (figs. 16A–16G) is from the CEAA edition of Herman Melville's works: *Mardi*, edited by Harrison Hayford, Hershel Parker, and G. Thomas Tanselle (Evanston: North-western UP; Chicago: Newberry Libr., 1970); and the fourth (figs. 17A–17B), an example of a documentary edition, is from Washington Irving's *Journals and Notebooks*, volume 1, 1803–06, edited by Nathalia Wright (Madison: U of Wis-consin P, 1969).

THE
DRAMATIC WORKS OF
THOMAS DEKKER

EDITED BY
FREDSON BOWERS
Professor of English Literature
University of Virginia

VOLUME III

THE ROARING GIRL
IF THIS BE NOT A GOOD PLAY, THE DEVIL IS IN IT
TROIA-NOVA TRIUMPHANS
MATCH ME IN LONDON
THE VIRGIN MARTYR
THE WITCH OF EDMONTON
THE WONDER OF A KINGDOM

CAMBRIDGE
AT THE UNIVERSITY PRESS
1958

FIG. 14A.   *Title page, volume 3 of Bowers's critical edition of Dekker.*

I. ii]   THE ROARING GIRL

Dauy.   Good tales do well,
In these bad dayes, where vice does so excell.
Adam.   Begin sir *Alexander.*
Alex.   Last day I met
An aged man vpon whose head was scor'd,
A debt of iust so many yeares as these,
Which I owe to my graue, the man you all know.
Omn.   His name I pray you sir.
Alex.   Nay you shall pardon me,   70
But when he saw me (with a sigh that brake,
Or seem'd to breake his heart-strings) thus he spake:
Oh my good knight, saies he, (and then his eies
Were richer euen by that which made them poore,
They had spent so many teares they had no more.)
Oh sir (saies he) you know it, for you ha seene
Blessings to raine vpon mine house and me:
Fortune (who slaues men) was my slaue: her wheele
Hath spun me golden threads, for I thanke heauen,
I nere had but one cause to curse my starres,   80
I ask't him then, what that one cause might be.
Omn.   So Sir.
Alex.   He paus'd, and as we often see,
A sea so much becalm'd, there can be found
No wrinckle on his brow, his waues being drownd
In their owne rage: but when th'imperious winds
Vse strange inuisible tyranny to shake
Both heauens and earths foundation: at their noyse
The seas swelling with wrath to part that fray,
Rise vp, and are more wild, more mad then they.
Euen so this good old man was by my question,   90
Stir'd vp to roughnesse, you might see his gall
Flow euen in's eies: then grew he fantasticall.
Dauy.   Fantasticall, ha, ha.
Alex.   Yes, and talkt odly.
Adam.   Pray sir proceed, how did this old man end?
Alex.   Mary sir thus.

     85 winds ̯] Scott; wind, Q   93 talkt] Dyce; talke Q

                              19   2-2

FIG. 14B. *Sample page of text from Bowers's Dekker.*

TEXTUAL NOTES

I.i

24 here presently, it shall]   All editors have placed a stop like a semi-colon after *here*, thus beginning a new clause with *presently*. The sense is indifferent whatever the modification, but if repetition of a cant phrase for comic effect is considered, then line 48 suggests the punctuation adopted here.

77 brow,]   Dyce and Bullen, of course, modernize to *brows* in consideration of the pronoun *them* in the next line. Nothing would be easier than for a compositor to fail to see a terminal *s*; on the other hand, Elizabethan grammar does not forbid reference of this sort.

II.ii

10 two leaud]   Collier confidently altered to *lewd*; Dyce printed *leav'd* but queried *loud;* Bullen retained *leav'd* and remarked only that the sense was intelligible. I take it that the primary sense intended is the comparison of the tongue to the two hinged parts of a door or gate, each of which can move independently and thus pronounce either slander or truth. The common phrase is 'double-tongued', or 'two-tongued', or 'fork-tongued'. The lines in Crashaw's *Hymn of the Nativity* doubtless do not apply here: 'Shee spreads the red leaves of thy Lips, | That in their Buds yet blushing lye' (*Poems*, ed. L. C. Martin [1927], p. 108).

III.iii

200 Honest Sir]   Q *Serieant* (*Seriant* [u]) is manifestly wrong. Dyce, followed by Bullen, emends to *Servant*. This is not much better, since there is small point in sounding the alarm to Gull before Jack Dapper. The odds are that the compositor mistook an abbreviation like S^r and expanded it wrongly.

IV.ii

49 Then they hang the head.]   Q prefixes the speech-heading *Mist. Open.*, which duplicates the same prefix at line 45. Line 49 begins a new page (sig. I1^v). There is about a third of a line of white space after the end of the last line on sig. I1^r, '...animalls they are', and the catchword is '*Mist. Open.*', repeated at the first line of the next page, as '*Mist. Open.* Then they hang the head.' This line does not join very smoothly to 'Lord what simple animalls they are.' and it would seem that some brief intervening remark by Mistress Gallipot has been dropped in error, but whether by the compositor or in the manuscript is not to be determined. However, if we may trust the evidence of the catchword, the manuscript could have been at fault.

102

PRESS-VARIANTS IN Q (1611)

[Copies collated: BM¹ (British Museum 162.d.35), BM² (Ashley 1159); Bodl (Bodleian Mal. 246[1]); Dyce (Victoria and Albert Museum); NLS (National Library of Scotland); CSmH (Henry E. Huntington Library); DFo (Folger Shakespeare Library); MB (Boston Public Library); Pforz (Carl H. Pforzheimer Collection); Taylor (Robert H. Taylor).]

SHEET A (*outer forme*)

Corrected: BM², Bodl, Dyce, NLS, CSmH, DFo, Pforz, Taylor.
Uncorrected: BM¹, MB.

Sig. A3.
  Dedication.
  15 cod-peece] cod-peice
  15 book] booke
Sig. A4ᵛ.
  Persons.
  Dramatis] Drammatis

SHEET B (*inner forme*)

Corrected: BM¹⁻², Bodl, Dyce, NLS, CSmH, MB, Pforz, Taylor.
Uncorrected: DFo.

Sig. B1ᵛ.
  I.i.22 in truth ſir] intruthſir
    33 ſlakes] ſlackes
    34 ſaiſt] ſaith
    35 *viua*] *viue*
    37 What] Wthat
    39 *Neatfoote*] *Neatfootte*
Sig. B2.
  I.i.54 Ha!] Ha:
    56 ſhape?] ſhape:
    59 prey] pray
    59 eyes] eyes,
    61 a loathed] aloathed
    78 gold] gold,
    82 heire?] heire,

104

FIG. 14D. *Sample page of press variants from Bowers's Dekker.*

EMENDATIONS OF ACCIDENTALS

Dedication

hd. *Comicke*ₐ] ~ ,
15 cod-peice] Q(u); cod-peece Q(c)

15 booke] Q(u); book Q(c)
18 ha's] *text*; has *cw*

Prologue

7 *Scœne,*] ~ .

Persons

DRAMMATIS] Q(u); DRAMATIS Q(c)

I.i

16 curle-pated] curle-|pated
33–34 The more...me !] *one line in*
        Q
50 When] | when
54 Ha:] Q(u); ~ ! Q(c)
54–55 Ha! | Life...] *one line* [life] *in*
        Q
56 shape:] Q(u); ~ ? Q(c)

58–59 waite ₐ ... both,] ~ , ...
        ~ ₐ
70 broke?] ~ ,
78 me:] ~ ,
89 ship-wracke?] ~ .
106 dangerous.] dangerours,
108 about?] ~ ,

I.ii

S.D. Goshawke] Goshake
4 (At] | (at
16 Y'are] Y are
20 seemes] seeemes
21 fill'd] fiil'd
29 rarely.] ~ ,
59 A stoole.] *run-on with line* 58
87 foundation: ... noyseₐ] ~ ₐ
        ... ~ :
88 fray,] Q(u); ~ ₐ Q(c)
89 madₐ] Q(u); ~ , Q(c)
90 question,] Q(u); ~ ₐ Q(c)
94 Pray...end?] Q *lines*: proceed, |
        How

109 roote —] ~ ,
109 sonne?] ~ ,
115 subtilty —] ~ .
119 foundation —] ~ ,
124 teeth —] ~ ,
143 aside —] ~ . —
185, 187 Ime] Q(u); I'me Q(c)
204 then?] ~ ,
207 ile] Q(u); Ile Q(c)
209 burnt.] Q(u); ~ ? Q(c)
222–223 hobby-|horse] hobbyhorse
223 towne to] to wneto
245 dangerous] dangerons
246 me —] ~ .

108

THE PLAYS AND
POEMS OF
Philip Massinger

EDITED BY
PHILIP EDWARDS
AND
COLIN GIBSON

VOLUME I

OXFORD
AT THE CLARENDON PRESS
1976

FIG. 15A. *Title page, volume 1 of Edwards and Gibson's critical edition of Massinger.*

I. ii. 43–73   *The Fatal Dowry*   23

Your Lordship will be pleasd to name the man,
Which you would haue your successor, and in me,
All promise to confirme it.
    Rochfort.   I embrace it,   45
As an assurance of their fauour to me,
And name my Lord *Nouall.*
    Du Croy.   The Court allows it.
    Rochfort. But there are suters waite heere, and their causes
May be of more necessity to be heard,
I therefore wish that mine may be defer'd,   50
And theirs haue hearing.
    Du Croy.   If your Lordship please
To take the place, we will proceed.
    Charmi.   The cause
We come to offer to your Lordships censure,
Is in it selfe so noble, that it needs not
Or Rhetorique in me that plead, or fauour   55
From your graue Lordships, to determine of it:
Since to the prayse of your impartiall iustice
(Which guilty, nay condemn'd men, dare not scandall)
Cı^v It will erect a trophy of your mercy
Which married to that Iustice—
    Nouall Senior.   Speake to the cause.   60
    Charmi. I will, my Lord: to say, the late dead Marshall
The father of this young Lord heere, my Clyent,
Hath done his Country great and faithfull seruice,
Might taske me of impertinence, to repeate
What your graue Lordships cannot but remember.   65
He in his life, became indebted to
These thriftie men, I will not wrong their credits,
By giuing them the attributes they now merit,
And fayling by the fortune of the warres,
Of meanes to free himselfe, from his ingagements,   70
He was arrested, and for want of bayle
Imprisond at their suite, and not long after
With losse of liberty ended his life.

---

50. I] *Gifford*; And *32*   56. it:] *Mason* (;) ; ~. *32*   60. Which] *Coxeter*;
With *32*   Iustice—] *Mason*; ~. *32*   64. impertinence, to repeate] *Coxeter*;
impertinence to repeate, *32*   65. remember.] *Gifford*; ~, *32*   66. became]
Mason; become *32*

FIG. 15B. *Sample page of text from Edwards and Gibson's Massinger.*

APPENDIX I

RUNNING CORRECTIONS TO THE TEXT

The Fatal Dowry

I. i

	Actus] Act.
10	runne] ~,
14	deserue] 32^2; deserne 32^1
17	Presidents] 32^2; presidents 32^1
29	you] 32^2; yon 32^1
33	dulnesse,] ~∧
36	*Charaloyes] Charloyes*
42	meriting] ~,
48	*Du Croye]* 32^2; *Dn ~* 32^1
57	eyes] ~,
69	innocence] ~,
70	that,] ~∧
99	goodnesse!] ~?
108	this,] ~∧
116	corruption,] ~;
	friend;] ~,
133	too.] 32^2; ~, 32^1
140	assurance] 32^2; assurauce 32^1
150	lawlesse,] ~;
151	That] that
159	inheritance] ~,
161	and] &
166	Luxury] *Luxury*
171 SD.	*Exeunt] Ex:*
173	sorrow] ~,
195	shelfe] ~,

I. ii

7	resigne,] ~∧
19	me] ~,
22	well] ~,
31	spent,] ~∧
90	boldnesse] bodldnesse
108	there,] ~∧
129	them,] ~;
134	soldyer,] ~:
146 SD.	*Exeunt] Ex.*

171	*Charaloyes] Charloyes*
174	patrimony] patri mony
177	after] After
181	peace.] 32^2; ~.; 32^1
182	liues] 32^2; liue 32^1
187	from] frõ
189	Sufficient] Sufficent
190	barre,] ~:
191	warre:] ~,
231	themselues] ~,
255 SD.	*Exeunt] Exit*
	and] &
288 SD.	*Exeunt] Ex.*
	and] &
289	Baumont!] ~.
293	*Charaloyes] Charloyes*

II. i

	Actus] Act.
10	'tis] 'Tis
14	old,] ~∧
28	inioy,] ~;
47 SD.	*speaks,] ~.*
	weeping.] ~,
	Musique.] ~,
49	sighes,] ~;
70	hath,] ~.
74	What,] ~∧
83	pillars,] ~∧
89	Bayes,] ~∧
94	Damn'd!] ~,
	ha, ha, ha.] ~! ~, ~.
95	wee'ld] weel'd
97	birth,] ~∧
	rogues!] ~.
114	Curace,] ~∧
127	house.] ~,
128	inheritance,] ~.
144	Iuly,] ~;

B

FIG. 15C. *Sample page of an appendix listing "corrections" (i.e., emendations) to the text, including only those not recorded at the foot of the text itself (fig. 15b), from Edwards and Gibson's Massinger.*

COMMENTARY

THE FATAL DOWRY

Cast

32 gives a list of the names of the characters only; the descriptions given here are based on Gifford, the first editor to supply them, but the order of *32*'s list has been retained. The 'Officers' vary in rank, from 'presidents' in Act I to bailiffs in Act V.

Act I

I. i. 1. *I may moue . . . your will*] 'I may make an application to the Court, in obedience to your will'.

9. *doe your parts*] do your part; cf. I. ii. 9, V. ii. 160.

19. *him selfe*] *32*'s 'your selfe' gives a most awkward change from third person to second person, followed in the next line by a return to the third person.

33. *This such a dulnesse*] 'this' for 'this is' can be paralleled, e.g. *Measure for Measure*, V. i. 131, 'this' a good Fryer' (Folio), and *King Lear*, IV. vi. 184, 'This a good block.' There is a strong pause before *This* which makes the rhythm sound.

36. *Charaloyes*] spelt *Charloyes* in *32*; see Introduction, p. 2.

37. *Marshall*] commander of the army, after the Duke of Burgundy.

37–8. *from whom he inherits . . . onely*] from the arguments of Arellius Fuscus in Seneca's *controversia*, which is the source of the play (see Introduction, p. 4): *Damnatus peculatus nihil aliud heredi suo reliquit quam se patrem.*

44–5 *satisfie . . . The summes*] The more usual construction would be 'of the sums', but *OED* remarks that the debt is occasionally found as a second object after 'satisfy'.

49. *Colonell*] three syllables, as it was usually spoken at this time, though on one or two occasions (e.g. III. i. 214) in this play it is slurred into two syllables.

70–1. *and in that, Assurance*] 'and in doing that (*flying to her succours*), having assurance'.

76. *sops*] for 'a sop to Cerberus', see Tilley, S 643; earliest usage, 1513.

87–9. *To drowne . . . against her*] 'to speak out against the oratory of a corrupt advocate and make him give back the money he took to oppose her'. A fee is returned by an outmanœuvred pleader in the next scene (220–4).

102 SD. *Enter . . . CREDITORS*] The stage-direction in *32* is crowded into the margin, beginning opposite ''Tis well', and editors have been puzzled, supposing the entry to follow that phrase. Gifford transferred ''Tis well' to Charalois; McIlwraith, leaving the words with Romont, thought they marked Romont's approval of a practice bow. But marginal entries are placed where they can conveniently be printed; ''Tis well' surely follows the entry and acknowledges Charalois' obeisance to the new arrivals.

Advocates leave the stage at line 139, and an entrance should be provided for them here. It is possible that the entrance had been struck out in the preparation of the prompt-book; the presence of the silent advocates adds nothing, and uses up actors.

FIG. 15D. *Sample page of textual and explanatory commentary from Edwards and Gibson's Massinger.*

Mardi

and

A Voyage Thither

HERMAN MELVILLE

NORTHWESTERN UNIVERSITY PRESS

and

THE NEWBERRY LIBRARY

Evanston and Chicago

1970

FIG. 16A. *Title page of the Northwestern-Newberry critical edition of Melville's* Mardi, *edited by Harrison Hayford, Hershel Parker, and G. Thomas Tanselle.*

LIBRARY OF CONGRESS CATALOG CARD NUMBER 67–21602

PRINTED IN THE UNITED STATES OF AMERICA

Cloth Edition, SBN 8101–0015–0
Paper Edition, SBN 8101–0014–2

CENTER FOR EDITIONS OF
AMERICAN AUTHORS
AN APPROVED TEXT
MODERN LANGUAGE
ASSOCIATION OF AMERICA

FIG. 16B. *Copyright page from the Northwestern-Newberry* Mardi, *with the CEAA seal.*

Chapter 75

Time and Temples

IN THE ORIENTAL Pilgrimage of the pious old Purchas, and in the fine old folio Voyages of Hakluyt, Thevenot, Ramusio, and De Bry, we read of many glorious old Asiatic temples, very long in erecting. And veracious Gaudentio di Lucca hath a wondrous narration of the time consumed in rearing that mighty three-hundred-and-sixty-five-pillared Temple of the Year, somewhere beyond Libya; whereof, the columns did signify days, and all round fronted upon concentric zones of palaces, cross-cut by twelve grand avenues symbolizing the signs of the zodiac, all radiating from the sun-dome in their midst. And in that wild eastern tale of his, Marco Polo tells us, how the Great Mogul began him a pleasure-palace on so imperial a scale, that his grandson had much ado to complete it.

But no matter for marveling all this: great towers take time to construct. And so of all else.

And that which long endures full-fledged, must have long lain in the germ. And duration is not of the future, but of the past; and eternity is eternal, because it has been; and though a strong new monument be builded to-day, it only is lasting because its blocks are old as the sun. It is not the Pyramids that are ancient, but the eternal granite whereof they are made; which had been equally ancient though yet in the quarry. For to make an eternity, we must build with eternities; whence, the vanity of the cry for

228

FIG. 16C. *Sample page of text from the Northwestern-Newberry* Mardi.

DISCUSSIONS OF READINGS   699

228.6   Gaudentio]   See note on 228.7.

228.7   -sixty-]   NN emends the A and E reading "three-hundred-and-seventy-five" to "three-hundred-and-sixty-five". Nathalia Wright called the editors' attention to this reading, pointing out that in Simon Berington's fictional *Memoirs of Sigr. Gaudentio di Lucca* (1737) the number of pillars in the "Temple of the Year," which is alluded to here, is appropriately 365. It is unlikely that in making the allusion Melville was not aware of the obvious point that the number of pillars corresponds to the number of days in the year and so wrote out the pointless number 375. Probably he saw the point and wrote out the proper number but in a way that induced a misreading by a copyist or compositor unaware of the point. Also corrected by NN is the A and E misspelling "Gaudentia" (228.6) for "Gaudentio", likewise on grounds of a probable misreading of Melville's manuscript.

248.2   *Donjalolo*]   The comma after "DONJALOLO" in A was removed in E; the change from "DONJALOLO" to "*Donjalolo*" is made in conformity with the styling of NN.

275.18–20   "The . . . hopes."]   This paragraph was not enclosed in quotation marks in A and E, but NN supplies the quotation marks since the comments are clearly the conclusion of Braid-Beard's speech.

281.34   above]   Both the A reading, retained by NN, and the E reading "about" make good sense in the context. As he "began over again" Yoomy either (as E has it) repeated the phrase "about ten hundred thousand moons" or (as A has it), having been challenged by Mohi the historian, he defiantly increased the time to "above ten hundred thousand moons". No ground exists for rejecting the copy-text reading.

298.5   them]   E repeats "stay-at-homes" in place of "them"; the change seems deliberately made to avoid the possible faulty reference of "them" to "travelers" rather than to "stay-at-homes". The change is not adopted by NN, however, since someone at Bentley's or even the compositor could have made it.

327.19   desire]   The E reading "require" somewhat strengthens Media's question, since in fact the old man does require, not merely desire, recompense. The change may be deliberate, not merely a compositorial misreading. Since, however, it cannot be taken as necessarily an authorial change, it is not adopted by NN.

368.1–2   enter many nations]   NN retains the A and E reading, assuming that the sense is merely that the speaker casually enters many nations, even as Mungo Park rested (or visited) in many African cots, and that no exact equivalence is intended between the number of nations and the number of cots (in which case "as" would be required after "enter").

FIG. 16D.   *Sample page of textual commentary from the Northwestern-Newberry edition of* Mardi. *(A = American edition, E = English edition, NN = Northwestern-Newberry edition.)*

	NN Reading	Copy-text Reading
4.32	symptoms E	symptons
6.1	Kamschatka NN	Kamschatska
15.4	reminiscences E	reminiscenses
22.17	the crew E	thc crew
40.6	Caribbean NN	Carribean
43.4	jackknife NN	jacknife
55.4	on E	an
62.10	brakes NN	breaks
66.28	Annatoo!" E	~ !ₐ
87.38	as E	of
*88.1	of NN	as
104.35	lunge NN	lounge
105.30	Crockett's NN	Crocket's
119.8	pump-brakes NN	pump-breaks
123.11	phosphorescence E	phosphoresence
147.9	philippic NN	phillipic
150.9	fish, we E	Fish, we
175.13	Archipelago. E	~ ₐ
175.25	transmissible NN	transmissable
185.4	twelve.ₐ E	~."
192.12	windrows NN	winrows
196.21	attendants. E	~,
203.26	itself. E	~,
210.12	us, E	~.
211.10	shall NN	Shall
212.13	Braid-Beard NN	Braid-beard
220.8	to the E	to tho
*228.6	Gaudentio NN	Gaudentia
*228.7	-sixty- NN	-seventy-
233.6	mouth E	month
246.21	nut. NN	~,
247.5	'Ah E	"~
247.5	fancy,' E	~,"

FIG. 16E. *Sample page of the list of emendations in the Northwestern-Newberry edition of* Mardi.

LINE-END HYPHENATION   713

178.19	jet-black	333.28	forty-seven
179.5	scroll-prowed	335.6	water-course
185.13	bulkheads	336.26	forest-tree
189.25	whirlpool	344.11	to-day
191.38	demi-god	344.28	anaconda-like
197.34	high-spirited	344.34	many-limbed
200.23	paddle-blades	352.10	stopping-places
200.26	shark's-mouth	366.16	vineyards
201.5	arrow-flights	367.24	land-locked
203.15	To-day	367.31	sea-side
212.13	Braid-Beard	372.8	cocoa-nut
217.27	sea-cavern	372.16	red-barked
225.3	†overarched	372.16	†net-work
226.29	†sweet-scented	372.20	†mouth-piece
231.15	overlooking	372.35	pipe-bowl
232.2	overlapping	373.10	pipe-bowls
237.37	balsam-dropping	374.15	black-letter
240.2	torch-light	374.23	coffin-lid
240.5	sea-girt	376.4	berry-brown
240.8	golden-rinded	376.25	skull-bowl
243.13	woe-begone	379.35	†foot-prints
243.28	burial-place	380.13	†swordfish
246.11	under-breeding	385.14	midmost
246.12	Arva-root	385.33	worm-eaten
253.17	milk-white	387.13	undertaker
256.38	lordly-looking	396.2	market-place
268.1	moss-roses	406.33	semi-transparent
271.10	overstepped	416.21	foot-prints
282.37	star-fish	418.21	cocoa-nuts
282.39	swordfish	423.20	rose-balm
283.16	moonbeams	426.39	†foreordained
285.14	close-grappling	446.5	purple-robed
286.8	overstrained	446.20	guava-rind
287.19	merry-making	456.39	after-birth
288.28	nursery-talk	463.23	oftentimes
289.1	tiger-sharks	467.34	snow-drifts
290.23	circumnavigated	467.35	ice-bergs
295.23	cocoa-nut	479.12	†river-horse
297.20	Commonwealth's	482.6	lord-mayor
330.9	palm-nuts	482.11	dragon-beaked
330.19	†halberd-shaped	482.18	sea-king
332.22	demi-gods	489.27	sword-hilt

FIG. 16F. *Sample page of the report of line-end hyphenations from the Northwestern-Newberry edition of* Mardi. *The list presents the editors' treatment of words hyphenated in the copy-text. (Daggered entries are words coincidentally hyphenated in the copy-text and Northwestern-Newberry edition and are recorded according to how the editors would have treated them had they not been broken at the end of a line.)*

SUBSTANTIVE VARIANTS 719

101.17–18	blue boundless A	boundless blue E
105.10	spiteful A	[*omitted*] E
106.18	could A	[*omitted*] E
106.18	see A	saw E
108.6	then A	[*omitted*] E
123.3	to A	by E
123.39	upon A	on E ·
125.16	And at A	At E
125.18	sedulously kept A	kept sedulously E
127.3	in A	[*omitted*] E
136.14	cheek A	cheeks E
144.12	as A	a E
150.32	the A	a E
153.14	was A	must have been E
157.14	would A	should E
176.37	one A	[*omitted*] E
192.26	over A	our E
202.22	loyal A	royal E
203.23	and A	an E
211.16	for A	that, for E
211.17	but A	[*omitted*] E
211.17	a A	a mere E
228.7	that A	the E
233.6	mouth NN	
	month A	mouth E
239.4	of the A	of E
246.13	then A	just then E
265.4	pass A	passed E
270.18	And . . . Mohi. A	[*omitted*] E
280.11	he A	the E
281.34	above A	about E
285.9	Kings A	King's E
289.4	a A	an E
297.9	swab A	to swab E

FIG. 16G. *Sample page of the list of substantive variants between the American edition (copy-text) and English edition, from the Northwestern-Newberry edition of* Mardi.

WASHINGTON
IRVING

JOURNALS AND
NOTEBOOKS

Volume I, 1803-1806

Edited by Nathalia Wright

The University of Wisconsin Press
Madison, Milwaukee, London
1969

FIG. 17A. *Title page, volume 1 of Wright's documentary edition of Irving's* Journals and Notebooks.

132   EUROPEAN JOURNAL, 1804–1805

November 16[290]

Yesterday we dined at Lord Shaftesbury's. There were but three or
four <strangers> ↑visitors↓ at table beside ourselves, but after dinner
in the evening more company came in and violins having been prepared we had a pleasant little dance. The Italians do not equal the
french in dancing altho' they have dancing masters of that nation. As
there are not many Gentlemen among the nobility who excel in dancing, they are obliged when they give balls to invite merchants clerks, to
assist in making up the dances[.] these they call "the dancers of the
city." & are considered much in the light of joint stools or arm chairs
sometimes used in <one> family dances to make up a set for a cotil-
lion or country dance. Ices & lemonades are handed about at the balls
continually – and the italians make no hesitation in eating the former
when in a state of the highest perspiration.

December 1

I have been for three or four days past engaged in examining <dif-
ferent> the paintings in several of the palaces. In this employment I
was accompanied by a Mr Wilson <a> the <S>Young Scotch man
who <has resided for some> I mentioned before as having seen at Mrs
Birds. He <?y?> very obligingly acted as cicerone and being ac-
quainted with every painting of merit in Genoa he acquitted himself
very well. To enter into a detail of the many fine peices I have seen
would be fatiguing[.] among the finest are a *holy family* by Reubens in
the palace of Giacomo Balbi.[291] Diogenes looking for an honest man –
Rape of the Sabines – Perseus with Medusa's head – <G>Je<s>za-
bel[292] <by> devourd by dogs – all four by Luca Giordano[293] a painter
of great merit. (It is one of the peculiarities of this painter that he continually changes his style in his different paintings.) Magdalene with a

290. Irving drew on this entry in his letter to William Irving, December 25,
1804–January 25, 1805.
291. The palace to which Irving refers is No. 6 Via Balbi, built in the seventeenth century by Bartolomeo Bianco (C. G. Ratti, *Instruzione di Quanto Può
Vedersi di Più Bello in Genova*, Genoa, 1780, I, 179 ff.). It was owned by Gacomo
Ignazio Balbi (d. 1796) until his death, then by his son Costantino (Staglieno,
"Genealogie di Famiglie Patrizie Genovesi," I, 46). A list of the paintings in it in
the period when Irving visited it is contained in [Giacomo Brusco?], *Description des
Beautés de Gênes et de ses Environs* (Genoa, 1788), pp. 139–45.
292. "J" and "z" are written in blue ink over "G" and "s."
293. Luca Giordano (1632–1705), who spent most of his life in Naples, formed
his style on that of Paolo Veronese and Pietro da Cortona.

F I G .   1 7 B .   *Sample page of text from Wright's Irving. Square brackets signal editorial*
                   insertions; angle brackets, restorations of canceled matter; question marks,
                   doubtful readings; and arrows, interlinear insertions.

Notes

[1] "Corrected" here refers not to rightness or wrongness but only to the making of a change, a correction.

[2] For discussion of modernization of accidentals, see McKerrow, *Prolegomena*; Parker; and Wells, *Modernizing*. A thoughtful and instructive debate focusing on the critical implications of modernizing Shakespeare's sonnet 129 may be followed in Graves and Riding; Booth's moderately modernized edition *Shakespeare's Sonnets*; and Greene.

APPENDIX ON
TEXTUAL NOTATION

Although scholarly publishers and scholarly editors have adopted various forms of textual notation over the years, the generally accepted style is that enunciated by R. B. McKerrow in his *Prolegomena for the Oxford Shakespeare*. It is a method adaptable for either horizontal or vertical variants as well as for the apparatus of the finished edition. Its basic principle is that the lemmatic reading—that reading found to the left-hand side of the open bracket—is always the reading of the base text (in working collational notes) or of the edited text (in the textual notes in an edition's apparatus) and that the readings to the right-hand side are the stemmatic readings. Thus simple variation is recorded as:

231. George] Iohn

"231" is the exact line reference to either the base text or edited text and can, of course, take whatever form is most convenient and conventional for recording an exact line location. For example, in plays it has been conventional to make reference by act, scene, and line: II.iii.231, although at least in Shakespeare's plays this is now regularly rendered as 2.3.231; in long subdivided poems, like *The Faerie Queene*, by book, canto, stanza, and line: III.i.13.6. Of course, for shorter poems a line number alone is sufficient. In recent years, however, editors have adopted the practice of through-line-numbering for all but the longest poems, ignoring act, scene, book, canto, stanza, and other divisions and assigning each line a sequential line number. For prose works the problem is slightly more difficult because line numbers are not constant, the lines varying from edition to edition in length and, therefore, in the material they contain. A common practice is to make reference by page and line number of the base text or edited text:

G1r.35, or 123.41.

In the example above "George" is the reading in line 231 of the base or edited text and "Iohn" the variant reading in another text. To identify the other text, a siglum must be added:

231. George] Iohn *B3*

"B3" is the identifying symbol for that particular copy or edition which contains that reading.

A swung dash (~) indicates that portions of the stemmatic reading agree with the lemmatic readings:

> 231. ran] ~, *B3*

An inferior caret indicates where the stemmatic readings lack punctuation found in the lemmatic reading:

> 231. ran,] ~ˌ *B3*

When the stemmatic readings lack material, it is indicated thus:

> 231. and Harry] *om. B3*

In cases where the lemmatic readings omit material or lack punctuation, the information is recorded thus:

> 231. Betty] ~ and Sally *B3*
> 231. sat] ~, *B3*

Placing these symbols (ˌ, ~, or *om*) to the left of the bracket would at least imply that the base or edited text contained those marks in it.

If no accidental or substantive variants save lineation occur, lineation changes in poetry are indicated thus:

> 232-3. They . . . down / Now . . . grown] They . . . dew / Help . . . hew *B3*

If other variants occur, the stemmatic readings, with line-division indication, must be fully written out. Of course, in prose no record is kept of lineation, although a record should be kept of line-end hyphenation for all those words that might be hyphenated even if they appeared in mid-line.

If several texts share a variant reading their sigla are added to the note:

> 231. George] Iohn *B3, B4, B8*

If there are several readings:

> 231. George] Iohn *B3, B4, B8*; John *B5, B6*

It is assumed that all sigla not shown as disagreeing with the lemmatic reading agree with it. If all subsequent texts share a variant, the plus sign is employed:

> 231. and Harry] *om. B3+*

These are the conventions and forms for recording variation. In the edited text it will also be necessary to record emendations in the copy-text. Again, the lemmatic reading is that found in the edited text, so that if the editor decides that the authoritative reading is different from that found in the copy-text, he or she must record that fact.

231. Iohn] *B5*; George *B1, B2, B7*; John *B3, B4, B8*

This note shows that the reading "Iohn" does not come from the copy-text, *B1*, that its earliest appearance is in *B5*, and that all other texts except *B6* have different readings. There is no need to record *B6* since we assume texts not found in the stemmatic readings agree with the lemmatic readings. If the editor must emend on his or her own authority the following form of note suffices:

231. Ralph] George *B1, B2, B7*; John *B3, B4, B8*; Iohn *B5, B6*

Some editors place the siglum of their own edition to the right of the bracket in such an instance.

Although readers of this book will find many variations from this notational system, it has proved itself the clearest, most useful, and most widely accepted of all methods of recording variations and emendations.

REFERENCE BIBLIOGRAPHY

Introduction and Definitions

In *Textual Scholarship: An Introduction* (New York: Garland, 1992), D. C. Greetham attempts to present (at greater length than we have) an overview of bibliographical and textual studies and includes topics that we slighted, including codicology, paleography, typography, and enumerative bibliography. *The Book Encompassed: Studies in Twentieth-Century Bibliography*, ed. Peter Davison (Cambridge: Cambridge UP, 1992), presents thirty essays in manuscript studies, paleography, typography, bookbinding, descriptive and analytical bibliography, book-trade history, textual criticism, and other subjects—most of the essays surveying the previous fifty years' developments, examining the present state of work in their subject, and offering guidance as to directions of future research.

Definitions of bibliography and its subdivisions appear in Fredson Bowers's "Bibliography, Pure Bibliography, and Literary Studies" and in the other five essays gathered under the heading "The Bibliographical Way" in his *Essays in Bibliography, Text, and Editing* (Charlottesville: UP of Virginia, 1975), 3–108. Other important essays in definition are Lloyd Hibberd's "Physical and Reference Bibliography," *Library* 5th ser. 20 (1965): 124–34; Rolf Du Rietz's "What Is Bibliography?" *Text* 1 (1974): 6–40; G. Thomas Tanselle's "Bibliography and Science" (1974) and "Descriptive Bibliography and Library Cataloguing" (1977), collected in his *Selected Studies in Bibliography* (Charlottesville: UP of Virginia, 1979), 1–92; and Ross Atkinson's "An Application of Semiotics to the Definition of Bibliography," *Studies in Bibliography* (*SB*) 33 (1980): 54–73. A history of the term *bibliography*, especially its European usage from the seventeenth through twentieth centuries, is provided by Rudolf Blum's *Bibliographia: An Inquiry into Its Definition and Designations* (1969), trans. Mathilde V. Rovelstad (Chicago: Amer. Lib. Assn.; Kent: Dawson, 1980).

Two influential works offering broad views of bibliographical and textual studies are Jerome J. McGann's essay "The Monks and the Giants: Textual and Bibliographical Studies and the Interpretation of Literary Works," *Textual Criticism and Literary Interpretation*, ed. McGann (Chicago: U of Chicago P, 1985), 180–99, and D. F. McKenzie's 1985 Panizzi Lectures, published as *Bibliography and the Sociology of Texts* (London: British Lib., 1986). McKenzie's lectures are reviewed at length in G. Thomas Tanselle's "Textual Criticism and Literary Sociology," *SB* 44 (1991): 83–143. Robert Darnton's "What Is the History of Books?" in *Books and Society in History*, ed. Kenneth E. Carpenter (New York: Bowker, 1983), 3–26, serves as an introduction to the interdisciplinary field of *l'histoire du livre.* It should be supplemented by Nicolas Barker's "Reflections on the History of the Book," *Book Collector* 39 (1990): 9–26, and Peter D. McDonald's "Implicit Structures and Explicit Interactions: Pierre Bourdieu and the History of the Book," *Library* 6th ser. 19 (1997): 105–21.

Among the basic means of access to bibliographical and textual studies are the *Dictionary Catalogue of the History of Printing from the John M. Wing Foundation in the Newberry Library*, 9 vols. (Boston: Hall, 1961, 1970); the volumes of T. H. Howard-Hill's *Index to British Literary Bibliography* (Oxford: Clarendon, 1969–80), including *Bibliography of British Literary Bibliographies* (1969; 2nd ed., 1987), *Shakespearian Bibliography and Textual Criticism* (1971), and *British Bibliography and Textual Criticism* (2 vols., 1979); and Robin Myers's *The British Book Trade from Caxton to the Present* (London: Deutsch, 1973). For British topics, these should be supplemented, of course, by the *New Cambridge Bibliography of English Literature*, 5 vols. (Cambridge: Cambridge UP, 1969–77); for American topics, by the bibliography volume of the *Literary History of the United States*, ed. Robert E. Spiller et al., 4th ed. (New York: Macmillan, 1974), and by G. Thomas Tanselle's *Guide to the Study of United States Imprints*, 2 vols. (Cambridge: Harvard UP, 1971). For the Association for Documentary Editing, Beth Luey compiled *Editing Documents and Texts: An Annotated Bibliography* (Madison: Madison House, 1990). The essays in *Scholarly Editing: A Guide to Research*, ed. D. C. Greetham (New York: MLA, 1995) survey developments in editing and serve as guides to further reading.

From 1950 through 1974 the annual *Studies in Bibliography* published checklists of bibliographical scholarship. The lists for 1949–55 were collected and indexed in *SB* 10 (1957); those for 1956–62, in *Selective Check Lists of Bibliographical Scholarship*, ser. B (Charlottesville: UP of Virginia, 1966). They may be supplemented by the *Index to Selected Bibliographical Journals, 1933–1970* (London: Bibliographical Soc., 1982). Among the current serial bibliographies that are especially useful are the *Annual Bibliography of the History of the Printed Book* (1973–), the *MLA International Bibliography* (1922–), and the *MHRA Annual Bibliography of English Language and Literature* (1921–). The most important periodicals in the field are *The Library, SB, Text, Papers of the Bibliographical Society of America* (*PBSA*), and *Analytical and Enumerative Bibliography* (*AEB*). The scholarly societies sponsoring these journals have Web sites that in some cases include archives and links to other relevant sites: the Bibliographical Society (London), <http://crane.ukc.ac.uk/semls/bibsoc>; the Bibliographical Society of the University of Virginia, <http://etext.lib.virginia.edu/

bsuva>; the Society for Textual Scholarship, <http://www.msstate.edu/Archives/TEXT/text.html>; and the Bibliographical Society of America, <http://www.cla.sc.edu/engl/bsa>. To these may be added the Society for the History of Authorship, Reading, and Publishing, <http://www.indiana.edu:80/~sharp>.

Analytical Bibliography

There is no standard, comprehensive treatment of analytical bibliography. Ronald B. McKerrow's *An Introduction to Bibliography for Literary Students* (Oxford: Clarendon, 1928), though much of it is outdated, remains a valuable primer, especially when combined with Philip Gaskell's *A New Introduction to Bibliography* (Oxford: Oxford UP, 1972), which emphasizes the materials and methods of printing and contains lists of primary and secondary works in historical bibliography, works essential for analytical bibliography. A number of works provide general and theoretical treatments of analytical bibliography. Fredson Bowers's *Bibliography and Textual Criticism* (Oxford: Clarendon, 1964), for example, deals with its relation to textual criticism and with its method of reasoning. D. F. McKenzie's "Printers of the Mind: Some Notes on Bibliographical Theories and Printing-House Practices," *SB* 22 (1969): 1–75, as well as his "Stretching a Point; or, The Case of the Spaced-Out Comps," *SB* 37 (1984): 106–21, questions assumptions about the normality and regularity of printing practices. In part an answer to McKenzie is G. Thomas Tanselle's "Bibliography and Science," *SB* 27 (1974): 55–89. In "The Selection and Presentation of Bibliographical Evidence," *Analytical and Enumerative Bibliography* 1 (1977): 101–36, Peter Davison deals with the same question and offers some practical suggestions in using and reporting bibliographical evidence.

An important dictionary of printing and publishing (and thus bibliographical) vocabulary is Geoffrey A. Glaister's *Encyclopedia of the Book*, 2nd ed. (1979), reprinted with a new introduction by Donald Farren (New Castle: Oak Knoll; London: British Lib., 1996). Useful especially for terms describing books is John Carter's *ABC for Book Collectors*, 7th ed. with corrections, additions, and an introduction by Nicolas Barker (London: Shaw, 1994; New Castle: Oak Knoll, 1995).

Because there is no comprehensive treatment of analytical bibliography, one must consult studies that focus on a particular type of evidence or on its application to a particular problem. Foremost among these studies is Charlton Hinman's *The Printing and Proof-reading of the First Folio of Shakespeare*, 2 vols. (Oxford: Clarendon, 1963), a model of analytical technique. For its use of watermark evidence, a similar model is A. H. Stevenson's *The Problem of the Missale Speciale* (London: Bibliographical Soc., 1967). And for both paper and typographical evidence, there are J. W. Carter and H. G. Pollard's *An Enquiry into the Nature of Certain Nineteenth-Century Pamphlets* (London: Constable,

1934; augmented ed., 1983) and Peter W. M. Blayney's *Nicholas Okes and the First Quarto*, vol. 1 of *The Texts of* King Lear *and Their Origins* (Cambridge: Cambridge UP, 1982).

As these titles suggest, many developments in analytical bibliography are contained in studies of particular books. To list any here is to slight a great many others; nonetheless, the following examples will indicate the nature and diversity of such studies: George R. Price, "The Printing of *Love's Labour's Lost* (1598)," *PBSA* 72 (1978): 405–34; D. F. McKenzie, "'Indenting the Stick' in the First Quarto of *King Lear* (1608)," *PBSA* 67 (1973): 125–30; James A. Riddell, "The Printing of the Plays in the Jonson Folio of 1616," *SB* 49 (1996): 149–68; W. Speed Hill, "Casting Off Copy and the Composition of Hooker's Book V," *SB* 33 (1980): 144–61; William B. Todd, "Concurrent Printing: An Analysis of Dodsley's Collection of Poems by Several Hands," *PBSA* 46 (1952): 45–57; Joseph Katz, "Analytical Bibliography and Literary History: The Writing and Printing of Wieland," *Proof* 1 (1971): 8–34; Peter L. Shillingsburg, "The Printing, Proof-Reading, and Publishing of Thackeray's *Vanity Fair*: The First Edition," *SB* 34 (1981): 118–45; Matthew Bruccoli and Charles A. Rheault, Jr., "Imposition Figures and Plate Gangs in *The Rescue*," *SB* 14 (1961): 258–62; William B. Todd, "The White House Transcripts," *PBSA* 68 (1974): 267–96.

Other studies focus primarily on a particular kind of evidence or method of analysis. For exemplary studies of ink as evidence, see Richard N. Schwab et al., "Cyclotron Analysis of the Ink in the Forty-Two Line Bible," *PBSA* 77 (1983): 285–315, and Philip M. Teigen, "Concurrent Printing of the Gutenberg Bible and the Proton Milliprobe Analysis of Its Ink," *PBSA* 87 (1993): 437–51. For paper, see Allan Stevenson, "Paper as Bibliographical Evidence," *Library* 5th ser. 17 (1962): 197–212; Paul Needham, "Allan Stevenson and the Bibliographical Uses of Paper," *SB* 47 (1994): 23–64; Stephen Spector, "Symmetry in Watermark Sequences," *SB* 31 (1978): 162–78; David L. Vander Meulen, "The Identification of Paper without Watermarks: The Example of Pope's *Dunciad*," *SB* 37 (1984): 58–81; Curt Buhler, "The Margins in Mediaeval Books," *PBSA* 40 (1946): 34–42.

For the analysis of evidence related to type and typesetting, see William H. Bond, "Casting Off Copy by Elizabethan Printers," *PBSA* 42 (1948): 281–91; R. A. Sayce, "Compositorial Practices and the Localization of Printed Books, 1530–1800," *Library* 5th ser. 21 (1966): 1–45; Adrian Weiss, "Font Analysis as a Bibliographical Method: The Elizabethan Play-Quarto Printers and Compositors," *SB* 43 (1990): 95–164; Robert K. Turner, Jr., "Reappearing Types as Bibliographical Evidence," *SB* 19 (1966): 198–209; Robin Dix and Trudi Laura Darby, "The Bibliographical Significance of the Turned Letter," *SB* 46 (1993): 263–70; Fredson Bowers, "Bibliographical Evidence from the Printer's Measure," *SB* 2 (1949–50): 153–67; George Walton Williams, "Setting by Formes in Quarto Printing," *SB* 11 (1958): 39–53; Kenneth Povey, "Working to Rule, 1600–1800: A Study of Pressmen's Practice," *Library* 20 (1965): 13–54.

For imposition and press work, see William H. Bond, "Imposition by Half-Sheets," *Library* 4th ser. 22 (1941–42): 163–67; Bowers, "Running-Title Evidence for Determining Half-Sheet Imposition," *SB* 1 (1948–49): 199–202; Povey, "On the Diagnosis of Half-Sheet Imposition," *Library* 5th ser. 11 (1956): 268–72; Oliver L. Steele, "Half-Sheet Imposition of Eight-Leaf Quires in Formes of Thirty-Two and Sixty-Four Pages," *SB* 15 (1962): 274–78; Povey, "Variant Formes in Elizabethan Printing," *Library* 5th ser. 10 (1955): 41–48; Povey, "The Optical Identification of First Formes," *SB* 13 (1960): 189–90; Joseph A. Dane, "Perfect Order and Perfected Order: The Evidence from Press-Variants of Early Seventeenth-Century Quartos," *PBSA* 90 (1996): 272–320; Ernest W. Sullivan II, "Marginal Rules as Evidence," *SB* 30 (1977): 171–80; D. F. Foxon, "On Printing 'At One Pull' and Distinguishing Impressions by Point-Holes," *Library* 5th ser. 11 (1956): 284–85; Peter L. Shillingsburg, "Register Measurement as a Method of Detecting Hidden Printings," *PBSA* 73 (1979): 484–88; William B. Todd, "Observations on the Incidence and Interpretation of Press Figures," *SB* 3 (1950–51): 171–205; Povey, "A Century of Press Figures," *Library* 5th ser. 14 (1959): 251–73; G. Thomas Tanselle, "Press Figures in America: Some Preliminary Observations," *SB* 19 (1966): 123–60; B. J. McMullin, "Press Figures and Concurrent Perfecting: Walker & Greig, Edinburgh, 1817–22," *Library* 6th ser. 12 (1990): 236–41; Todd, "Recurrent Printing," *SB* 12 (1959): 189–98; Craig Abbott, "Offset Slur as Bibliographical Evidence," *PBSA* 70 (1976): 538–41; Matthew J. Bruccoli, "A Mirror for Bibliographers: Duplicate Plates in Modern Printing," *PBSA* 54 (1960): 83–88. And, of course, descriptive bibliographies and textual studies (including critical editions) should be consulted for their application of analytical bibliography.

Increasingly in recent years, analytical bibliography and literary criticism have come together in the concern for the "materiality of texts." Especially influential have been McGann's *The Beauty of Inflections: Literary Investigations in Historical Method and Theory* (Oxford: Clarendon, 1988) and *The Textual Condition* (Princeton: Princeton UP, 1991). Some representative studies that take account of what McGann calls "bibliographical codes" are David McKitterick's "Old Faces and New Acquaintances: Typography and the Association of Ideas," *PBSA* 87 (1993): 163–86; Evelyn Tribble's *Margins and Marginality: The Printed Page in Early Modern England* (Charlottesville: UP of Virginia, 1993); and some of the essays in *Cultural Artifacts and the Production of Meaning: The Page, the Image, and the Body*, ed. J. M. Ezell and Katherine O'Brien O'Keeffe (Ann Arbor: U of Michigan P, 1994) and in *Reading Books: Essays on the Material Text and Literature in America*, ed. Michele Moylan and Lane Stiles (Amherst: U of Massachusetts P, 1996).

Descriptive Bibliography

The standard treatment is Fredson Bowers's *Principles of Bibliographical Description* (Princeton: Princeton UP, 1949; rpt. New York: Russell, 1962), the reading of which may be prefaced by David L. Vander Meulen's "The History and Future of Bowers's *Principles*," *PBSA* 79 (1985): 197–219, and by G. Thomas Tanselle's "A Description of Descriptive Bibliography," *SB* 45 (1992): 1–30.

More extended treatment of the degressive principle, the purposes of description, and the need to adjust description to the materials examined is offered by Bowers in "Purposes of Descriptive Bibliography, with Some Remarks on Methods" (1952) and "Bibliography Revisited" (1969), both reprinted in his *Essays in Bibliography, Text, and Editing* (Charlottesville: UP of Virginia, 1975), 111–34, 151–95. G. Thomas Tanselle deals with the problem of degree of accuracy in "Tolerances in Bibliographical Description," *Library* 5th ser. 23 (1968): 1–12; with ideal copy in "The Concept of Ideal Copy," *SB* 33 (1980): 18–53; and with the distinction between describing a single copy and describing ideal copy in "Descriptive Bibliography and Library Cataloguing," *SB* 30 (1977): 1–56.

In a number of articles, Tanselle has proposed elaborations, refinements, and modifications of Bowers's *Principles*: "A System of Color Identification for Bibliographical Description" (1967); "The Bibliographical Description of Patterns" (1970); "The Bibliographical Description of Paper" (1971); "The Identification of Type Faces in Bibliographical Description," *Library* 5th ser. 23 (1968): 1–12; "The Use of Type Damage as Evidence in Bibliographical Description," *Library* 5th ser. 23 (1968): 328–51; "Book-Jackets, Blurbs, and Bibliographers," *Library* 5th ser. 26 (1971): 91–134; "The Description of Non-Letterpress Material in Books," *SB* 35 (1982): 1–42; "Title-Page Transcription and Signature Collation Reconsidered," *SB* 38 (1985): 45–81; and "A Sample Bibliographical Description, with Commentary," *SB* 40 (1987): 1–30. The first three of these are reprinted from *SB* in his *Selected Studies in Bibliography* (Charlottesville: UP of Virginia, 1979), 139–243.

In "Descriptive Bibliography and the Victorian Periodical," *SB* 49 (1996): 61–94, Maura Ives discusses, with examples, the application of descriptive methods to periodicals. Bibliographical taxonomy, treated at length in Bowers's *Principles*, has also been discussed in James B. Meriwether and Joseph Katz's "A Redefinition of 'Issue,'" *Proof* 2 (1972): 61–70; in Tanselle's "The Bibliographical Concept of 'Issue' and 'State,'" *PBSA* 69 (1975): 17–66, and his "The Arrangement of Descriptive Bibliographies," *SB* 37 (1984): 1–38; and in James L. W. West III's "The Bibliographical Concept of Plating," *SB* 36 (1983): 252–66.

Of course, the various theoretical and methodological approaches are applied and tested in bibliographies. Thus a person interested in descriptive bibliography should consult actual bibliographies and examine their successes and failures. The following are a few notable examples: Warner Barnes, *A Bibliography of Elizabeth Barrett Browning* (Austin: Humanities Research Center; Waco: Armstrong Browning Library, 1967); Jacob Blanck, *Bibliography of American Literature* (New Haven: Yale UP, 1955–); B. C. Bloomfield and Edward Mendelson, *W. H. Auden: A Bibliography, 1924–1969,* 2nd ed. (Charlottesville: UP of Virginia, 1972); Edwin Bowden, *James Thurber: A Bibliography* (Columbus: Ohio State UP, 1968); Matthew J. Bruccoli, *F. Scott Fitzgerald: A Descriptive Bibliography* (Pittsburgh: U of Pittsburgh P, 1972); C. E. Frazer Clark, Jr., *Nathaniel Hawthorne: A Descriptive Bibliography* (Pittsburgh: U of Pittsburgh P, 1978); Philip Gaskell, *A Bibliography of the Foulis Press* (London: Hart-Davis, 1964); David Gilson, *A Bibliography of Jane Austen* (New York: Clarendon, 1982); W. W. Greg, *A Bibliography of the English Printed Drama to the Restoration,* 4 vols. (London: Bibliographical Soc., 1939–59); Geoffrey Keynes, *A Bibliography of George Berkeley* (Oxford: Clarendon, 1976); D. F. McKenzie, *Cambridge University Press, 1696–1712: A Bibliographical Survey* (Cambridge: Cambridge UP, 1966), vol. 1, app. 1; Joel Myerson, *Ralph Waldo Emerson: A Descriptive Bibliography* (Pittsburgh: U of Pittsburgh P, 1982); William B. Todd, *A Bibliography of Edmund Burke* (London: Hart-Davis, 1964); James L. W. West III, *William Styron: A Descriptive Bibliography* (Boston: Hall, 1977).

Textual Criticism

Three concise introductions to textual study, especially its editorial aspect, are Fredson Bowers's "Textual Criticism," in *The Aims and Methods of Scholarship in Modern Languages and Literatures,* ed. James Thorpe (New York: MLA, 1963), 23–42; G. Thomas Tanselle's "Textual Scholarship," in *Introduction to Scholarship in Modern Languages and Literatures,* ed. Joseph Gibaldi (New York: MLA, 1981), 29–52; and D. C. Greetham's "Textual Scholarship," in the 2nd edition (1991) of the *MLA Introduction to Scholarship,* 103–37. An invaluable survey of scholarship in textual criticism, especially as it relates to editing, is contained in *The Center for Scholarly Editions: An Introductory Statement* (New York: MLA, 1977), issued with periodically updated supplements.

Among recent treatments of the theoretical foundations of textual criticism the two most influential are Jerome J. McGann's *A Critique of Modern Textual Criticism* (Chicago: U of Chicago P, 1983) and G. Thomas Tanselle's *A Rationale of Textual Criticism* (Philadelphia: U of Pennsylvania P, 1989). Peter L. Shillingsburg's *Scholarly Editing in the Computer Age: Theory and Practice,* 3rd ed. (Ann Arbor: U of Michigan P, 1996) usefully relates editorial practices to theoretical perspectives. The relation between textual criticism and other fields, particularly literary theory, is explored in D. C. Greetham's "Textual and Literary Theory: Redrawing the Matrix," *SB* 42 (1989): 1–30; Michael Groden's "Contemporary Textual and Literary Theory," *Representing Modernist Texts:*

Editing as Interpretation, ed. George Bornstein (Ann Arbor: U of Michigan P, 1991), 259–86; Jerome J. McGann's "The Text, the Poem, and the Problem of Historical Method" (1981), in his *The Beauty of Inflections: Literary Investigations in Historical Method and Theory* (Oxford: Clarendon, 1985), 111–32; Hershel Parker's "The 'New Scholarship': Textual Evidence and Its Implications for Criticism, Literary Theory, and Aesthetics," *Studies in American Fiction* 9 (1981): 181–97; Morse Peckham's "Reflections on the Foundations of Modern Textual Editing," *Proof* 1 (1971): 122–55; G. Thomas Tanselle's "Textual Criticism and Deconstruction," *SB* 43 (1990): 1–33; James Thorpe's "The Aesthetics of Textual Criticism" (1965), reprinted in his *Principles of Textual Criticism* (San Marino: Huntington Library, 1972), 3–49; and in the essays gathered in *Devils and Angels: Textual Editing and Literary Theory,* ed. Philip Cohen (Charlottesville: UP of Virginia, 1991). The role of analytical bibliography and literary criticism in editing is discussed in Bowers's *Bibliography and Textual Criticism* (Oxford: Clarendon, 1964) and *Textual and Literary Criticism* (Cambridge: Cambridge UP, 1959) and in Tanselle's "Textual Study and Literary Judgment," *PBSA* 65 (1971): 109–22.

Among the many works on the study and editing of classical texts (and other texts with long manuscript traditions) are Edward J. Kenney's *The Classical Text* (Berkeley: U of California P, 1974); Paul Maas's *Textual Criticism,* trans. Barbara Flower (Oxford: Clarendon, 1958); Martin L. West's *Textual Criticism and Editorial Technique* (Stuttgart: Teubner, 1973); W. W. Greg's *The Calculus of Variants* (Oxford: Clarendon, 1927); Vinton Dearing's *Principles and Practice of Textual Analysis* (Berkeley: U of California P, 1974); and Charles Moorman's *Editing the Middle English Manuscript* (Jackson: UP of Mississippi, 1975). A review of developments in classical textual studies may be found in Georg Luck's "Textual Criticism Today," *American Journal of Philology* 102 (1981): 164–94. In "Classical, Biblical, and Medieval Textual Criticism and Modern Editing," *SB* 36 (1983): 21–68, Tanselle explores the relations between the editing of classical and modern texts. For surveys of textual criticism as applied to classical and biblical works and by scholars of French, German, Italian, Spanish, Russian, Arabic, Sanskrit, and folk literatures (as well as American and English), see the essays in *Scholarly Editing: A Guide to Research,* ed. D. C. Greetham (New York: MLA, 1995). In "A New Approach to the Critical Constitution of Literary Texts," *SB* 28 (1975): 231–64, Hans Zeller explains the rationale and methods of historical-critical editing as practiced in Germany; see also *Contemporary German Editorial Theory,* ed. Hans Walter Gabler, George Bornstein, and Gillian Borland Pierce (Ann Arbor: U of Michigan P, 1995).

A thorough and influential survey of documentary editing is provided by Tanselle in "The Editing of Historical Documents," *SB* 31 (1978): 1–56, reprinted in his *Selected Studies in Bibliography* (Charlottesville: UP of Virginia, 1979), 451–506. Its theory and practice are described in Mary-Jo Kline's *A*

Guide to Documentary Editing (Baltimore: Johns Hopkins UP, 1987). Recent developments may be followed in the journal *Documentary Editing* (formerly the *ADE Newsletter*), published by the Association for Documentary Editing, and in the annual bibliographical review in *American Archivist.*

A seminal document for modern critical editing is W. W. Greg's "The Rationale of Copy-Text," *SB* 3 (1950–51): 19–36, reprinted in his *Collected Papers*, ed. J. C. Maxwell (Oxford: Clarendon, 1966), 374–91. Recent debate in textual criticism has been centered on such issues as copy-text, authorial intention, the distinction between accidentals and substantives, multiple versions of works, editorial eclecticism, textual instability, and the collaborative or social nature of literary production. As a pioneer in the application of Greg's rationale to both Renaissance and post-Renaissance texts, Fredson Bowers has been a key figure in the debate. Some of his most important contributions to it are reprinted in his *Essays in Bibliography, Text, and Editing* (Charlottesville: UP of Virginia, 1975); to them may be added "Scholarship and Editing," *PBSA* 70 (1976): 161–88, and "Greg's 'Rationale of Copy-Text' Revisited," *SB* 31 (1978): 90–161. Among those taking exception to Greg's rationale are Paul Baender in "The Meaning of Copy-Text," *SB* 22 (1969): 311–18; Vinton A. Dearing in "Concepts of Copy-Text Old and New," *Library* 5th ser. 28 (1973): 281–93; and Jerome J. McGann in *A Critique of Modern Textual Criticism* (Chicago: U of Chicago P, 1983). For well-documented critical surveys of this and other issues in textual criticism, see G. Thomas Tanselle's essays collected in his *Textual Criticism since Greg: A Chronicle, 1950–1985* (Charlottesville: UP of Virginia, 1987) and his essays "Textual Criticism and Literary Sociology," *SB* 44 (1991): 83–143; "Editing without a Copy-Text," *SB* 47 (1994): 1–22; and "Textual Criticism and Editorial Idealism," *SB* 49 (1996): 1–60.

Several collections reprint some of the essays mentioned above or present other valuable essays on matters practical and theoretical: O M Brack, Jr., and Warner Barnes, eds., *Bibliography and Textual Criticism: English and American Literature, 1700 to the Present* (Chicago: U of Chicago P, 1969); Ronald Gottesman and Scott Bennett, eds., *Art and Error: Modern Textual Editing* (Bloomington: Indiana UP, 1970); Warner Barnes and James T. Cox, eds., "Textual Studies in the Novel," a special issue of *Studies in the Novel* 7 (1975): 317–471; Jerome J. McGann, ed., *Textual Criticism and Literary Interpretation* (Chicago: U of Chicago P, 1985); Dave Oliphant and Robin Bradford, eds., *New Directions in Textual Studies* (Austin: Ransom Humanities Research Center, 1990); George Bornstein, ed., *Representing Modernist Texts: Editing as Interpretation* (Ann Arbor: U of Michigan P, 1991); Ian Small and Marcus Welsh, eds., *The Theory and Practice of Text-Editing* (Cambridge: Cambridge UP, 1991); George Bornstein and Ralph G. Williams, eds., *Palimpsest: Editorial Theory in the Humanities* (Ann Arbor: U of Michigan P, 1993); Alexander Pettit, ed., *Editing Novels and Novelists, Now*, a special issue of *Studies in the Novel* 37 (1995):

247–454; D. C. Greetham, ed., *The Margins of the Text* (Ann Arbor: U of Michigan P, 1997); and the series of volumes from the Editorial Conference, University of Toronto (1966–).

A procedure for textual collation is briefly described in the Center for Editions of American Authors (CEAA) *Statement of Editorial Principles and Procedures*, rev. ed. (New York: MLA, 1972). In "A Sampling Theory for Bibliographical Research," *Library* 5th ser. 27 (1972): 310–19, David Shaw applies statistical methods to the problem of determining the number of copies that should be collated. Charlton Hinman describes his collating machine in "Mechanized Collation at the Houghton Library," *Harvard Library Bulletin* 9 (1955): 132–34; and Gordon Lindstrand describes his in "Mechanized Textual Collation and Recent Designs," *SB* 24 (1971): 204–14. In connection with these articles, one should consult George Guffey's "Standardization of Photographic Reproductions for Mechanical Collation," *PBSA* 62 (1968): 237–40.

For discussion of the use of computers for collation, textual analysis, and preparation of an edition, see Peter M. W. Robinson's "Collation, Textual Criticism, Publication, and the Computer," *Text* 7 (1994): 77–94, and Peter L. Shillingsburg's *Scholarly Editing in the Computer Age: Theory and Practice*, 3rd ed. (Ann Arbor: U of Michigan P, 1996). For electronic editions, see also the essays in *The Politics of the Electronic Text*, ed. Warren Chernaik, Caroline Davis, and Marilyn Deegan, Office for Humanities Communication Publications 3 (Oxford: Office for Humanities Communication, 1993); in *The Text Encoding Initiative: Background and Contexts*, ed. Nancy Ide and Jean Véronis, special issues of *Computers and the Humanities* 29.1–3 (1995); and the article by John Lavagnino, "Reading, Scholarship, and Hypertext Editions," *Text* 8 (1995): 109–24.

McKerrow's *Prolegomena for the Oxford Shakespeare* presents a method for recording textual variants in an editorial apparatus. A more recent discussion is Tanselle's "Some Principles for Editorial Apparatus" (1972), in his *Selected Studies*, 403–50. Both genetic and descriptive systems for recording manuscript variants are described in Bowers's "Transcription of Manuscripts: The Record of Variants," *SB* 29 (1976): 212–64. A proposal for presenting texts and apparatus for multiple versions of a work appears in Ted-Larry Pebworth and Ernest Sullivan II, "Rational Presentation of Multiple Textual Traditions," *PBSA* 83 (1989): 43–60.

In *From Writer to Reader: Studies in Editorial Method* (Oxford: Clarendon, 1978), Philip Gaskell provides examples of textual histories and the editorial problems they present. And, of course, as examples of editorial method, scholarly editions of various kinds can be consulted. Notable among critical editions are Fredson Bowers's editions of Dekker, Beaumont and Fletcher, Dryden, Fielding, and Marlowe, and the editions completed under the supervision or guidance of the CEAA (1964–76), the Center for Scholarly Editions (1976–), and Committee on Scholarly Editions: for example, of Crane, Dewey, Donne,

Emerson, Hawthorne, Howells, Irving, Melville, Thoreau, and Twain. Also of note are Hans Walter Gabler's critical and synoptic edition of Joyce's *Ulysses*; the Folger Library edition of the works of Richard Hooker under the general editorship of W. Speed Hill; George Kane and E. T. Donaldson's editions of *Piers Plowman*; the Oxford Standard Editions such as William Ringler's edition of Sidney's poetry and Philip Edwards and Colin Gibson's edition of the plays and poems of Philip Massinger; and the Clarendon editions of Dickens and the Brontës. Among documentary editions are David L. Vander Meulen's facsimile edition of Pope's *Dunciad* of 1728, Michael J. Warren's parallel-text facsimile edition of the quarto and folio versions of *King Lear*, the Yale edition of the complete works of St. Thomas More, and Charles E. Robinson's edition of Mary Shelley Wollstonecraft's *Frankenstein Notebooks* (in facsimile and genetic transcription). Links to Web sites of projects using the Text Encoding Initiative guidelines for electronic texts may be found through the TEI home page, <http://www.uic.edu:80/orgs/tei/>.

GLOSSARY OF BIBLIOGRAPHICAL AND TEXTUAL TERMS

ABRIDGMENT. The process or product of shortening a text or reducing the size of a book through condensation or omission.

ACCIDENTALS. In textual criticism, such formal features of a text as capitalization, spelling, word division, punctuation, and italicization, as opposed to wording. See *substantives.*

ADVANCE. Monies paid to an author before publication of a book and later deducted from the royalties earned on its sale.

ADVANCE COPIES. Copies of a book released by a publisher before the date of publication—for example, to book-club selection committees, book reviewers, and sales personnel. They may differ from copies offered to the public.

ANA. A collection of sayings, anecdotes, or other information by or about a person or about a subject. Also used as a suffix to indicate materials about a subject, as in *Americana, Boswelliana,* and *Johnsoniana.*

ANALYTICAL BIBLIOGRAPHY. The branch of bibliography devoted to determining the circumstances of books' production through examining such physical evidence as ink, paper, typography, format, and arrangement of text.

ANNOTATED BIBLIOGRAPHY. An enumeration of works, as on a particular subject or by a particular author, along with notes on the content of those works.

ANNUAL. A book or journal published as part of a yearly series.

ANTHOLOGY. A book containing a collection of texts or portions of texts by one author or several.

APOGRAPH. In classical textual criticism, a manuscript containing a text copied from another manuscript (the exemplar).

APPARATUS. In textual criticism, the notes, tables, and other items that describe the texts and explain what editors have done to the text.

ARCHETYPE. In textual criticism, especially classical textual criticism, a text no longer surviving in any document but reconstructed or postulated on the basis of surviving later states of the text, which are witnesses to it.

ASCENDER. The part of a lowercase letter extending above the x-height, or main body, of the letter, as in *b, d, h,* and *k.*

ASCII FILE. An electronic text file coded according to the American Standard Code for Information Interchange, a system that codes letters, numerals, punctuation, some special characters, carriage returns, tabs, line feeds, and end-of-line marks. Also called DOS text and used to transfer information between programs.

ASSOCIATION COPY. A copy owned and perhaps annotated by the author or by someone closely connected with the author or subject matter.

ATTRIBUTION. The ascription of a work—for instance, one published anonymously or pseudonymously—to an author.

AUTHOR BIBLIOGRAPHY. An enumerative, annotated, or descriptive bibliography concerning the works by or about, or by and about, an author or group of authors.

AUTHORITY. In textual criticism, the principle by which one judges readings of a text; also, the quality ascribed to a documentary text that is judged to contain readings sanctioned by that principle.

AUTOGRAPH. Written in the author's own hand; used in such phrases as "autograph manuscript" and "autograph letter."

BAD BREAK. A general term for the various unsightly arrangements of type that printers seek to avoid at the beginnings or ends of lines, paragraphs, columns, and pages, such as a single word occupying the first line of a column or page (a widow) or a subheading occupying the last line of a page.

BALLS. In printing, leather-covered pads fitted with handles and used in the handpress period to ink type.

BASE TEXT. A text against which others are compared during collation; or a text in reference to which textual variation and annotation is reported, as in a variorum edition.

BASTARD TITLE. See *half title*.

BED. The part of a press on which type is placed for printing.

BEST-TEXT. In textual criticism, the extant documentary text thought to best represent the author's intention.

BIBLIOGRAPHICAL CODES. Bibliographical features, including paper, typography, and design, considered signifying elements in the reading of a book.

BIBLIOGRAPHY. The study of books, including their texts, materials, history, production, and distribution; also an account, list, or description of books or works.

BIBLIOMETRICS. The statistical study of book production, book distribution, readership, library use, or patterns of citation.

BIBLIOPEGY. The art of binding books.

BIBLIOPHILE. A lover of books.

BINDER'S LEAVES. Leaves not integral to a book's printed sheets but added to the book during binding.

BINDER'S TICKET. A stamped or printed identification of a book's binder, generally appearing (if used) on a paste-down endpaper.

BINDING. The process or product of folding, gathering, and fastening together the printed sheets of a book and enclosing them in covers.

BINDING CLOTH. Cloth used in binding, especially since the 1820s, when publishers began issuing books in prefabricated casings rather than leaving binding to the bookseller or purchaser. The cloth may be embossed with a variety of patterns, or grains, that in descriptive bibliography may be designated diaper, rib, ripple, bead, sand, pansy, and beaded-line cloth.

BLACK LETTER TYPE. A group of angular, scriptlike typefaces represented by textura, rotunda, and bastarda and no longer commonly used, although one bastarda type (fraktur) was used in Germany until the mid-1900s. *Gothic type* is sometimes used as a synonym but confusingly also refers to recent sans-serif typefaces.

BLEED. Printing, generally of an illustration, that extends beyond the trimmed edge of a page.

BLIND STAMP. An inkless design or lettering impressed into paper or binding.

BLIND STRIKE. A type printing without being inked, an obvious printing fault, but one which testifies to the existence of the type in the original setting. Also called blind impression.

BLOCK BOOKS. Books printed from woodcuts; also known as xylographs. If text has been added by hand, xylographs become chiroxylographs.

BLOCKS, WOOD. Engraved or etched wooden plates used for printing, especially of illustrations.

BLURB. Advertising or descriptive text, often in the form of quotation, appearing on a dust jacket or in a publisher's catalogue or advertisement.

BOARDS. The wood, cardboard, or other material used as stiff covers or to stiffen the covers of a binding.

BODKIN. In printing, a slender pointed instrument used to prize type from the forme for corrections.

BODY. The piece of metal (or shank) on which a type letter or other character is cast; also, body size, which is a measurement in points indicating the height of the body of type and which may be the same as or smaller than the size of the typeface (the measurement, from ascender to descender, of the printed letters of a particular font).

BOOK PLATE. A slip, often decorated, pasted to an endpaper to show ownership of a book.

BOOK SCRIPT. A handwriting used in manuscript books and formal documents, consisting of carefully formed letters and few ligatures. Also called book hand.

BORDER. A printed frame or compartment enclosing matter on title pages or elsewhere in a book. A border printed from printer's rules is called a frame or rule frame; one from separate printer's cuts or ornaments is also a frame; and one from a single engraved or cast piece or from several pieces made to be used together as a single design is a compartment.

BOWDLERIZE. To expurgate by omitting or modifying supposedly offensive passages, as Thomas Bowdler did in his edition of Shakespeare (1818).

BROADSIDE. A sheet printed to produce one large page (if printed on one side only) or less commonly two (if both sides) and not folded. Used, for example, for the leaves of large books of plates, for royal proclamations, and for ballads. Also called broadsheet.

CALENDAR. In bibliography, a list and physical description of manuscripts.

CALENDER. The steel rollers of a papermaking machine that smooth the paper. Paper thus smoothed is said to be calendered; supercalendered if smoothed to glossiness.

CALF. Leather used in binding made from the hide of a calf; the most common leather used in binding.

CAMERA-READY COPY. Type proofs, artwork, and other graphic material ready to be photographed for the production of printing plates.

CANCEL. One leaf or more or a slip pasted to a page to replace what was originally printed, as for correction or for insertion of a title page with another publisher's or bookseller's imprint. That which is replaced may be called the cancelland; that which replaces, the cancellans (or simply cancel). To cancel is to cut out printed or blank pages.

CASE. A compartmented tray in which type is kept for composition; a type case. Also, a cover or binding; used especially to refer to bindings made up separately and subsequently affixed to books. See fig. 18, a type case from Joseph Moxon, *Mechanick Exercises on the Whole Art of Printing* (1683–84).

CASTING OFF. Estimating the space, including number of pages, to be occupied by copy when it has been set into type; see *copyfitting*.

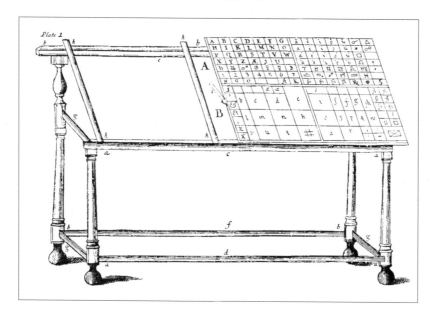

FIG. 18. *Case.*

CATALOGUE or **CATALOG**. A listing, often with annotation or description, of documents (books, periodicals, manuscripts, etc.) in a particular collection or, as in a union catalogue, in several collections. The collection may be, for example, that of a library, a publisher, or bookseller.

CATCHWORD. The first word of a page, appearing also at the foot of the preceding page as a guide to assembling the pages in correct order. Catchwords were in common use in English printed books from the mid-sixteenth century until the later eighteenth century.

CHAIN LINES. Lines, roughly twenty-five millimeters apart, created by the mold in which laid paper was made and running parallel to the shorter sides of the sheet. Chain lines may also be impressed into machine-made paper by a dandy roll. See *wire lines*.

CHASE. A metal frame in which pages of type are arranged and locked up for printing or for making plates.

CHECKLIST. An enumerative bibliography or a descriptive bibliography with minimal descriptive detail.

CHI. The Greek letter χ, used in a collational formula to indicate unsigned leaves or gatherings inserted within a sequence of signatures and not inferable as part of that sequence.

CIP DATA. Library of Congress Cataloging-in-Publication data, arrayed as in a library catalog and printed on the copyright page of many books since 1971.

CLEAR TEXT. A text, as in a scholarly edition, presented without interruption by editorial annotation, symbols, or interpolation, the editorial apparatus having been separated from the edited text.

CODEX. A book (as opposed, say, to a papyrus roll); in particular a manuscript book. The plural is *codices*.

CODICOLOGY. The study of manuscripts as physical objects.

COLLATE. In book production, to assemble sheets or gatherings for binding. In bibliography, to analyze and record (as in a collational formula) the number, order, and arrangement of leaves and gatherings in a book. In textual criticism, to compare one text with another to discover textual variation.

COLLATION FORMULA. An abbreviated form for recording the number, order, and arrangement of leaves and gatherings in a book, using signatures to represent gatherings and superscript figures to indicate the number of leaves in a gathering.

COLLOTYPE. In printing, a photolithographic process of printing from a plate coated with gelatin; developed in the 1860s and used especially for illustrations. Also, a printing plate made by this process, and the printed matter resulting from its use.

COLONIAL EDITION. In British publishing, the production of a cheaper edition for sale in the rest of the Empire.

COLOPHON. Notes at the end of manuscripts and printed books giving information about production, usually including date, place, and producer (scribe or printer). The note may be accompanied by a printer's device. Information in these notes is not always reliable.

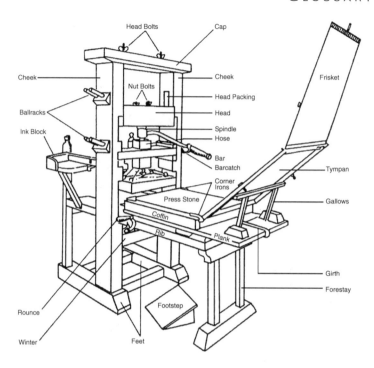

FIG. 19. *Common press.*

COMMON PRESS. The wood handpress in use throughout the handpress period (1450–1800), consisting of a wood frame in which a screw-driven platen impressed the paper onto an inked forme of type. See fig. 19.

COMPOSING STICK. A handheld tray into which the compositor places the types from his cases according to his copy. In early printing the length of the stick was fixed so a compositor would have to have several of various standard lengths. Later composing sticks had an adjustable end that allowed one stick to serve for setting lines of varying lengths. See fig. 20, a composing stick from Joseph Moxon, *Mechanick Exercises on the Whole Art of Printing* (1683–84).

COMPOSITION. The process of setting type, spaces, rules, headings, and the like.

COMPOSITOR. A person who sets type.

CONCORDANCE. An index to the individual words in a text or group of texts, often with an indication of the immediate linguistic context of each occurrence of the words.

CONJUGATE LEAVES. Leaves that form a pair joined by an inner fold. Thus, in a sheet folded to form a quarto, leaf 1 is conjugate with leaf 4, leaf 2 with leaf 3. Leaves that are not conjugate are disjunct.

CONTAMINATION. In textual criticism, the process by which a scribe or typesetter produces a copy of a text by consulting two or more previous copies, or exemplars; also called conflation.

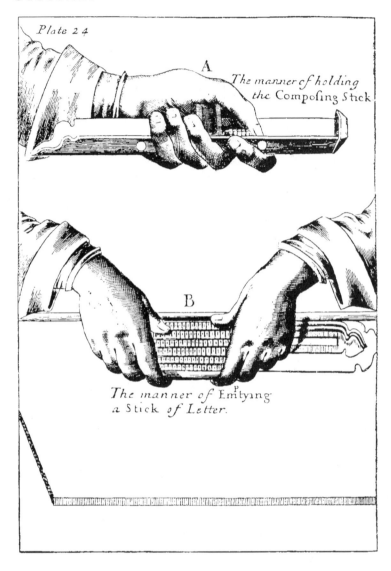

FIG. 20. *Composing stick.*

COPY. In printing, the material to be set in type.

COPYEDITING. The editing of copy, as by a publisher, before it is set in type.

COPYFITTING. The process of estimating the space to be occupied when copy is set in type. Also called casting off copy.

COPYRIGHT. A legal right to reproduce and publish the text of a work.

COPY-TEXT. In critical editing, the text (generally of a particular document) whose readings, because of the circumstances of its production, are presumed authoritative in the absence of contrary evidence. An editor follows its readings except when they are determined to be in error or when there is evidence for the superior authority of variant readings in another text.

CORPUS. A body of writings, as of an individual author, on a given subject, in a particular language, or from a particular period or region.

CORRUPT. Said of a documentary text containing textual error or other nonauthoritative textual alteration.

COUNTERMARK. A sort of supplemental watermark, appearing in the opposite half of the sheet from the larger watermark proper. Used in the handpress period, often to indicate the mill producing the paper.

CRITICAL EDITION. A scholarly edition that presents a text constructed by adopting readings from one document or more and by correcting readings determined to be errors. The critical text thus constructed is accompanied by an apparatus that explains the editorial principles and procedures, lists the textual emendations, and provides a historical collation of the text. Critical editing often resorts to an expedient known as copy-text.

CROPPED. The cutting down of the edges of the leaves by a binder's knife. This is often done so extensively that it affects the printed page.

CRT COMPOSITION. A form of phototypesetting in which digitally stored information produces an image on a cathode-ray tube that is in contact with film or photosensitive paper.

CRUX. A textual reading that is the subject of critical and editorial question and controversy.

CURSIVE SCRIPT. A handwriting in which the pen is not lifted from the paper as it proceeds from one letter to another and in which the letter forms tend to be rounded rather than angular.

CUT. Originally, in letterpress printing, a woodcut. By extension, also a zinc etching, halftone engraving, or other cut or engraved illustration. See *linecut* and *halftone*.

CYLINDER PRESS. A press that prints from a flat forme against which a cylinder revolves to make the impression.

DANDY ROLL. In papermaking machines, a wire cylinder that is used to create the texture of the paper and that may be used to impress wire lines, chain lines, and watermarks on paper.

DECKLE EDGE. The untrimmed, uneven edge of a sheet of paper as it comes from the mold in papermaking by hand or from the web in papermaking by machine. The deckle is the frame around the mold used in making paper by hand; it is a rubber dam or strap in papermaking machines.

DEFINITIVE EDITION. A scholarly edition that provides a thorough record of a text and its history and presents a critical text based on the evidence of that record. The term is no longer in favor, except as an object of derision.

DEGRESSIVE PRINCIPLE. In descriptive bibliography, the adjustment of descriptive method to the period or importance of the books being described.

DESCENDER. The part of a lowercase letter extending below the x-height, or main body, of the letter, as in *g, j, p, q,* and *y.*

DESCRIPTIVE BIBLIOGRAPHY. The branch of bibliography concerned with the principles and practice of describing the physical materials and forms of books (and other printed documents). Also, the product of such study, such as a description of the books that have presented texts of an individual author's works.

DESKTOP PUBLISHING. The use of microcomputer hardware and software to create, edit, and design documents and to print them (in small quantities) or to produce camera-ready copy or electronic files used in typesetting (for larger quantities).

DEVICE. A design or emblem (such as the Aldine Anchor and Knopf Borzoi) used by a printer or publisher as an identifying mark, as on a title page or final page of a book.

DIGITIZATION. The conversion of nondigital information into digital format (binary bits), as when a graphic image is scanned so that it may be displayed on a computer monitor.

DIGRAPH. Two letters combined into one printed or written character, such as Æ, æ, and œ.

DIPLOMATIC EDITION. See *documentary edition.*

DIPLOMATICS. The study of documents, especially legal manuscripts.

DIRECTION LINE. At the foot of a page, a line containing such matter as the catchword, signature, and page number.

DISBOUND. Pamphlets or small books removed from composite volumes into which they have been bound.

DISJUNCT LEAVES. See *conjugate leaves.*

DISPLAY TYPE. Type larger than the body type, used for title pages, half titles, chapter heads, and the like.

DISTRIBUTION. The process of removing pieces of type from the chase and returning them to the type case.

DITTOGRAPHY. Inadvertent repetition, as by a scribe or compositor, of letters, words, or lines. See *haplography.*

DIVINATIO. In classical textual criticism, a synonym for conjectural emendation.

DOCUMENT. A manuscript, printed book, or other form embodying a text.

DOCUMENTARY EDITION. A scholarly edition that presents, without emendation, the text of a particular document. The text is accompanied by an apparatus that generally includes a description of the document transcribed, the basis for its selection, the principles of transcription employed, and lists of variant readings found in other documents. Also called diplomatic edition.

DOCUMENTARY TEXT. A text as it appears in a particular book, manuscript, or other material form.

DUMMY. A sketched layout showing the design of a book or other document to be printed; or an unprinted or partially printed version that shows the size, shape, and general design of the planned final product. A dummy made from galley proofs is called a paste-up dummy.

DUODECIMO. A book format in which the sheets are printed so that each sheet, after being folded, produces twelve leaves (twenty-four pages). Also, a book printed with this format. Also called twelvemo. Abbreviated 12° and 12mo.

DUST JACKET. A protective and usually promotional paper wrapper that folds around the front and back covers of a book. Also called dust wrapper.

ECLECTIC TEXT. A text constructed by selecting readings from several texts.

EDGES. The three outer edges of the leaves (top, bottom, and fore), which may be trimmed, gilded, stained, marbled, painted, or otherwise decorated.

EDITION. In the strict bibliographical sense, all copies of a book printed from substantially the same setting of type or from plates made from that type or type-image. Publishers use the term more loosely and variously, often to distinguish among copies identifiable by publishing format (such as paperback and hardback), change of publisher, textual revision, or some other feature, even if all the copies belong to the same edition in a bibliographical sense.

EDITION BINDING. The binding up of books before the publisher supplies them to booksellers. The practice became common in the early nineteenth century.

ÉDITION DE LUXE. Any book produced to be valued for its appearance rather than content.

ELECTRONIC EDITION. An edition, scholarly or not, consisting of computer files and perhaps of hypertext links between and within the files.

ELECTROTYPE. A metal printing plate cast from a wax, lead, or plastic mold of set type or illustrations and, through electrolysis, faced with copper, nickel, or steel.

ELIMINATIO. In classical textual criticism, the elimination of certain manuscript readings or texts from consideration as witnesses to earlier readings of a text. *Eliminatio codicum descriptorum* is elimination of manuscript texts derived from other extant manuscripts; *eliminatio lectionum singularium* is elimination of a unique reading in the face of a differing reading common to two or more independent witnesses.

EM. In typesetting, a unit of measurement equal to the type size in question; thus, for example, one em in twelve-point type is twelve points. Also, a shortened form of *em-quad*; that is, a quad that is the square of the type size in question.

EMENDATIO. In classical textual criticism, the use of conjecture to emend the text reconstructed from surviving witnesses, thereby removing errors.

EMENDATION. In modern editing, the editorial alteration of the copy-text or base-text to adopt readings from other documentary texts or to adopt readings not present in any document but arrived at through editorial conjecture (conjectural emendation).

EN. In typesetting, a unit of measurement equal to one-half an em.

ENDPAPER. The leaf pasted to the inside of a cover (the paste-down endpaper) and the conjugate, unpasted leaf (the free endpaper, or flyleaf).

ENGRAVING. An illustration printed from metal plates into which a design or lettering has been incised.

EPIGRAPHY. The study of inscriptions, that is, the writing on coins, medals, stones, wax tablets, pottery, and the like. Also, that writing itself.

ERRATA. A list of errors or misprints noted after printing, printed with the preliminaries, separately printed and tipped in or laid in the completed book, or, as in multivolume books, printed in a later volume. Also called corrigenda.

ETCHING. A process of making an image, as on a printing plate, by allowing an acid or other chemical to eat, or etch, areas that will print in intaglio printing. The non-printing areas are protected from the acid, as by a coating of paraffin or varnish. Also, a print taken from etched plates.

EXEMPLAR. A copy (in the sense of "individual specimen," rather than "reproduction") of a manuscript or book; more specifically, the manuscript from which a scribe copied another.

EX-LIBRARY COPIES. Copies of a book that have been owned by a lending library and that thus bear traces of this ownership, such as call numbers, labels, and stampings.

EXPLICIT. The final words of an early manuscript or book, sometimes including pious thoughts; relief at completing the work; the title of the work; the name of the author, scribe, or printer; and the place of copying or printing.

EXPURGATION. The process or product of revising a text to expunge passages considered offensive or morally objectionable.

FACE. The printing surface of a piece of type. See *typeface.*

FACSIMILE EDITION. An edition that reproduces an earlier edition's text and its typographical appearance.

FACTOTUM. A printer's ornament containing a space into which may be inserted a letter; used for printing an initial.

FAIR COPY. A corrected and cleanly written manuscript, produced by its author or by a scribe. See *foul papers.*

FELT SIDE. The side of handmade paper not lying on the wires and chains of the paper mold during its manufacture; so called because the paper would be turned out of the mold onto a piece of felt. (Opposite the felt side is the mold, or wire, side.) Also, the upper side of a sheet of paper formed on the wire of a papermaking machine.

FIRST EDITION. The first printed edition of a book. Book collectors often use the term to mean the first impression of the first edition.

FLAT. In offset printing, the assemblage of film negatives or positives arranged for the production of a printing plate.

FLOWERS. In printing, floral type ornaments, often combined to create borders. Also called florets and printer's flowers.

FLYLEAF. An additional blank leaf inserted by the binder between the integral printed leaves of a book and the book's front free endpaper. Also, the front free endpaper.

FLY TITLE. A second half title, usually found after the title page and other preliminaries and before the main body of the book.

FOLIATION. The numbering of the leaves rather than the pages of a book or manuscript.

FOLIO. A book format in which sheets are printed for folding once, each sheet thus producing two leaves (four pages). Abbreviated 2° and F. Also, a leaf, especially one numbered on its front; the number on a leaf; the number on a page; and a book made up of folio sheets.

FONT. A complete assortment of type in a particular size and design, or face, generally including capitals, small capitals, lowercase letters, punctuation, and common diacritical marks.

FOOT. The bottom of a page, especially the margin or lower edge of the leaf. Also, the lower surface of a type.

FORE-EDGE. The outer edge of a book's leaves, opposite the spine.

FORE-EDGE PAINTING. A painting made on the splayed fore-edge of a book and visible only when the edge, which may be gilded or marbled, is again splayed.

FORGERY. A fraudulently made text or inscription, manuscript, book, or other document.

FORMAT. In the most general sense, the design and layout of a book. More particularly, the scheme by which type pages have been arranged (imposed) within a forme so that when a printed sheet is folded it produces a particular number and sequence of leaves. See *duodecimo, folio, octavo, quarto,* and *sixteenmo.* Also, a designation of book size, since the size depends on the number of times a sheet is folded (and the size of the full sheet).

FORME. The assemblage, or imposition, of type pages for the printing of one side of a sheet. The outer forme includes the two pages that will come first and last when the sheet is printed; the inner forme is the opposite side. Also, especially in American usage, *form.*

FOUL CASE. A compositor's case in which some pieces of type have been distributed into the wrong compartments and wait for the opportunity to create a typographical error.

FOUL COPY. A manuscript or other document that has been used as by a printer in setting type and thus has likely been fouled by marks of correction and design. Also called dead copy.

FOUL PAPERS. An author's original uncorrected manuscript, especially play manuscripts such as those postulated to have been used as setting copy of some of Shakespeare's quartos. See *fair copy.*

FOXING. A brownish spotted discoloration of paper; caused by chemical reaction in the paper, especially when exposed to dampness.

FRAME. Enclosures, typically of title pages, made of separate type ornaments, woodcuts, or rules pieced together.

FRISKET. A frame covered with parchment or paper in which holes have been cut to expose the areas to be printed and to mask the areas of the chase that are not to be printed (the *furniture*, q.v.).

FRONTISPIECE. An illustration, often an engraving, that faces a title page.

FRONT MATTER. See *preliminaries.*

FULL BOUND. All the outer surface of the boards and spine are covered with a particular binding material (e.g., calf, cloth).

FURNITURE. In printing, wood or metal spacing material placed around type pages within a chase.

GALLEY. A metal tray into which set type is placed before it is divided into pages.

GALLEY PROOF. A proof printed from type while still in the galley.

GATHERING. A book section consisting of a folded sheet, folded portions of a sheet, or quired sheets. Also called *signature* (q.v.).

GENEALOGICAL METHOD. An approach to editing associated with classical textual criticism but also applied to modern. It makes use largely of internal evidence (such as shared and unique errors) to establish relations, or affiliations, between surviving manuscript texts. The affiliations may be represented in a stemma. They aid in recension, the construction of an earlier state of the text.

GENETIC EDITION. A scholarly edition that has the chief goal of establishing and displaying a text's development rather than constructing an authoritative text, the premise often being that a work is best represented not by a single text but by a series of texts reflecting its textual history or versions. In this sense, synonymous with *synoptic edition.* The term may also be restricted to an edition showing the development of the text or texts in a single document, as opposed to a synoptic edition, which shows the development as it appears in several documents. All genetic editions use inclusive-text presentations.

GHOST. In bibliography, a book that has been said to have existed but that in fact has never existed.

GILT or **GILDED.** Of a book, having gold leaf applied to its edges; sometimes used to refer to various kinds of stamping on bindings.

GLOSS. A marginal or interlinear annotation of a portion of a text, especially one that translates or offers a synonym for a word in the text.

GOTHIC TYPE. A general term for type based originally on a twelfth-century German book script and characterized by angular forms (for example, bastarda, fraktur, and rotunda). Also called *black letter* (q.v.) and text. Modern printers use the term *gothic* to refer to sans serif type.

GRANGERIZED. Of a book, having plates, prints, manuscripts, letters, printed documents, and other illustrative material added after publication. This is usually done by the owner but is sometimes done professionally, as with James Granger's *Biographical History of England* (1769), which was bound with blank leaves for the addition of such things.

GRAVURE. Intaglio printing from large copper-surfaced cylinders on which the printing image is etched after passing through a mesh screen. Also called photogravure. The process was perfected for commercial application in the 1890s.

GUIDE LETTER. A small letter placed in the space provided for the later insertion of a rubricated or illuminated initial of that letter.

GUTTER. See *margins.*

HALF-BOUND. Bound with one material (often leather) around the spine and the outer corners and another (often cloth or paper) on the remaining portion of the front and back covers. Half-cloth designates a binding with cloth around the spine (and sometimes the outer corners) and with the remainder in paper. Quarter-bound designates a binding with leather on the spine but not on the corners.

HALF-SHEET IMPOSITION. The arrangement of type within a forme so that it produces from one sheet two identical units for folding after the sheet is cut in half. For example, to produce two half-sheets of eight pages each, all eight pages are imposed in one forme, one side of the sheet is printed, the sheet is turned left to right, the other side of the sheet is printed, and finally the sheet is cut in half to yield two duplicate eight-page units. See *work-and-turn.* See fig. 21, an example of half-sheet imposition from Joseph Moxon, *Mechanick Exercises on the Whole Art of Printing* (1683–84).

HALF TITLE. The title of a book, minus subtitle and author's name, printed on the leaf preceding the title page and sometimes again on a leaf following the preliminaries, at which position it is sometimes called a *fly title* (q.v.), bastard title, or second half title.

HALFTONE. A continuous-tone illustration, such as a photograph, produced by projecting an image through a screen onto a photosensitive plate, resulting in an image made up of a pattern of varying-sized dots.

HAND. The handwriting of a particular person, as in "the author's hand." Also, a type or style of handwriting, as in "a book hand," although the term *script* (q.v.) is also used in this sense.

HANDPRESS PERIOD. In historical bibliography, the period 1500–1800, during which printing became well established although the technology remained relatively stable, employing the common handpress and movable type.

HAPLOGRAPHY. The writing or setting once of what should have been written or set twice. See *dittography.*

HEAD. The top or top margin of a page.

HEADLINE. The line at the top of a page bearing such matter as the running title and page number.

Plate 28.

Impoſing a Folio Half Sheet.   *Impoſing a Quarto Half Sheet.*

Impoſing an Octavo Half Sheet.   *Impoſing a Twelves Half Sheet.*

FIG. 21.   *Half-sheet imposition.*

HEADPIECE. A printer's ornament used at the beginning of a text or textual division (such as a chapter).

HINMAN COLLATOR. A device, developed by Charlton Hinman, for comparing, or collating, pages from two copies of an edition through optics that superimpose the two images and then alternately illuminate one page and then the other. Textual variation or movement of type appears to blink on the continuous image.

HISTORIATION. The embellishment of manuscript or printed initials with illustrative drawings.

HISTORICAL COLLATION. In textual criticism, a listing of variant readings (stemmatic readings) of all or some documentary texts of a work, generally keyed to the readings (lemmatic readings) of one particular text.

HISTORICAL-CRITICAL EDITING. A form of critical editing that regards each documentary text as representing a separate version of a work and that restricts critical judgment to the correction of unauthorized errors within that text.

HOLOGRAPH MANUSCRIPT. A manuscript in the author's handwriting.

HOUSE STYLE. The conventions of such matters as design, typography, grammar, punctuation, spelling, and usage followed by a publisher in preparing copy for printing or by a compositor in setting type.

HYPARCHETYPE. In classical textual criticism, a reconstructed text from which a group of manuscript texts have descended and which in turn is used as a witness in the reconstruction of an earlier archetype.

HYPERTEXT. Electronic text or texts with links that allow nonlinear reading. When hypertext includes sounds, images, animation, and the like, it is sometimes called hypermedia.

IDEAL COPY. In descriptive bibliography, the form of a book as published or as intended for publication, as that form has been deduced from examination of surviving copies.

ILLUMINATION. The decoration by hand of a manuscript or book by adding illustrations, initials, and ornaments in gold or silver or, more generally, in any colors.

IMPOSING STONE. A large flat piece of stone or, later, iron forming the surface of a table on which type pages were arranged in formes.

IMPOSITION. The arrangement of pages in the chase to print one forme so that when the sheets are properly folded the pages run in the correct order.

IMPRESSION. All copies of a book produced by one pressrun, or printing. Also, each operation, or cycle, of the press that prints an inked image, used in measuring the speed of a press, as in two thousand impressions an hour.

IMPRINT. The printed name of publisher or printer (often with the date and place of publication or printing) appearing in books, as on the title page or copyright page or as a colophon.

INCIPIT. The beginning words of a text, used to identify early manuscripts and incunables, especially those lacking title pages.

INCLUSIVE TEXT. In a scholarly edition, an edited text that incorporates editorial symbols, interpolations, and the like rather than being presented in clear text.

INCUNABLE or **INCUNABULUM.** A book printed from movable type during the infancy of printing, especially before 1501. The plural is *incunables* or *incunabula.*

INDEX. A usually alphabetical listing of terms, subjects, names, titles, authors, linguistic forms, or the like in a particular text, group of texts, or corpus, with the listed items keyed to their appearance (as by page numbers). Also, the character alternatively known as a fist (☞).

INITIAL. A large, sometimes fancy letter at the beginning of a chapter or other section of a text.

INSCRIPTION. In bibliography, a name and sometimes a note and date written in a book (often on an endpaper or title page) by the author, owner, or person giving it as a gift.

INTAGLIO. Printing not from relief (see *letterpress*) but from depressed areas in an engraved or etched surface that has been inked and wiped so that ink remains in the depressions.

INTERLINEATION. The placement or addition of notes, revisions, translations, and the like between the lines of a book or manuscript text.

ISBN. International Standard Book Number, assigned to a book by the publisher according to an international standard and consisting of ten digits identifying the publisher and book.

ISSN. International Standard Serial Number, the equivalent of the ISBN for serials.

ISSUE. In bibliographical taxonomy, all copies of an impression that bear some distinctive feature (such as a variant title page) marking them as a unit of sale distinct from that of other copies of the impression. Also, as a verb, to release to the public, to publish.

ITALIC TYPE. A cursive-like version of roman type.

JUSTIFICATION. In printing, the setting of lines so that each occupies the same measure and aligns with the others at the right and left margin, thus producing the typical rectangular type page of books. A type page justified at the left margin but not at the right is called ragged right.

JUVENILIA. Writings produced by an author in his or her youth.

KERN. A part of a type that overhangs its body and may overlap a neighboring type.

LACUNA. A gap in a text, as when a portion of a document is missing.

LAID PAPER. Paper made by hand and showing the wire and chain lines of the paper mold. Also, machine-made paper showing these lines as made by a dandy roll. See *wove paper*.

LARGE-PAPER COPY. Within an impression, one of probably a small number of copies printed on larger paper than the bulk of copies and sold at a higher price or used for presentation.

LAY. The arrangement of the compartments for sorts in a typecase.

LAYOUT. A plan for the design of a book or other printed document, showing such features as spacing, placement of text and headings, and type specifications.

LEADING. The spacing between lines of type, created by inserting thin strips of metal (leads) the length of the line or by using type cast on body larger than its face (for example, a ten-point face on a twelve-point body). The term is also used for such spacing when no actual leads or metal type have been used, as in photocomposition.

LEAF. A piece of paper consisting of one page on its front (*recto*) and one on its back (*verso*).

LECTIO. In textual criticism, a reading; that is, the wording at a particular point in a text. Used in such phrases as *lectio brevior* 'shorter reading,' *lectio difficilior* 'harder reading,' *lectio facilior* 'easier reading,' and *lectio singularis* 'unique reading.'

LEMMATA. In classical and medieval commentaries and scholia, as well as in the apparatus of modern scholarly editions, the quoted words of the text that serve as headings or points of reference for commentary, gloss, lists of variants, or other annotation. The singular is *lemma*.

LETTERPRESS. Relief printing; that is, printing from an inked raised surface such as that of type, stereotypes, woodcuts, and photoengravings. Also, the material so printed. Now frequently used to mean that portion of the page printed to appear to be made by types, no matter what method of printing is employed.

LIGATURE. The stroke connecting two letters. Also, a type containing two or more connected (ligatured) letters, such as ffl.

LIMITED EDITION. An edition restricted to a particular number of copies; often each copy is numbered and signed.

LINDSTRAND COMPARATOR. A device, developed by Gordon Lindstrand, that allows textual comparison, or collation, of the pages of two copies of an edition by requiring the user to view each with a different eye, forcing the nervous system to superimpose them. Textual variation or movement of type causes a stereoscopic effect or a failure of superimposition.

LINEATION. The arrangement or division of text into lines.

LINECUT. A photoengraving of a line drawing, made by photographically transferring its image to a zinc or copper plate and etching away the plate's metal surface not protected by the drawing. Also called line block, line engraving, line etching, and line plate.

LINOTYPE. A typesetting machine, introduced in the 1890s, that cast not individual pieces of type but whole lines (called slugs). Operation of its keyboard assembled matrices in which molten metal was cast to make the slug. Other slug-casting machines were manufactured under the names Intertype and Typograph.

LITHOGRAPHY. A planographic printing process using a printing surface treated so that its image areas are ink-receptive and nonimage areas are ink-repellent. Originally, in 1798, the surface was a dampened (and abraded or slightly etched) stone on which a greased image took ink but the wet surrounding portion did not. In the nineteenth century, metal plates replaced stones in commercial applications. Chromolithography makes use of multiple surfaces, each taking a different colored ink. Photolithography produces the image on a thin metal plate by photochemical means. See *photo-offset*.

LOGOTYPE. A single piece of type with two or more nonligatured characters on it. Also, especially as *logo*, an identifying symbol of a company or product.

LOWER CASE. The typecase placed beneath the upper case in a frame used by compositors. The lower case held noncapital letters, that is, lowercase letters.

MACHINE-PRESS PERIOD. In historical bibliography, the period 1800–1950, during which iron presses replaced wooden ones, machine-driven presses replaced hand-powered ones, printing increasingly employed plates rather than type, and typesetting and binding became mechanized. There is no generally accepted term for the period or periods since 1950, in which setting of metal type has given way to photocomposition and computer typesetting and in which photo-offset printing has been dominant.

MAJUSCULE. In paleography, a form of handwriting in which all letters are of the same height. Also, a capital letter.

MAKEREADY. The final preparation of a press and forme for printing, especially the adjustment of the forme or tympan so that all portions of the type print evenly.

MANUSCRIPT. A handwritten or typewritten document.

MARBLING. Decoration in a marble pattern, as on book edges and on paper used for endpapers. Created by touching paper to the surface of a liquid on which pigments have been floated.

MARGINALIA. Matter written in the margin of a document, generally by someone other than the author.

MARGINS. The spaces surrounding the printed area of a page, consisting of the head or top margin; outer or outside margin; tail, foot, or bottom margin; and inner margin. The margin between the printed areas of two conjugate leaves is the gutter margin.

MEASURE. In printing, the width to which a page or column of type is set. The width is reckoned in ems or picas.

MINUSCULE. In paleography, a class of handwriting in which some strokes (ascenders and descenders) extend beyond the main body of a letter. Also, a lowercase letter.

MISPRINT. An error in printing, as that resulting from a compositor's inadvertent departure from copy or from the shifting of type within a chase during printing.

MOLD SIDE. See *felt side.*

MONOTYPE. A typesetting and casting machine developed in the 1890s and consisting of two units: a keyboard unit to code the typesetting by perforating a strip of paper, and a casting unit to translate the codes into matrices in which the individual type characters were cast from molten metal.

NATIONAL BIBLIOGRAPHY. A list of books published in or otherwise related to a particular country, such as A. W. Pollard and G. R. Redgrave's *A Short-Title Catalogue of Books Printed in England, Scotland, and Ireland, and of English Books Printed Abroad, 1475–1640* and Charles Evans's *American Bibliography: A Chronological Dictionary of All Books, Pamphlets, and Periodical Publications Printed in the United States of America from the Genesis of Printing in 1639 Down to and Including the Year 1800.*

NORMALIZATION. The alteration of a text to bring its punctuation, spelling, capitalization, metrics, or similar features into conformance with the conventions of its time or, as in modernization, a later time.

OCTAVO. A book format in which the sheets are printed for folding three times, each sheet thus producing eight leaves (sixteen pages). Also, a book printed with this format. Abbreviated 8° and 8vo.

OFFSET. A printing process in which the inked image is transferred from type or plates to a surface and from it to the paper being printed. See *photo-offset*.

OLD-SPELLING EDITION. An edition that preserves the spelling contemporary with its text.

OLD STYLE. See *roman type*.

ORNAMENT. In printing, a broad term for decorative items such as borders, initials, flourishes, flowers, rules, and tailpieces.

ORTHOGRAPHY. Spelling or the study of spelling.

PAGE. One side of a leaf of a book.

PAGINATION. The numbering of pages. See *foliation*.

PALEOGRAPHY. The study of handwriting from former times, certainly from ancient times, and perhaps from as late as the Renaissance.

PALIMPSEST. A writing surface, such as a parchment or tablet, from which one text has been scraped away and another written in its place.

PAPERBACK. A book bound in paper not covering boards.

PAPER SIZES. The dimensions of sheets used in printing. Sizes have varied—even sizes bearing the same name—over time and at the same time. Here are some names and approximate sizes from nineteenth-century England: foolscap (17″ × 13″), crown (20″ × 15″), demy (22½″ × 17½″), royal (25″ × 20″), double royal (40″ × 25″). Combining paper size and imposition format produces names for book sizes, such as foolscap folio, foolscap quarto, and crown octavo.

PAPYRUS. A reed cut into strips that, layered and pressed, form a writing material of the same name, as in ancient Greek and Roman rolls.

PARALLEL TEXT. In scholarly editing, two or more texts presented together, as in columns or on facing pages.

PARATEXT. The peritext, consisting of such items as titles, authors' names, forewords, dedications, prefaces, epigraphs, notes, and afterwords, all of which frame a text, and the epitext, consisting of texts not physically appended to the text in question but associated with its public and private history, such as advertisements, reviews, author's statements and correspondence about it, and records of its production and publication.

PARCHMENT. Writing material made from the skin of a sheep or goat. Also, paper resembling such material in its smoothness, translucence, and toughness.

PART PUBLICATION. Publication of a book in installments, or parts, each installment usually printed on one sheet or more, folded, and provided with paper wrappers.

PART TITLE. The title of a major division of a text, often appearing on a separate recto page. Also called divisional half title.

PASTEDOWN. An endpaper pasted to the inner side of the front or back cover of a book.

PERFECT BINDING. An unsewn binding, common in paperbacks, in which the inner folds of a book's gatherings have been cut and the leaves secured to the binding with a flexible glue.

PERFECTING. Printing the second side of a sheet. Also called backing up.

PHOTOENGRAVING. A photomechanical process of making linecuts, halftones, and plates by exposing an image on a photosensitive surface and then etching away nonprinting areas from the surface.

PHOTOLITHOGRAPHY. See *lithography*.

PHOTO-OFFSET. A printing process in which an inked image from a photolithographic plate on one cylinder is transferred (offset) to a blanket that runs over another cylinder and that then transfers the image to paper. Also called offset lithography. See *lithography*.

PHOTOTYPESETTING. A type of direct-image composition: in one version, light is projected through a photomatrix arrayed with type characters to produce an image on photographic paper; in another, a cathode-ray tube or a laser beam is used to expose film or photosensitive paper. Also called photocomposition.

PHYSICAL BIBLIOGRAPHY. Analytical and descriptive bibliography.

PI. The Greek letter π, used in a collation formula to indicate initial unsigned leaves or gatherings that are not inferable as part of the sequence of signed gatherings that follow. Also, set type that has been spilled or otherwise disordered.

PICA. A printer's unit of measure equal to twelve points (about ⅙″) and used to measure width and depth of typeset material and of margins. See *type size*.

PIRACY. Printing and publishing a book without authorization or legal right; a violation of copyright.

PLANOGRAPHY. Printing from a plane surface, as in photo-offset, rather than from a raised surface (as in letterpress) or an engraved one (as in intaglio).

PLATE. A solid surface that bears an intaglio, relief, or planographic image that, when inked, will print a whole page or forme; for example, electrotype, stereotype, collotype, and photo-offset plates. Also, a full-page book illustration printed separately from the book's text.

PLATEN. On a printing press, the flat plate that presses paper against inked type. Not all presses have platens; see *cylinder press* and *rotary press*.

POINT. A unit of type measurement equal to 0.01384 inches, or about ½₂ of an inch. A ten-point typeface measures ten points from the highest ascender to the lowest descender. Type with a ten-point face may appear on, say, a twelve-point body, in which case the type is said to be ten on twelve point. Also, in descriptive bibliography, a feature of a book or group of books (such as a misprint, a textual variant, or a watermark) serving to distinguish them from others and thus as a quick means of identification.

PRELIMINARIES. The material preceding the main text in a book, such as title page, dedication, preface, and table of contents. Also called prelims and front matter.

PRESENTATION COPY. A book given someone by the author (or sometimes the illustrator or publisher) and usually containing a signed inscription to that effect.

PRESS CORRECTION. Correction made during the process of printing; also called stop-press correction.

PRESS FIGURE. A number appearing in the bottom margin of a leaf, especially in books from the late seventeenth through early nineteenth century, identifying the forme in which it appears as the work of a particular press or press operator.

PRESS VARIANT. A textual variant that arises during a pressrun, such as that caused by a stop-press correction (although the variant need not be a correction and often is not).

PRESSWORK. In book production, the actual printing of the book, excluding the preceding composition and the subsequent binding.

PRIMARY BIBLIOGRAPHY. A list or description of books or works that are the subject of study, as opposed to books or works that are *about* the subject. Often used to designate bibliography devoted to works by an author rather than to works written about an author. See *secondary bibliography*.

PRINTOUT. Hard-copy output from a printer driven by a computer.

PROMPTBOOK. A manuscript or printed copy used to stage a play.

PROOF. An impression taken, or "pulled," from type or plates or a printout from a computer file for examination and correction, that is, for proofreading. Galley proofs are pulled from type that is not yet arranged into pages; page proofs, from pages already imposed; press proofs, from type or plates about to be used for a pressrun; foundry proofs, from type before it is used to make stereotypes or electrotypes. Reproduction proofs, or repros, are pulled for use in photoengraving or for photo-offset lithography or are the final photocomposed typesetting. A revise is a proof taken to check corrections made after a previous proof.

PROVENANCE. The postproduction history (especially ownership) of one copy of a book or other document.

PUBLISH. To issue printed (or otherwise reproduced) textual or graphic material for sale or public distribution.

PULP. Fibrous material (such as rags and wood) mechanically or chemically softened and mixed with water and sizing, such as gelatin or resin, to form the material from which paper is made. Also, a book or magazine printed on paper made from mechanically pulped wood.

QUAD. Short for *quadrat*, which is a blank piece of type used for spacing and measured in ems.

QUARTO. A book format in which the sheets are printed for folding twice, each sheet thus producing four leaves (eight pages). Abbreviated 4°, 4to, Q, and Qto. Also, a book printed in this format.

QUASI FACSIMILE. In bibliography, a descriptive transcription of printed matter (such as that on a title page), one that presents the text and describes or reproduces some features of its physical appearance, such as line endings, capitalization, decoration, and type style.

QUIRE. One-twentieth of a ream of paper; thus twenty-four sheets of a 480-count ream or twenty-five sheets of a 500-count ream. Also, a gathering, especially one of four sheets folded once to produce eight leaves. As a verb, to quire is to insert one sheet or more within another to create a gathering. Finally, a book in quires is a book whose sheets have been printed but not yet folded and gathered.

QUOIN. In printing, wedges of wood or metal used to lock type within a chase.

RECENSIO or RECENSION. In classical textual criticism, the reconstruction of the lost common ancestor of surviving texts through the examination of manuscripts and the texts they contain and through the construction of a stemma showing the relations among the texts.

RECTO. The front of a leaf; the right-hand page. Compare *verso*.

REDACTION. The process or product of abridging, adapting, or otherwise altering a text.

REFERENCE BIBLIOGRAPHY. The branch of bibliography concerned primarily with enumerating, describing, and providing access to works as opposed to books (or other documentary forms).

REGISTER. (1) In early books, a list, appearing at the end or in the preliminaries, giving the book's signatures for gathering and binding; (2) the entry of a claim for copyright, as in the Stationer's Register; (3) in printing, the correspondence in position of the type pages on the two sides of a leaf; (4) in color printing, the alignment of superimposed images from the plates used for each color.

REGULARIZATION. In editing, the imposition of uniformity in such textual details as spelling, punctuation, word division, and capitalization.

REMAINDERS. Books sold at reduced price after demand has waned, sheets of such books sold to a wholesaler who issues them in a cheap (remainder) binding, or books or sheets pulped for lack of demand.

REPRINT. A printing of something previously printed. A reprint may be from the same typesetting or from a new one.

REPRODUCTION PROOFS. Proofs, from type or photocomposition, used to produce photo-offset or gravure printing plates. Also called repros.

ROMAN TYPE. A broad class of type originally modeled on the script of early fifteenth-century Italian humanistic scribes and commonly used in books since. Old-style roman is characterized by a left-inclined axis of curves, oblique bracketed serifs, and alternating thick and thin strokes (e.g., Bembo, Garamond, and Granjon). Transitional roman, developed in the eighteenth century, is characterized by a more nearly vertical axis of curves and bracketed serifs (e.g., Baskerville and Caledonia). Modern roman, of the eighteenth and nineteenth centuries, is characterized by more geometric letters that have a vertical axis of curves; horizontal, often unbracketed serifs; and abruptly alternating thick and thin strokes (e.g., Bodoni and Corvinus).

ROTARY PRESS. A press that prints from a revolving cylindrical forme.

ROYALTIES. Payments made to authors for publication, generally as a percentage of a book's price and based on the number of copies sold.

RUBRICATION. A form of decoration in early books and manuscripts, consisting of painted headings (rubrics), initials, paragraph marks, and the like. Especially used for these decorations when they are painted red.

RULE. A strip of metal used to print a line. Also, such a line whether printed from metal or from some other composition process (such as photocomposition). Rules are commonly used to divide or frame text on the title page or elsewhere. Rules may be wavy, double, centrally swelled, or otherwise made decorative.

RUNNING TITLE. The book title, chapter or other division title, or subject heading appearing in the headline (sometimes in the direction line) of a page. Also called running head.

SANS SERIF. Type or hand lettering without serifs, as in the typefaces Futura and Helvetica. Also called block letter and *gothic type*. See *black letter type*.

SCRIBE. A public official or functionary charged with the writing, copying, and keeping of documents; a copyist, especially of classical and medieval manuscripts.

SCRIPT. In paleography, a form or style of handwriting, used in such phrases as *secretary script* and *majuscule script*. See *hand*. In typography, a type style resembling cursive handwriting.

SCRIPTORIUM. A writing room, as that set aside in monasteries for the copying of manuscripts.

SECONDARY BIBLIOGRAPHY. A list or description of books or works about a subject, especially an author. See *primary bibliography*.

SECRETARY SCRIPT. A form of cursive handwriting, also known as English hand and gradually replaced after 1580 by the italic, or Italian, script.

SERIAL. A publication issued in successive parts, generally at regular intervals and without an announced or projected date of cessation, such as newspapers, magazines, annuals, monograph series, proceedings, and scholarly journals.

SERIALIZATION. Publication in installments in a magazine or newspaper.

SERIATIM. In series, as in setting the text of a book in page order (e.g., pp. 1, 2, 3, 4) as opposed to setting the text by formes.

SERIF. A short line projecting at an angle from the upper or lower end of a main stroke of a handwritten or type letter.

SETOFF. Ink transferred accidentally by the contact of one printed sheet with another sheet or by contact of a sheet with a tympan sheet or cloth bearing wet ink.

SGML. Standard Generalized Markup Language, an international standard introduced in the 1980s and used for tagging, or coding, the structure of electronic texts, including such structural features as titles, chapters, headings, subheads, and paragraphs. Various programs can convert marked structures according to desired formats, as for printing or electronic publication.

SHEET. A rectangular piece of paper used in printing and then folded to produce the leaves of a book. See *paper sizes*.

SHEETWISE. The method of printing in which one side of a sheet is printed from one forme and the other side from another. Compare *work-and-turn*.

SHOW-THROUGH. A printing fault in which printed matter from one side of a leaf is visible on the other side.

SIGLUM. In textual criticism, a letter, figure, or other symbol used as a shorthand reference to a book or manuscript, as in a stemma, historical collation, or list of emendations. The plural is *sigla.*

SIGNATURE. A letter, figure, or other symbol appearing in the direction line, usually on the first page of a sheet and often on additional pages, and used as an aid to the binder in arranging and gathering the sheets and as a system of reference to a book's leaves. Also, a folded sheet, half-sheet, or quarter-sheet.

SIXTEENMO. A book format in which sheets are printed to produce sixteen leaves (thirty-two pages). Also, a book printed in this format. Abbreviated 16° and 16mo.

SKELETON FORME. In printing, the chase, furniture, running titles, quoins, and so forth in which type pages have been arranged for printing a forme.

SORTS. The individual characters that make up a font of type; thus, within a font, all pieces of type for the lowercase letter *a* compose one sort, lowercase *b*, another sort, and so on. The printer's type-case is divided into compartments, one compartment for each sort. Confusingly, the term sometimes refers to an individual piece of type.

SPINE. The part of the binding that covers the inner folds of a book's gatherings.

STANDING TYPE. Type that has been set and printed from but not distributed, as when stored in anticipation of a subsequent impression.

STATE. A part of a book (for example, a leaf or forme) exhibiting variation (especially in typesetting or makeup) from the same part in other copies of the same impression, such as the variation resulting from stop-press corrections.

STATIONER. A tradesperson, especially a bookseller, with a shop, or station, as opposed to one who is itinerant. Later and more specifically, a member of the Company of Stationers, which was incorporated by royal charter in 1557 and comprised printers, publishers, booksellers, bookbinders, and dealers in writing material.

STEMMA. A diagrammatic representation of the genetic relations among texts of a work; thus a sort of family tree of the texts.

STEMMATICS. The principles and practice of representing, in a stemma, the relations among texts of a work.

STEREOTYPE. A printing plate cast from a plaster or a paper (flong) mold of a forme of type.

STRIPPING. The process of arranging film negatives or positives in a flat for the production of an offset plate.

SUBEDITION. In bibliographical taxonomy, an impression or impressions (of the same edition) bearing a publisher's imprint different from that of another impression or impressions.

SUBSTANTIVES. In textual criticism, the words of a text, as opposed to such formal features as spelling and punctuation. See *accidentals.*

SWASH LETTERS. Italic capital letters with strokes ending in a flourish.

SYNOPTIC EDITION. See *genetic edition.*

SYSTEMATIC BIBLIOGRAPHY. Enumerative bibliography, with especial concern for the classification and arrangement of the items listed.

TAILPIECE. An ornament or other decorative device used at the end of the text of a poem, chapter, or other division of a book.

TEI. Text Encoding Initiative, a project that developed a system of SGML-conformant codes used to mark electronic texts for textual analysis and manipulation, as in editing.

TEXT. The sequence or array of words and graphic images transmitted in a document or documents or through other media; the term has also been used more broadly to refer to nonverbal forms such as painting and dance. A documentary text is the text within a particular document. The text of a work may be represented, more or less accurately, in several documents.

TEXTUAL BIBLIOGRAPHY. A term sometimes used to refer to the application of analytical bibliography to textual criticism.

TEXTUAL CRITICISM. The study of the transmission of texts and the application of this study to scholarly editing.

TEXTUS RECEPTUS. The received text; that is, the text of a work that has gained favor or at least familiarity through long and common use.

TIP IN. The process or product of pasting a leaf or slip of paper within or between gatherings, as may be done with errata slips, separately printed illustrations, or inserted leaves.

TITLE PAGE. An early page in a book giving (not always accurately) such information as author, title, subtitle, publisher, printer, place of publication, and date, and sometimes bearing illustration or decoration.

TOLERANCE. In descriptive bibliography the degree of specificity employed in measurements, color designation, quasi-facsimile transcriptions, and other description.

TRADE BIBLIOGRAPHY. Lists of books offered for sale, such as the *English Catalogue of Books* and the *Publisher's Trade List Annual*. More accurately called trade catalogs.

TRADE EDITION. An edition or portion of an edition sold through retail booksellers, as distinguished from an edition offered by a book club or prepared especially for libraries, for example.

TRANSCRIPT. A written, typed, or printed document recording a spoken text. Or, more generally, a copy made of a text contained in another document.

TRANSLITERATION. The process of transcribing a text in an alphabet different from its own, for example, rendering the Cyrillic alphabet in the roman.

TRIM SIZE. The vertical and horizontal dimensions of a book's leaves after the folds of the gatherings are trimmed or cut away.

TRIVIALIZATION. The tendency of scribes, copyists, and compositors to substitute more familiar words, meaning, and grammatical or metrical forms for more difficult ones. Also known as banalization.

TYMPAN. In printing, the cloth or paper placed between the platen of the press and the paper to be printed. In hand printing, the parchment- or paper-covered frame that presses the paper to be printed onto the type by the force of the platen. Also, the frame holding the cloth or paper.

TYPE. A piece of metal on which a character (letter, figure, punctuation, etc.) appears as a raised surface that when inked will transfer its mirror image. Also, by extension, such characters when printed by other means, as in phototypesetting.

TYPE BATTER. Wear or damage to type that may occur during storage or use.

TYPEFACE. The face of a printing type, that is, the printing surface of the type. Also, the classification or name of a particular design of the face, such as Baskerville, Caslon, and Times New Roman.

TYPE ORNAMENT. Printers' ornaments that are cast and set as type, such as borders, flowers, flourishes, headbands, initials, and tailpieces.

TYPE PAGE. The type assembled for printing a page. Also, the area of a page occupied by print.

TYPESCRIPT. A typewritten manuscript.

TYPE SIZE. The dimension of a type, measured from the front to the back of the body of the type. More or less standard type sizes designated by name began to be developed early in the sixteenth century, and standardization was aided in the nineteenth century by the development of the point system and of mechanical typesetting machines. Some early designations and their approximate equivalents in points: nonpareil (6 pts.), brevier (8 pts.), long primer (10 pts.), small pica (11 pts.), pica (12 pts.), english (14 pts.), great primer (18 pts.), double pica (22 pts.).

TYPOGRAPHY. The style, design, arrangement, and appearance of typeset material. Also, the craft of type design and use, and the study of type.

UPPER CASE. The typecase placed in the superior position (above the lower case) in a frame used by compositors. The upper case held capital, or uppercase, letters.

UR-TEXT. The original text of a work.

VARIANT. A text or portion of a text that differs from another of the same work.

VARIORUM EDITION. A scholarly edition in which a base text (not necessarily critically edited) is annotated with a record of critical and textual commentary on particular passages, of editors' emendations, or of variant readings present in other texts. A critical variorum reports primarily critical commentary; a textual variorum, primarily textual variation.

VELLUM. Writing or binding material made from the skin of a calf, kid, or lamb. Also, a sturdy, smooth cream-colored paper.

VERSION. In textual criticism, a form of a work (as represented by a variant text or texts) judged to be sufficiently different from another form to be regarded as a variant of that work; thus, for example, an acting version of a play may be distinguished from a reading version.

VERSO. A left-hand page of a book; also, the side of a manuscript leaf to be read second. Compare *recto*.

VIGNETTE. An illustration that lacks a border and clearly defined edge and thus shades into the surrounding area of the page. Also, a printer's ornament of vines, leaves, tendrils, and perhaps grapes.

WATERMARK. A lettering or design visible when paper is held up to light. In laid paper, the watermark is produced from wire sewn to the wire-and-chain paper mold; in machine-made paper, it may be impressed into the paper by a dandy roll.

WEB-FED PRESS. A press that prints not sheets but reels of paper.

WIDOW. A short line at the beginning of a page or column, carried over from the previous page or column. Considered a design fault to be avoided or corrected by compositors.

WIRE LINES. Lines roughly one millimeter or less apart created by a papermaking mold and running parallel to the longer sides of a sheet of handmade, or laid, paper. In machine-made paper they may be created by a dandy roll. See *chain lines*.

WITNESS. In textual criticism, a manuscript or other documentary text considered as evidence in the reconstruction of an earlier text.

WOODCUT. An illustration printed from an inked image cut in the plank side of a piece of wood, producing a bold printed area against a white background. The term is sometimes used for *wood engraving* as well.

WOOD ENGRAVING. An illustration printed from an inked image cut in the end grain of a piece of wood, the image appearing in white against a black background.

WORK. In textual criticism, a poem, play, novel, short story, essay, letter, treatise, or other construction represented and transmitted by a text or texts.

WORK-AND-TURN. A method of printing in which a forme is imposed so that one side of a sheet is printed, turned left to right, and printed on the other side from the same forme, thereby producing two copies from a single sheet. If the sheet is turned from front to back, the process is called work-and-tumble. See *half-sheet imposition*; compare *sheetwise*.

WORMHOLES. The holes made by bookworms, the bibliophagous larvae of various insects.

WOVE PAPER. Paper, whether made by hand or machine, bearing not the wire and chain lines of laid paper but rather a fine regular pattern of woven or meshed wires, as in most book paper today. See *laid paper*.

WRAPPERS. Paper covers of a book.

WRONG FONT. An error (or an expediency when a printer is short of type) consisting of the use of a typeface or type size different from that of the font with which neighboring text is set.

XEROGRAPHY. A photocopying process in which a latent image is created through an electrostatic charge that attracts a resinous powder.

X-HEIGHT. The height of the lowercase letters (excluding ascenders and descenders) of a particular font.

XYLOGRAPH. See *block books*.

WORKS CITED

Abbott, Craig S. *John Crowe Ransom: A Descriptive Bibliography*. Troy: Whitston, forthcoming.

Aubrey, John. *Aubrey's Brief Lives*. Ed. Oliver Lawson Dick. London: Secker, 1950.

Barker, Nicolas, and John Collins. *A Sequel to* An Enquiry into the Nature of Certain Nineteenth- Century Pamphlets: *The Forgeries of H. Buxton Forman and T. J. Wise Re-examined*. London: Scolar, 1983.

Barnes, Warner. "Film Experimentation in Beta-Radiography." *Direction Line* 1 (1975): 3–4.

Bentley, Richard. *Milton's* Paradise Lost: *A New Edition*. London, 1732.

Bishop, Edward. "Re:Covering Modernism: Format and Function in the Little Magazines." *Modernist Writers and the Marketplace*. Ed. Ian Willison, Warwick Gould, and Warren Chernaik. London: Macmillan; New York: St. Martin's, 1996. 287–319.

Blayney, Peter W. M. *Nicholas Okes and the First Quarto*. Vol. 1 of *The Texts of* King Lear *and Their Origins*. Cambridge: Cambridge UP, 1982.

Booth, Stephen. *Shakespeare's Sonnets*. New Haven: Yale UP, 1980.

Bowers, Fredson. The Bibliographical Way. Lecture. U of Kansas. 14 Nov. 1958. Lawrence: U of Kansas Libraries, 1959. Rpt. in Bowers, *Essays* 54–74.

———. *Bibliography and Textual Criticism*. Oxford: Clarendon, 1964.

———. "Bibliography Revisited." *Library* 5th ser. 24 (1969): 84–128. Rpt. in Bowers, *Essays* 151–95.

———. "Elizabethan Proofing." 1948. Bowers, *Essays* 240–53.

———. *Essays in Bibliography, Text, and Editing*. Charlottesville: UP of Virginia, 1975.

———. *Principles of Bibliographical Description*. 1949. New York: Russell, 1962.

———. "Purposes of Descriptive Bibliography with Some Remarks on Methods." 1953. Rpt. in his *Essays* 111–34.

———. Textual introd. *The Centenary Edition of the Works of Nathaniel Hawthorne*. Ed. William Charvat et al. Vol. 2. Columbus: Ohio State UP, 1962. xlix–lxv.

———. Textual introd. *Edward II. The Complete Works of Christopher Marlowe*. Ed. Bowers. 2nd ed. Cambridge: Cambridge UP, 1981. 2: 3–12.

———. "Was There a Lost 1593 Edition of Marlowe's *Edward II*?" *Studies in Bibliography* 25 (1972): 143-48.

Bradley, Sculley, et al., eds. Leaves of Grass: *A Textual Variorum of the Printed Poems*. 3 vols. New York: New York UP, 1980.

Browning, B. L. *Analysis of Paper*. 2nd ed. New York: Dekker, 1977.

Bruccoli, Matthew. "Getting It Right: The Publishing Process and the Correction of Factual Errors—with Reference to *The Great Gatsby*." *Essays in Honor of Wil-*

liam B. Todd. Comp. Warner Barnes and Larry Carter. Ed. Dave Oliphant. Austin: Harry Ransom Humanities Research Center, 1991. 41–59.

Cahill, T. A., et al. "The Vinland Map, Revisited: New Compositional Evidence on Its Ink and Parchment." *Analytical Chemistry* 59 (1987): 829–33.

Carter, John, and Graham Pollard. *An Enquiry into the Nature of Certain Nineteenth-Century Pamphlets*. London: Constable, 1934. 2nd ed. Ed. Nicolas Barker and John Collins. London: Scolar, 1983.

Center for Editions of American Authors. *Professional Standards and American Editions*. New York: MLA, 1969.

Clark, C. E. Frazer, Jr. *Nathaniel Hawthorne: A Descriptive Bibliography*. Pittsburgh: U of Pittsburgh P, 1978.

Colwell, Ernest C. "Text and Ancient Versions of the New Testament." *The Interpreter's Bible*. Ed. George Arthur Buttrick et al. Vol. 1. New York: Abingdon, 1952. 72–83.

Crews, Frederick C. *The Pooh Perplex: A Freshman Casebook*. New York: Dutton, 1963.

Croll, Morris. "The Baroque Style in Prose." *"Attic" and Baroque Prose Style*. Ed. J. Max Patrick, Robert O. Evans, and John M. Wallace. Princeton: Princeton UP, 1969. 230–33.

Darnton, Robert. *The Business of Enlightenment: A Publishing History of the* Encyclopédie, *1775–1800*. Cambridge: Belknap–Harvard UP, 1979.

———. *The Forbidden Best-Sellers of Pre-revolutionary France*. London: Harper, 1996.

Davison, Peter, ed. *The Book Encompassed: Studies in Twentieth-Century Bibliography*. Cambridge: Cambridge UP, 1992.

Dearing, Vinton A. "The Poor Man's Mark IV or Ersatz Hinman Collator." *Papers of the Bibliographical Society of America* 60 (1966): 149–58.

———. *Principles and Practice of Textual Analysis*. Berkeley: U of California P, 1974.

Derrida, Jacques. "Limited Inc. ABC." *Glyph* 2 (1977): 162–254.

Duggan, Hoyt N. *The* Piers Plowman *Electronic Archive*. 1994. Institute for Advanced Technology in the Humanities Research Reports, 2nd ser. 19 Oct. 1998. <http://jefferson.village.virginia.edu/piers/archive.goal.html>.

Edel, Leon. "The Text of *The Ambassadors*." *Harvard Library Bulletin* 14 (1960): 453–60.

Eisenstein, Elizabeth L. *The Printing Press as an Agent of Change*. Cambridge: Cambridge UP, 1979.

Empson, William. Letter. *Times Literary Supplement* 24 Aug. 1973: 978.

Evans, G. Blakemore, et al., eds. *The Riverside Shakespeare*. Boston: Houghton, 1974.

Febvre, Lucien, and Henri-Jean Martin. *The Coming of the Book: The Impact of Printing, 1450–1800*. Trans. David Gerard. Ed. Geoffrey Nowell-Smith and David Wootton. Atlantic Highlands: Humanities, 1976.

Gabler, Hans Walter, ed. *Ulysses: A Critical and Synoptic Edition*. 3 vols. New York: Garland, 1984.

Gabler, Hans Walter, George Bornstein, and Gillian Pierce, eds. *Contemporary German Editorial Theory*. Ann Arbor: U of Michigan P, 1995.

Gaskell, Philip. *From Writer to Reader: Studies in Editorial Method*. Oxford: Clarendon, 1978.

———. *A New Introduction to Bibliography*. Oxford: Oxford UP, 1972.

Graves, Robert, and Laura Riding. "A Study in Original Punctuation and Spelling." 1927. Rev. *The Common Asphodel.* By Graves. London: Hamilton, 1949. 84–95.

Greenblatt, Stephen, et al., eds. *The Norton Shakespeare.* New York: Norton, 1997.

Greene, Thomas M. "Anti-hermeneutics: The Case of Shakespeare's Sonnet 129." *Poetic Traditions of the English Renaissance.* Ed. Maynard Mack and George deForest Lord. New Haven: Yale UP, 1982. 142–61.

Greetham, D. C. "Textual and Literary Theory: Redrawing the Matrix." *Studies in Bibliography* 42 (1989): 1–24.

Greg, W. W. *The Calculus of Variants.* Oxford: Clarendon, 1927.

———. "On Certain False Dates in Shakesperian Quartos." *Library* 2nd ser. 9 (1908): 113–31, 381–409.

———. "The Rationale of Copy-Text." *Studies in Bibliography* 3 (1950–51): 19–36. Rpt. in *Collected Papers.* By Greg. Ed. J. C. Maxwell. Oxford: Clarendon, 1966. 374–91.

Guffey, George. "Standardization of Photographic Reproductions for Mechanical Collation." *Papers of the Bibliographical Society of America* 62 (1968): 237–40.

Harner, James L. *On Compiling an Annotated Bibliography.* New York: MLA, 1985.

Hayford, Harrison, et al., eds. *Typee: A Peep at Polynesian Life.* Vol. 1 of *The Writings of Herman Melville.* Evanston: Northwestern UP; Chicago: Newberry, 1968.

Hayford, Harrison, and Merton M. Sealts, Jr., eds. *Billy Budd Sailor (An Inside Narrative).* By Herman Melville. Chicago: U of Chicago P, 1962.

Hinman, Charlton, ed. *The First Folio of Shakespeare: The Norton Facsimile.* New York: Norton, 1968.

———. *The Printing and Proof-reading of the First Folio of Shakespeare.* 2 vols. Oxford: Clarendon, 1963.

Housman, A. E. "The Application of Thought to Textual Criticism." 1922. *The Classical Papers of A. E. Housman.* Ed. J. Diggle and F. R. D. Goodyear. Vol. 3. Cambridge: Cambridge UP, 1972. 1058–69.

Ide, Nancy, and Jean Véronis, eds. *The Text Encoding Initiative: Background and Contexts.* Spec. issues of *Computers and the Humanities* 29.1–3 (1995): 1–231.

"Information about Project Gutenberg." Project Gutenberg. 19 Oct. 1998 <http://www.astro.indiana.edu/personnel/link/guttext.html>.

Kappel, Andrew J. "Complete with Omissions: The Text of Marianne Moore's *Complete Poems.*" *Representing Modernist Texts: Editing as Interpretation.* Ed. George Bornstein. Ann Arbor: U of Michigan P, 1991. 125–56.

Krueger, Robert, ed. *The Poems of Sir John Davies.* Oxford: Clarendon, 1975.

Lancashire, Ian. "Renaissance Electronic Texts: Encoding Guidelines." *Renaissance Electronic Texts Supplementary Studies* 1 (1994). <http://www.library.utoronto.ca/utel/ret/GUIDELINESO.HTML>.

Levenston, E. A. *The Stuff of Literature: Physical Aspects of Texts and Their Relation to Meaning.* Albany: SUNY P, 1992.

MacMahon, Candace W. *Elizabeth Bishop: A Bibliography, 1927–1979.* Charlottesville: UP of Virginia, 1980.

Madan, Falconer. "Degressive Bibliography: A Memorandum." *Transactions of the Bibliographical Society* 9 (1906–08): 53–65.

A Manual of Style Containing Typographical Rules Governing the Publications of the University of Chicago, Together with Specimens of Type Used at the University Press. Chicago: U of Chicago P, 1925.

Matthiessen, F. O. *American Renaissance: Art and Expression in the Age of Emerson and Whitman.* New York: Oxford UP, 1941.

McCrone, Walter C. "Authenticity of Medieval Document Tested by Small Particle Analysis." *Analytical Chemistry* 48 (1976): 676A–79A.

McDonald, Peter D. "Implicit Structures and Explicit Interactions: Pierre Bourdieu and the History of the Book." *Library* 6th ser. 19 (1997): 105–21.

McGann, Jerome J. *The Beauty of Inflections: Literary Investigations in Historical Method and Theory.* Oxford: Clarendon, 1988.

———. "The Complete Writings and Pictures of Dante Gabriel Rossetti: A Hypermedia Research Archive." *Text* 7 (1994): 95–105.

———. *A Critique of Modern Textual Criticism.* Chicago: U of Chicago P, 1983.

———. "Revision, Rewriting, Rereading; or, 'An Error [Not] in *The Ambassadors.'*" *American Literature* 64 (1992): 95–110.

———. *The Textual Condition.* Princeton: Princeton UP, 1991.

McKenzie, D. F. *Bibliography and the Sociology of Texts.* London: British Lib., 1986.

———. "Printers of the Mind: Some Notes on Bibliographical Theories and Printing-House Practices." *Studies in Bibliography* 22 (1969): 1–75.

McKerrow, Ronald B. *An Introduction to Bibliography for Literary Students.* Oxford: Clarendon, 1928.

———. *Prolegomena for the Oxford Shakespeare: A Study in Editorial Method.* Oxford: Clarendon, 1939.

McKerrow, Ronald B., and F. S. Ferguson. *Title-Page Borders Used in England and Scotland, 1485–1640.* London: Bibliographical Soc., 1932.

McLeod, Randall. "Spellbound." *Play-Texts in Old Spelling.* Ed. G. B. Shand and Raymond C. Shady. New York: AMS, 1984. 81–96.

Rev. of *Modern Heroism,* by Roger Sale. *Times Literary Supplement* 27 July 1973: 848.

Moore, Marianne. *The Complete Poems of Marianne Moore.* New York: Macmillan-Viking, 1967.

Motley, Willard. *Knock on Any Door.* New York: Appleton, 1947.

Moxon, Joseph. *Mechanick Exercises on the Whole Art of Printing.* 1683–84. Ed. Herbert Davis and Harry Carter. 2nd ed. New York: Dover, 1962.

Moyles, R. G. *The Text of* Paradise Lost: *A Study in Editorial Procedure.* Toronto: U of Toronto P, 1985.

Mumford, Lewis. "Emerson behind Barbed Wire." *New York Review of Books* 18 Jan. 1968: 4.

Needham, Paul. "The Compositor's Hand in the Gutenberg Bible: A Review of the Todd Thesis." *Papers of the Bibliographical Society of America* 77 (1983): 341–71.

Neidig, William. "The Shakespeare Quartos of 1619." *Modern Philology* 8 (1910): 145–63.

Nelson, Cary. *Repression and Recovery: Modern American Poetry and the Politics of Cultural Memory, 1910–1945.* Madison: U of Wisconsin P, 1989.

Nichol, John W. "Melville's '"Soiled" Fish of the Sea.'" *American Literature* 21 (1949): 338–39.

Nunberg, Geoffrey, ed. *The Future of the Book.* Berkeley: U of California P, 1996.

Parker, Hershel. "Regularizing Accidentals: The Latest Form of Infidelity." *Proof* 3 (1973): 1–20.

Pearsall, Derek. "Editing Medieval Texts: Some Developments and Some Problems." *Textual Criticism and Literary Interpretation.* Ed. Jerome J. McGann. Chicago: U of Chicago P, 1985. 92–106.

Poe, Charmian. "Byron and Byroniana at Northern Illinois University: A Descriptive Catalogue." Diss. Northern Illinois U, 1980.

Pollard, A. W. *Shakespeare Folios and Quartos: A Study in the Bibliography of Shakespeare's Plays, 1594–1685.* London: Methuen, 1909.

Pollard, A. W., and G. R. Redgrave. *A Short-Title Catalogue of Books Printed in England, Scotland, and Ireland, and of English Books Printed Abroad, 1475–1640.* Rev. Katherine F. Pantzer, W. A. Jackson, and F. S. Ferguson. 2nd ed. 3 vols. London: Bibliographical Soc., 1976, 1986, and 1991.

Potter, Lois. Rev. of *The Complete Works,* by William Shakespeare, ed. Stanley Wells and Gary Taylor. *Times Literary Supplement* 10 April 1987: 389–90.

"Practical Editions." *Proof* 2 (1972): 283–318, 3 (1973): 369–94, 4 (1975): 165–82.

Prosser, Eleanor. *Shakespeare's Anonymous Editors: Scribe and Compositor in the Folio Text of 2 Henry IV.* Stanford: Stanford UP, 1981.

Ransom, John Crowe. *Selected Poems.* New York: Knopf, 1969.

The Rossetti Archive. University of Virginia Institute for Advanced Technology in the Humanities, Research Reports, First Series 1993. <http://jefferson.village.virginia.edu/rossetti/rossetti.html>. 19 Oct. 1998.

Sayce, R. A. "Compositorial Practices and the Localization of Printed Books, 1530–1800." *Library* 5th ser. 21 (1966): 1–45.

Shef, Roger. "How Many *T*s Had Ezra Pound's Printer?" *Studies in Bibliography* 49 (1996): 277–83.

Shillingsburg, Peter L. "Detecting the Use of Stereotype Plates." *Editorial Quarterly* 1 (1975): 2–3.

———. *Scholarly Editing in the Computer Age: Theory and Practice.* 3rd ed. Ann Arbor: U of Michigan P, 1996.

Simmons, J. S. G. "The Delft Method of Watermark Reproduction." *Book Collector* 18 (1969): 514–15.

———. "The Leningrad Method of Watermark Reproduction." *Book Collector* 10 (1961): 329–30.

Simpson, Percy. *Proof-Reading in the Sixteenth, Seventeenth, and Eighteenth Centuries.* 1935. New foreword. London: Oxford UP, 1970.

Smith, Barbara Herrnstein. *Poetic Closure: A Study of How Poems End.* Chicago: U of Chicago P, 1968.

Sprague, Arthur Colby, ed. *Samuel Daniel: Poems and A Defence of Ryme.* Cambridge: Harvard UP, 1930.

Staton, Walter F., Jr., and W. E. Simeone, eds. *A Critical Edition of Sir Richard Fanshawe's 1647 Translation of Giovanni Battista Guarini's* Il Pastor Fido. Oxford: Clarendon, 1964.

Sternberg, Paul R., and John M. Brayer. "Composite Imaging: A New Technique in Bibliographic Research." *Papers of the Bibliographical Society of America* 77 (1983): 431–45.

Stevenson, A. H. *The Problem of the Missale Speciale*. London: Bibliographical Soc., 1967.

Tanselle, G. Thomas. "The Concept of Ideal Copy." *Studies in Bibliography* 33 (1980): 18–53.

———. "Greg's Theory of Copy-Text and the Editing of American Literature." *Studies in Bibliography* 28 (1975): 167–229. Rpt. in Tanselle, *Selected Studies* 245–307.

———. "Historicism and Critical Editing." *Studies in Bibliography* 39 (1986): 1–46.

———. "The Recording of Press Figures." *Library* 5th ser. 21 (1966): 318–25.

———. "A Sample Bibliographic Description with Commentary." *Studies in Bibliography* 40 (1987): 1–30.

———. *Selected Studies in Bibliography*. Charlottesville: UP of Virginia, 1979.

———. "Textual Criticism and Literary Sociology." *Studies in Bibliography* 44 (1991): 83–143.

———. "Tolerances in Bibliographical Description." *Library* 5th ser. 23 (1968): 1–12.

Taylor, Charles B. "A Critical Old Spelling Edition of Sir John Davies' *Nosce Teipsum.*" Diss. Northern Illinois U, 1971.

Taylor, Gary, and Michael Warren, eds. *The Division of the Kingdoms: Shakespeare's Two Versions of* King Lear. Oxford: Oxford UP, 1983.

Text Encoding Initiative. 1998. <http://www.uic.edu:80/orgs/tei>. 19 Oct. 1998.

Todd, William B. "Concealed Editions of Samuel Johnson." *Book Collector* 2 (1953): 59–65.

———. *The Gutenberg Bible: New Evidence of the Original Printing*. 3rd Hanes Lecture. Chapel Hill: U of North Carolina P, 1982.

University of London School of Advanced Study. Advertisement. *Times Literary Supplement* 31 March 1998: 34.

Vander Meulen, David. *Pope's* Dunciad *of 1728: A History and Facsimile*. Charlottesville: UP of Virginia, 1991.

Walker, Alice. *Textual Problems of the First Folio*. Cambridge: Cambridge UP, 1953.

Webster, John. *The Tragedy of the Dutchesse of Malfy*. London, 1623.

Wellek, René, and Austin Warren. *Theory of Literature*. 3rd ed. New York: Harcourt, 1956.

Wells, Stanley. *Modernizing Shakespeare's Spelling*. Oxford: Clarendon, 1979.

———, ed. *Shakespeare: Select Bibliographical Guides*. Oxford: Oxford UP, 1973.

Wells, Stanley, et al., eds. *The Complete Works*. By William Shakespeare. Modern-spelling ed. Oxford: Clarendon, 1986. Original-spelling ed. Oxford: Clarendon, 1988.

Werstine, Paul. "Shakespeare." *Scholarly Editing: A Guide to Research*. Ed. D. C. Greetham. New York: MLA, 1995. 253–82.

West, James L. W., III. *William Styron: A Descriptive Bibliography*. Boston: Hall, 1977.

Williams, George Walton, and Thomas L. Berger. "Variants in the Quarto of Shakespeare's *2 Henry IV.*" *Library* 6th ser. 3 (1981): 111–15.

Williams, W. P. "A Critical Edition of Jeremy Taylor's *The Liberty of Prophesying.*" Diss. Kansas State U, 1968.

Wilson, Edmund, "The Fruits of the MLA." *New York Review of Books* 26 Sept. 1968: 7+; 10 Oct. 1968: 6+. Rpt. as *The Fruits of the MLA*. New York: New York Review, 1968.

Zeller, Hans. "A New Approach to the Critical Constitution of Literary Texts." *Studies in Bibliography* 28 (1975): 231–64.

INDEX

Page numbers in italics indicate illustrations.

bibliographical taxonomy, in descriptive
bibliographies, 26, 36, 37, 130; and
textual stemma, 28–29, 94. *See also*
edition; impression; issue; state
bibliography, bibliography of, 126–27;
criticism of, 4, 10; definitions of,
125; history of, 1–4, 125; studies
in, 125–27. *See also* analytical
bibliography; annotated
bibliography; author bibliography;
descriptive bibliography; enumerative
bibliography; historical bibliography;
physical bibliography; reference
bibliography; textual bibliography
binding, 45–46
Bishop, Edward, 32
Bishop, Elizabeth, 76
black-letter type, 38
Blake, William, 65
Blayney, Peter W. M., 25, 128
Blanck, Jacob, 131
blind stamp, 46
Bloomfield, B. C., 131
Blum, Rudolf, 125
blurb, 46
Bond, William H., 128, 129
Book Encompassed, The (ed. Davison), 9
bookplate, 45
Books in Print, 16
Booth, Stephen, 121n2
borders, title-page, 39
Bornstein, George, 85n5, 132, 133
Bowden, Edwin, 131
Bowers, Fredson, 14, 15, 36, 82, 83,
85n4, 133, 134; "Running-Title
Evidence," 129; "Bibliographical
Evidence," 128; *Bibliography and
Textual Criticism*, 15, 70, 127, 132;
*The Dramatic Works of Thomas
Dekker*, 103–07; *Essays in
Bibliography*, 125, 130, 133;
Edward II, 30; "Elizabethan
Proofing," 22, 95; *Principles of
Bibliographical Description*, 36–37,
39–40, 47n2, 130; *Scarlet Letter, The*,

31; *Textual and Literary Criticism*,
132; "Textual Criticism," 131
Brack, O M, Jr., 133
brackets, square, in bibliographical
description, 39, 42–43; in
pagination, 20
Bradford, Robin, 133
Bradley, Sculley, 72
Brayer, John M., 91
brevior lectio potior, 76
Browning, B. L., 16
Browning, E. B., 15, 17, 18
Brown Women Writers Project, 75
Bruccoli, Matthew J., 78, 128, 129, 131
Buhler, Curt, 128
Byron, Lord, 19

Cahill, T. A., 18
Cairncross, Andrew, 10
camera-ready copy, 65
cancel, in collation formula, 43;
detection of, 23; and issue, 27; of
title page, 57
Carpenter, Kenneth E., 126
Carter, John, 16–17, 18, 127
case, type, 24, 25, *139*
casting off, 24–25, 55, 98, 128
Catalog of Copyright Entries, 16
catchwords, 32, 44
Center for Editions of American
Authors, 4, 82, 102, 113, 134
Center for Scholarly Editions, 131, 134
chain lines, 17, 40–41, 45
chase, 21
Chaucer, Geoffrey, 84, 100
Chernaik, Warren, 134
chi (χ), 42
Chicago Manual of Style, The, 8, 31
cladistics, 76
Clark, C. E. Frazer, Jr., 37–38, 131
Clark Library (Univ. of California), 91
clear text, 100, 101
cloth, binding, 46
codicology, 14
Cohen, Philip, 132
collation, textual, and computers,
90–91, 134; in critical editing,